INSIDERS' GUIDE®

QUICK ESCAPES® SERIES

Quick Escapes®
los angeles

getaways from the metro area

SEVENTH EDITION

Eleanor Harris
and
Claudia Harris Lichtig

INSIDERS' GUIDE®

GUILFORD, CONNECTICUT

AN IMPRINT OF THE GLOBE PEQUOT PRESS

To Ben, the very best person in the world to escape with

To buy books in quantity for corporate use
or incentives, call **(800) 962–0973, ext. 4551,**
or e-mail **premiums@GlobePequot.com.**

INSIDERS' GUIDE®

Text design by Casey Shain
Maps by M. A. Dubé © Morris Book Publishing, LLC.
Photo credits: p. 119: Hearst Castle®/California State Parks; p. 214: Justine Rathbun. All other photos by the author.

ISSN 1540-2096
ISBN-13: 978-0-7627-4219-6
ISBN-10 0-7627-4219-4

Manufactured in the United States of America
Seventh Edition/First Printing

CONTENTS

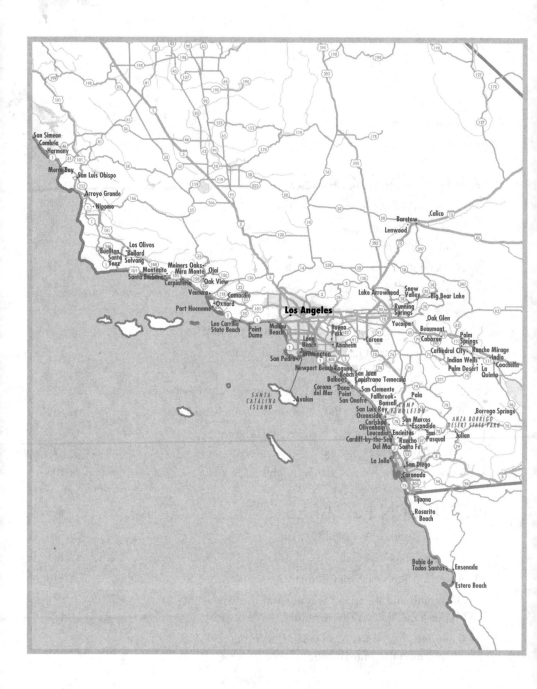

EASTERN ESCAPES......175

The prices and rates listed in this guidebook were confirmed at press time. We recommend, however, that you call establishments before traveling to obtain current information.

ACKNOWLEDGMENTS

any thanks to the kind people in various visitor bureaus and chambers of commerce, the patient staff at our local National Automobile Club, public relations personnel, and others who graciously shared local lore and helped us with the research and development of this book.

INTRODUCTION

This is a Southern California guide to select destinations of particular scenic beauty and year-round outdoor recreational attractions for overnight, weekend, or longer getaways. Each has something special to recommend it. Some places are deservedly well known, and others—small towns and villages—may be new discoveries you can claim for your own.

Each "escape" is presented as a detailed itinerary for the best of sightseeing, dining, and overnight accommodation in the featured area. Easy-to-follow, road-tested directions, including driving time and distance, get you there and back with the easiest, most direct route.

In all areas of its spectacular countryside, Southern California is an enchanting, carefree, warm, and sunny vacationland. The mild Mediterranean-like climate and weather are unfailingly wonderful. Usually there's no rain from mid-April to mid-October, so you can pretty much depend on blue skies for perfect vacations almost year-round.

Few places in the world are as beautiful and abundantly rich in natural scenic and geographic diversity. This book escorts you to the mile-high snowcapped mountains, sun-kissed deserts, romantic secluded beaches, sleepy rural villages, peaceful farmlands, and quiet harbors that are Southern California—all ideal change-of-pace getaways, where you can have fun, unwind, and relax.

You'll visit parks, boat-filled marinas, zoos, a popular offshore island in the Pacific, avocado and orange groves, museums, a sunny all-Danish city, world-famous amusement parks, art colonies, world-class championship golf and tennis resorts, famous beauty-health spas, a gold camp town, missions, a legendary private art-filled castle, a rural mile-high apple-growing community, and gaming casinos in imaginatively themed luxe megaresorts. A bonus is the region's proximity to Mexico, a foreign country just a few hours' drive from Los Angeles. One escape takes you to the world's most popular and exciting border city (a duty-free zone), and another continues farther south into the "real" Mexico to a lively bayside resort town along the seductive Mexican Riviera. (Please note that you need either a passport or birth certificate to reenter the United States. A driver's license is not an acceptable form of identification for reentry.)

Hotels and resorts range from upscale, world-class, and glamorous with unlimited amenities to cozy, quiet hideaways, all first-rate and nontouristy. Sports and fitness enthusiasts will find plenty of golf, tennis, bicycling, horseback riding, water sports, skiing, and hiking. The gourmet and the wine maven will be delighted, as will the sun-worshiper, the nature lover, and the culture-vulture. Shoppers and gamblers will find nirvana, and children will find warm welcomes and much to keep them busy.

Since Southern California is the heart of the world's entertainment industry, film stars, celebrities, movies, and TV have long been an important part of its glamour and lifestyle. Many picturesque locales showcased throughout the years in films are highlighted in passing. Besides serendipitous spotting of celebrities at any time, anywhere, you're also apt to come upon film crews at work on location throughout the area, shooting a TV episode, a commercial, or a movie.

Additionally, Southern California has a wealth of romance and history associated with its past and with its Spanish and Mexican heritage: the great rancheros, pioneer settlers, the Wild West, cowboys, missions, stagecoaches, gold strikes, and gold camp towns. History is kept alive and celebrated in many of the small cities with museum exhibits, living-history events, and other special year-round presentations.

The Los Angeles region has the finest freeway system in the world, enabling motorists to drive long distances in the shortest of times. Get to know the freeways and their routes as well as their traffic patterns. Odd-numbered freeways travel north and south; even numbered, east and west. Read maps and plot out your routes beforehand.

Take advantage of the seasons and what they offer. Contrary to what most people believe, Southern California has four distinct seasons. There's spring, when the air is soft and fragrant with lilacs and apple blossoms and the deserts are ablaze with wildflowers as far as one can see. In summer's long, lazy afternoons you can travel longer distances or linger indefinitely at the beaches and lakesides to watch the sunsets. In fall the days become shorter, the air is brisk, and the landscape turns russet as golden leaves flutter to the ground and aromatic wisps of smoke curl from chimneys during apple harvests and merry Oktoberfests. Mild winter months bring a blustery nip to the breeze; crisp, clear air; and endless vistas. The brief rainy season begins, and snowy mountain winter sports beckon, while the sunbaked desert, with warmer temperatures and less rain, is a brilliant color wheel of lavender mountains, green golf courses, and blue swimming pools. Energetic vacationers can spend a morning skiing in a mountain resort and then bask in the warm desert sun or swim in the ocean a few hours later.

Throughout the year these getaways offer a happy grab bag full of colorful regional, seasonal, historical, and holiday festivals, carnivals, fiestas, cook-offs, sports tournaments, ethnic and cultural celebrations, pageants, and other long-running events and activities of every kind to attend and enjoy.

There are actually forty escapes from Los Angeles in these twenty chapters, since many chapters include more than one destination. We have pointed out many places of interest and other cities along the way you may wish to visit as a side trip or mark for future exploration. Further, the destination cities follow in logical geographic and freeway sequence, so they're easy to revisit en route or returning from another getaway in the same general direction.

All the time-consuming and pesky details have been researched in each custom itinerary to offer the maximum freedom from stress during your escapes. Look for the special headings at the end of each chapter. *There's More* points out additional attractions to investigate this time or next visit. *Special Events* highlights local happenings and festivities that may be of interest. *Other Recommended Restaurants and Lodgings* offers fine alternative dining and accommodations not mentioned in the itinerary. Last, *For More Information* lists sources to contact for brochures, city maps, and further attractions in each destination.

Fees and fares are mentioned but not quoted, as they are subject to change. Prices are reasonable unless otherwise indicated. While missions and museums usually charge admission, special "free" days are noted. Hotel reservations are definitely recommended (midweek is less crowded than weekends). Be sure to make your plans as early as possible for holidays and busy seasons. We recommend that you call establishments before traveling to obtain current information.

Maps provided at the beginning of each section are for reference only and should be used in conjunction with a road map. Distances suggested are approximate.

All directions given in this book originate from downtown Los Angeles.

SOUTHERN
ESCAPES

Living on the Water

Newport Beach, Balboa / 1 Night

This two-day getaway to a nearby exclusive resort city is short on mileage but long on diversion and year-round appeal. Catering to an elite lifestyle, about 9,000 sumptuous yachts preen in sparkling bays surrounded by miles of whitesand beaches. The friendly coastal city is a collection of several small villages offering water sports, world-class hotels, gourmet dining in some 300 restaurants, and fanciful shopping. Exploring individual islands and piers, you'll go on harbor cruises, lunch on a Mississippi-style paddle wheeler, visit museums, relax at a waterfront amusement park, eat chocolate-dipped frozen bananas, and dine in bayside bistros.

☐ Beach

☐ Piers

☐ Boating

☐ Harbor cruise

☐ Museums

☐ Decorative gardens

☐ Shopping

☐ Amusement park

Day 1 / Morning

Take San Diego Freeway 405 south past the small beach cities—Manhattan Beach, Huntington Beach, and others—to Corona del Mar Freeway 55, which becomes Newport Boulevard. Continue on Newport Boulevard, cross the Pacific Coast Highway to Via Lido, and turn left to Lido Marina Village at the entrance to Balboa Peninsula, about 55 miles.

In **Lido Marina Village** stroll down Via Oporto, an attractive, curving redbrick-paved street of flowers, fountains, and flower baskets hanging from decorative streetlamps. In this delightful European-style waterfront area, dozens of shops and galleries back up to the boardwalk cafes, which face the water and offer pleasant outdoor dining on little tables overlooking the luxe yachts bobbing in their slips. Among the eateries, look for Bayfront Cafe's tasty gyros, shish kebab, and a great egg-salad sandwich; Le Bistro's fruit and cheese plate with a glass of wine; Mama Mia's Pizza; and others.

LUNCH: The Camelot Restaurant, 3420 Via Oporto, #2, Newport Beach. (949) 673–3233. You'll like the generous portions and menu variety from eggs Benedict, excellent seafood linguini, and Cobb salad to homemade French onion soup. Full bar. Waterfront or inside dining.

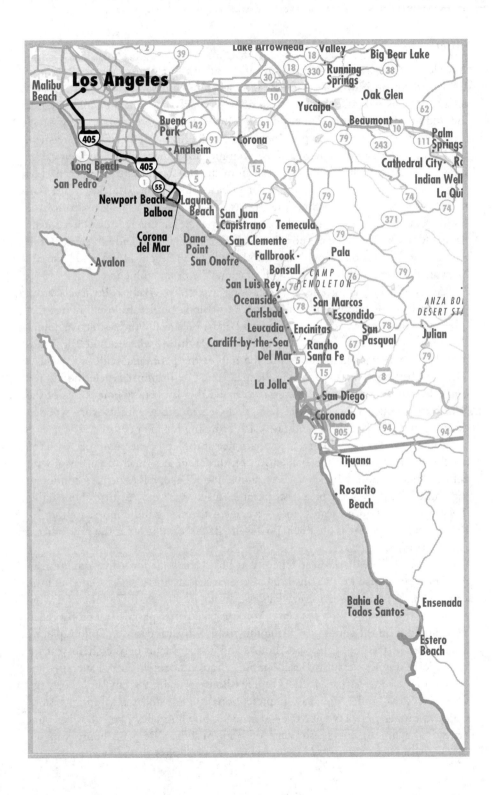

Afternoon

After lunch drive around the posh Lido Isle residential section. Then take Newport Boulevard to the **Newport Pier** area, passing the landmark 1952 Crab Cooker restaurant in its red building with a tall sidewalk clock out front, and continue past the Old Spaghetti Factory and popular Woody's Wharf, where some hungry guests arrive for lunch by boat. Newport Pier is where the historic Dory Fleet fishermen, the last on the West Coast, have arrived each morning since 1891 with their catch. Early risers can watch the dories roll in from the ocean and onto the beach, then watch the Dorymen prepare the fish for public sale in a small, enclosed open-air fish market on the sand behind their boats, where large gray pelicans patrol the rooftops waiting for handouts and gulls hover even closer. Lively McFadden Square has many snack places that are popular for fresh clam chowder and fish tacos. In this area along Oceanfront, you'll also find Portofino Beach Hotel and restored Doryman's Oceanfront Inn B&B with gracious Victorian ambience.

As you drive along the 2.5-mile-long stretch of Balboa Peninsula from Newport Pier, Newport Boulevard changes to Balboa Boulevard. You'll notice that it becomes more crowded as you approach Balboa Village and the distinctive dome-shaped cupola silhouette of the famous **Balboa Pavilion,** where all the Big Bands played in the 1930s and 1940s. It was the hub of the peninsula, built in 1906 as a Victorian bathhouse and the Pacific Electric Red Car Terminal, where the big red cars delivered visitors from Los Angeles to spend the day. It now houses Tale of the Whale restaurant. The adjacent old-fashioned General Store, with its worn wooden flooring and large barrels of candy, is worth browsing for mementos.

Appealing **Balboa Village,** a compact area at the tip of the peninsula, with the pavilion on one side and the Balboa Inn on the other, has small-town flavor, with tall ficus trees, wooden benches, cafes, shops, and a bakery. Residents recommend the Shore House Cafe for breakfast, and it seems busy all day. At small shops across the street you'll find postcards, above-average souvenirs, wind chimes, and books. Buy a postcard, sit down on a bench to write it, and drop it off at the post office a few doors away.

Next to Balboa Pavilion is where you board for your forty-five-minute nar-rated **harbor cruise** on the Mississippi-style riverboats, the *Pavilion Queen* and the *Pavilion Paddy,* which depart every half hour from 10:00 A.M. to 7:00 P.M. (in win-ter from 11:00 A.M. to 3:00 P.M.; fare). You can take better photos and probably see a bit more up on the sundeck. During the cruise, which focuses on famous past or present movie stars' and celebrities' homes and luxury yachts berthed here, you see where John Wayne, Newport Beach's most famous resident, lived and anchored his boat, the *Wild Goose;* pass James Cagney's house and Joan Crawford's boat, the *Queen of Sheba;* and cruise past unpretentious million-dollar bayfront mansions with swimming pools, twenty-five-car garages, bowling alleys, and the like built beneath the homes due to shortage of land. At Edgar Bergen's house you see daughter Candice's (*Murphy Brown*) playhouse, a dollhouse-size sailboat.

Car ferries cross Newport Harbor in four minutes.

Drifting along on the bay, you'll see the sailboarder school with students in the water and note where Jack Benny, George Burns, and Roy Rogers and Dale Evans lived. It's a lovely cruise, with the sun dancing on the water and kayaks and other boats of all sizes crisscrossing your path. The longer, ninety-minute cruise goes out of the harbor, where the seals cavort offshore and where *Gilligan's Island* and *Treasure Island* were filmed. This is one of the country's largest marinas and the launching site of the spectacular annual Newport-Ensenada race of more than 500 yachts of all sizes.

After your harbor cruise, turn right and stroll down the oceanfront boardwalk to the **Balboa Fun Zone,** a miniature waterfront amusement park built in 1936 as an old-fashioned California seaside attraction. Watch the arcade games, ride the bumper cars, or take a turn on the Ferris wheel and small merry-go-round with its unmistakable calliope music. You'll find snack bars for ice cream and frozen yogurt as well as benches to sit on to watch the ocean or the Fun Zone action. Stop for a slice of pizza or the whole pie at Gina's Pizza or, if it's crowded, walk back a few steps to Bay Burger or Cold Stone Creamery. It's a happy scene, with boats in the water, people licking Balboa's famous chocolate-covered ice cream bars, pigeons fluttering about, skateboarders, rollerskaters, children, and strollers.

At Palm Avenue you can watch the historic Balboa ferry arrive at the pier and unload its three cars and its thirty passengers and bicyclists and pick up more of the same to sail back across the harbor for the four-minute ride to **Balboa Island** for a

modest fee. This is a nostalgic way to get to the island. The privately owned car ferries date from 1916, and probably the line of cars waiting to board began then, too.

Following Main Street back toward Balboa Beach, **Kites, Etc.,** at 711 East
Bay, is a marvel of kites of all sizes, shapes, and colors. Closed Tuesday January
through March. Across the boulevard at Balboa Pier's end, the original Ruby's
Diner has been a popular eatery since 1982. The broad beach is uncrowded, and
the water is tempting. Stretch out on the sand around the pier and watch the waves
or go for a swim. This beautiful, clean beach can be yours for the afternoon.

Along Main Street at beachside, you'll find more restaurants and shops. Balboa
Inn, at 105 Main Street, built in 1929 on the beach, with Spanish-style architecture,
was belle of the coast, a place where Errol Flynn, Howard Hughes, and other *bons
vivants* overnighted. It's been remodeled and modernized many times and is still a
popular hostelry.

DINNER: Fleming's Prime Steakhouse & Wine Bar, 455 Newport Center
Drive, Newport Beach. (949) 720–9633. Fleming's specializes in delicious steaks,
seafood, and chicken and serves more than one hundred different varieties of wine
by the glass. Dinner only.

LODGING: Newport Beach Marriott Hotel and Spa, 900 Newport Center
Drive, Newport Beach. (800) 228–9290 (reservations only); (949) 640–4000. Excellent central location near Fashion Island, with 532 large, nicely furnished guest
rooms and twenty suites with sitting areas, private patios, or balconies with views.
TV with free in-room movies, clock, hair dryer, iron and ironing board, three heated
swimming pools with spas, sauna, health club free to guests, eight lighted tennis
courts, restaurant, lounges, sushi bar, business center, and complimentary shuttle to
John Wayne Airport.

Day 2 / Morning

BREAKFAST: At **Sam and Harry's Steakhouse** at Newport Beach Marriott
Hotel and Spa. Don't let the name fool you. Enjoy the daily breakfast buffet or
order waffles, pancakes, French toast, and all types of egg dishes a la carte. Or visit
Coco's in Fashion Island, 151 Newport Center Drive, for more reasonably priced
breakfast fare, with friendly but slow service—better bring a book or your knitting
to keep you awake until your order arrives. Besides eggs and pancakes, there are
many interesting breakfast specialties and lower-priced senior specials.

Fashion Island, in sleek Newport Center and marked by Mediterranean-style
architecture, fountains, courtyards, and tree-lined walkways, features major upscale
department stores, hundreds of specialty shops, cinemas, boutiques, and many
restaurants.

The soaring, dramatic Farmer's Market Atrium Court, rimmed with fast-
fooderies, sweetshops, a deli, and a bakery, is a convenient and popular meeting
place. Shop Fashion Island Monday through Friday from 10:00 A.M. to 9:00 P.M.,

Saturday from 10:00 A.M. to 6:00 P.M., and Sunday from noon to 5:00 P.M. (800) 495–4753; (949) 721–2000 (concierge desk).

Take Newport Center Drive to the Coast Highway, turn right to Jamboree Road, and then turn left. Go over the short bridge to the small, lighthearted world of Balboa Island, which has seventy shops, galleries, cafes, and restaurants along its one main street, Marine Avenue—a funky, crowded, youth-oriented area where car traffic barely moves and parking spaces are hard to come by. Along Marine Avenue, with its tall, thick eucalyptus trees, munch on the island treat, frozen bananas dipped in chocolate, as you browse the small, trendy shops and cafes. Amelia's, with fancy grillwork, is a longtime local dinner favorite, serving fine Italian cuisine. Starbucks is always available when you need a coffee break. Also here are Hershey's market on the corner of Park, a post office, boutique, bookstore, and jewelry, souvenir, and clothing shops. Strollers stand in line for the house specialty at Dad's Donut Shop & Bakery, watch the car ferries land, or stroll around the whole island, with its small beach cottages.

LUNCH: Bayside Restaurant, 900 Bayside Drive, (949) 721–1222. American Contemporary is the flavor as you feast on the two-course "wine and dine." The excellent chicken chop-chop salad has an Asian influence. Other good dishes include the open-faced grilled chicken sandwich, salmon, salads, and pastas. Open Monday through Wednesday 11:30 A.M. to 10:00 P.M., Thursday until 10:30 P.M., Friday, Saturday, and Sunday until 11:00 P.M. Sunday Champagne brunch.

Afternoon

A special place to visit any time of year is **Roger's Gardens,** 2301 San Joaquin Hills Road, Corona del Mar. (949) 640–5800. Take Pacific Coast Highway south to MacArthur Boulevard and turn left to San Joaquin Hills Road; at the corner turn right, into the entrance. Even non-gardeners appreciate the spectacular beauty of the hundreds of colorful hanging flower baskets for which the nursery is famous. Its seasonal holiday decor in the large, well-stocked gift shop is inspiring. Pick up a brochure and garden map for self-guided tours of this seven-and-a-half-acre botanical showplace.

From here go back on MacArthur to Pacific Coast Highway and turn left (south) for a few blocks to the small, exclusive beach community of **Corona del Mar,** with its warm sands and parks that provide fine places to lounge, catch some sun, and watch Technicolor sunsets. East Coast Highway, the main street of this little city, is a long, browsable strip of boutiques, galleries, and restaurants, including noted silversmith Allan Adler's shop and the landmark, Five Crowns award-winning dinner house.

Next is **Sherman Library and Gardens,** 2647 East Pacific Coast Highway, Corona del Mar (949–673–2261), which covers an entire block in low-rise, California residential-style tan buildings. The library is a research center focusing on the development of the region. The gardens are stunning, showcasing more than 2,000 plant species in attractive settings of hanging baskets; fountains; a lattice-covered, shady planting, growing area; a serene tea garden; reflecting pools; fountains; sculptures; and tall trees—a lovely escape from the city. The gift shop has cards, baskets, and books. Admission. Open daily 10:30 A.M. to 4:00 P.M. Cafe Jardin (tea garden restaurant) open 11:30 A.M. to 2:00 P.M. Sunday brunch. Reservations are strongly suggested. Call (949) 673–0033.

Retrace your way back to Los Angeles.

There's More

Golf. Many courses open to the public, including:

Newport Beach Golf Course, 3100 Irvine Avenue, Newport Beach. (949) 852–8681. Near the airport; 18-hole executive course lighted for night play, driving range, pro golf shop, restaurant, lounge.

Hyatt Regency Newport Beach Back Bay Golf Course, 1107 Jamboree Road, Newport Beach. (949) 729–1234. This nine-hole course is perfect for a quick round of golf.

Boller Studio's Art Affairs at Sea. (949) 566–0009. Ladies! Just for you! Relax and learn how to paint as you cruise Newport Bay and the coastline. Create your own fantasy landscape and masterpiece on scheduled trips that leave from the Fun Zone. Each "art affair" is limited to six participants (women only). All art supplies provided. Four-hour cruise from 10:00 A.M. to 2:00 P.M.; includes refreshments, gourmet lunch, wines, and treats. Fee. No painting experience necessary.

Harbor cruises, whale-watching, Catalina Island cruise. Balboa Pavilion Ticket Office, Balboa. (949) 673–5245.

Orange County Museum of Art, 850 San Clemente Drive, Newport Beach. (949) 759–1122; www.ocma.net. Modern and contemporary art featured in changing exhibitions. Permanent collection focuses on post–World War II California art, including works by Richard Diebenkorn, Joe Goode, and Billy Al Bengtsen. Bookstore offers art books, artisan showcase puppets. Museum open Tuesday through Sunday, 11:00 A.M. to 5:00 P.M.; free admission on Tuesday.

Newport Harbor Nautical Museum, 151 East Coast Highway, Newport Beach. (949) 673–7863. The thematic galleries hold nearly a century of Newport Beach history in photographs, artifacts, navigational and nautical instruments, boat models, and ships in bottles. Gift shop. Open Tuesday through Sunday, 10:00 A.M. to 5:00 P.M. Donations accepted.

Newport Sports Museum. 100 Newport Center Drive, (949) 721–9333. Eight different sports-themed rooms and an interactive gym. Featured items worn by athletes of the past and present make you feel as if you are in your own "field of dreams." Open Tuesday through Sunday 10:00 A.M. to 5:00 P.M. Admission.

Marconi Automotive Museum & Foundation for Kids. 1302 Industrial Drive, (714) 258–3001. More than seventy exotic cars and motorcycles including one of a kind Ferraris, Lamborghinis, Jaguars, and Formula Race cars. This place is for all car enthusiasts who want to live life in the fast lane. Tours by appointment Monday through Friday 9:00 A.M. to 5:00 P.M. Also available for rental and special occasions.

Upper Newport Bay Ecological Preserve and Nature Preserve, Jamboree Road and Back Bay Drive. Surrounded by bluffs and cliffs that encircle Newport Back Bay, this 752-acre coastal wetland is a designated wildlife preserve. Bird-watchers can spot nearly 200 bird species; additionally, from August to April up to 30,000 birds are present, including many endangered species. Popular for biking, hiking, fishing, boating, and horseback riding, with nature trails and free guided walking tours Saturday and Sunday. Information: Friends of Newport Bay, (949) 923–2290.

Special Events

January–April. Whale-watching excursions. Newport Beach. (949) 673–1434.

January. Newport Beach Restaurant Association, Restaurant Week. (877) 4NB–DINE

Mid-February. Annual Newport Beach Jazz Party. Newport Beach. (949) 759–5003.

Mid-March. Newport Beach International Film Festival. (949) 253–2880.

Toshiba Classic Golf Tournament. Newport Beach Country Club. (949) 644–9550.

April. Toshiba Senior Classic, Newport Beach Country Club. (949) 644–9550.

Newport Beach–to–Ensenada, Mexico, Yacht Race. The world's largest international yachting event. More than 500 yachts participate in this spectacular 125-mile race; watch them start from the cliffs or beach. (949) 644–1023.

May. Newport Harbor Boat Show, Newport Dunes Resort. (949) 757–5959.

Newport Beach Jazz Festival, Hyatt Regency. Advance tickets available. (949) 729–6057.

July–August. Summer concert series. Fashion Island. (949) 721–2000.

Old Glory Boat Parade. Decorated boats tour Newport Harbor. (949) 673–5070.

September. Taste of Newport, Fashion Island. (949) 729–4400.

November. Menorah-lighting ceremony. Fashion Island. (949) 721–2000.

Tree Lighting Ceremony, Fashion Island. (949) 721–2000.

November 6. Christmas Fantasy at Roger's Gardens. (949) 640–5800.

Mid-December. Newport Harbor Christmas Boat Parade. More than 200 color-fully decorated and lighted boats tour the harbor. (949) 729–4400.

Other Recommended Restaurants and Lodgings

Newport Beach

The Cannery Restaurant, 3010 Lafayette Avenue. (949) 566–0000. The old cannery was razed and reopened as an architectural-award-winning restaurant using recy-cled machinery, catwalks, and other equipment as authentic decor. Dine over Newport Harbor and watch boats drift dreamily past as you enjoy steaks, seafood, or items from the sushi bar. Sunday champagne brunch. Later, browse the Cannery Village shops and galleries.

The Arches, 3334 West Coast Highway. (949) 645–7077. Handsome, comfortable restaurant—a local tradition since 1922 for good food, though a bit pricey. New York steak sandwich, seafood specialties, Caesar salad prepared tableside.

Hyatt Regency Newport Beach, 1107 Jamboree Road. (800) 233–1234; (949) 729–1234. Lush tropical landscaping and relaxed feeling in rambling low-rise build-ings built in 1961 on twenty-six acres overlooking Newport's Back Bay. Newly renovated; offers 403 nicely furnished rooms, twelve suites with minibar and refrig-erator, TV, free in-room movies, room service, three swimming pools, whirlpools, 9-hole executive golf course, sixteen lighted tennis courts, fitness room, jogging paths, two restaurants, two lounges. Seasonal golf and getaway packages. Complimentary airport shuttle to John Wayne Airport.

The Balboa Bay Club & Resort, 1221 West Coast Highway. (888) 445–7153; (949) 654–5000. Nostalgic, elegant resort, beautifully refurbished, offers 160 rooms, including ten suites, swimming pool, spa with a variety of treatments. One restau-rant, lounge, fitness center, TV, DVD, and Internet access.

Newport Dunes Waterfront Resort, 1131 Back Bay Drive. (800) 765–7661; (949) 729–3863. Upscale RV park on one hundred acres, with full hookups, marina, indi-vidual picnic areas, swimming pool and spa, fitness center, clubhouse, showers, laun-dry facilities, restrooms. There's a grocery store/marketplace, and satellite twenty-four-hour security. Launch area; bring your own boat or rent one here.

For More Information

Newport Beach Conference and Visitors Bureau, 3300 West Coast Highway, Newport Beach, CA 92663. (800) 942–6278; (949) 722–1611; www.newport beach-cob.com.

SOUTHERN ESCAPE TWO

Swallows and Sunshine

Laguna Beach, Dana Point, San Juan Capistrano / 1 Night

This two-day seaside jaunt takes you to Southern California's most popular artists' enclave. In this small, friendly oceanside village, you'll visit galleries and a museum, enjoy superb water sports and wide beaches, go shopping, and relax in a coffee pub. You'll also wander through a romantic, historic port and continue on to the world-famous mission where the swallows return every year.

☐ Beaches

☐ Surfing

☐ Art galleries

☐ Museum

☐ Water sports

☐ Historic Port

☐ Marinas

☐ Mission

Day 1 / Morning

Drive south on I–5, Santa Ana Freeway, passing the **Citadel Outlet Stores,** where you can pick up some designer bargains. You pass Anaheim and Disneyland. After Tustin, exit onto Highway 133 south, which becomes Laguna Canyon Road and winds down to Pacific Coast Highway and Laguna Beach.

Laguna Beach has been called the quintessential casual Southern California beach town, a small, unfettered, happy, and sunny place where houses roost atop steep ocean cliffs and where curving, narrow streets are graced with tall eucalyptus trees planted by pioneer homesteaders.

Busy Pacific Coast Highway, the main thoroughfare cutting through the city alongside the ocean, is flanked by a multitude of shops, restaurants, hotels, and businesses. Laguna Beach is as well known for its beautiful beaches and nonpareil surfing and other water sports as it is for its art galleries.

With its mild climate and windblown landscape of ocean and bluffs, Laguna Beach has been a successful artists' enclave since the early 1900s, when thirty or so artists began straggling in by horse and buggy or stagecoach. They came to paint the spectacularly scenic hills and untamed surf, and they tried to capture the clear and changing light in the manner of the French impressionists. But one doesn't have to be a Gauguin to appreciate the considerable natural beauty of Laguna Beach's 7-mile rocky canyon and craggy cliffs, which plunge dramatically some 40 feet down to the restless ocean. Though lively throughout the year, the little city fairly overflows with throngs of visitors during its annual eight-week summer art

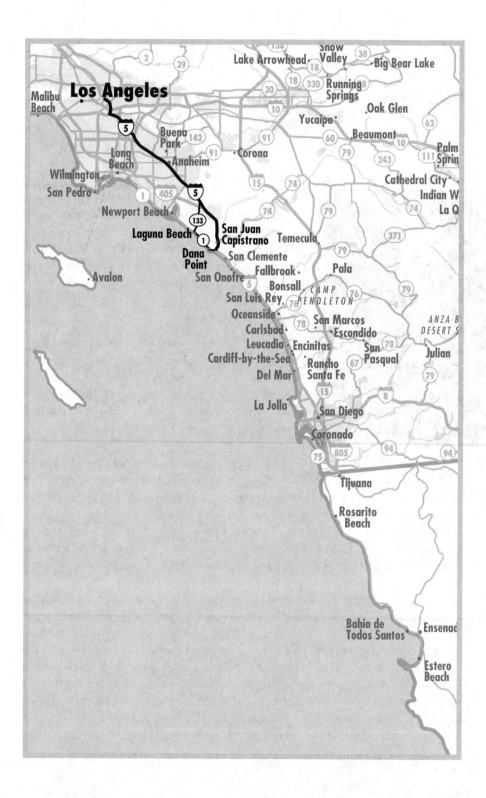

festivals, which attract about three million people (see "Special Events" at the end of this chapter).

LUNCH: The Terrace Cafe, Hotel Laguna, 425 South Coast Highway, Laguna Beach. (949) 494–1151. In the middle of the village, the sun-filled cafe, mere yards from the bounding surf, is unbeatable for a midday break and sunset viewing. Menu selections range from hamburgers, pizza, and salads to seafood and sautéed chicken.

Afternoon

One of Laguna Beach's most pleasant small-town aspects is its intimate size. You can walk everywhere, which is a good thing since parking spaces are hard to find. Stroll **Forest Avenue,** Laguna Beach's tree-shaded main street and gallery row, which expresses the city's friendly atmosphere in its bustle of people, flowers, sidewalk cafes, architecturally attractive multistory plazas, art galleries, restaurants, and boutiques. Banana Republic has women's fashions, and Thee Foxes Trot, at 260, features handcrafted home and personal accessories. Scandia Bakery and Deli, which sells bulk coffees and lunch, buzzes with hungry patrons.

Hollywood discovered Laguna Beach's photogenic attributes during the silent-film era, when moviemakers D. W. Griffith, Mack Sennett, and other legendary innovators substituted its craggy coastline for such foreign locales as the French Riviera, Hawaii, and Italian and Greek coastal villages. Errol Flynn's *Captain Blood* was shot near Three Arch Bay, *Robinson Crusoe* was filmed here in 1922, and many scenes in Harold Lloyd's movies took place on Forest Avenue. Between 1913 and 1930 more than fifty silent movies were filmed in Laguna Beach.

Through the years many Hollywood stars, authors, and other creative people have found the city to be a perfect escape. Among former residents are Mary Pickford, Bette Davis, Judy Garland, Rudolph Valentino, Charlie Chaplin, and Mickey Rooney. John Steinbeck wrote *Tortilla Flat* while hunkered down at 540 Park Avenue; Tennessee Williams was a pinsetter at the bowling alley. Many prominent celebrities still call Laguna home.

In the heart of downtown, at Broadway and Coast Highway, **Main Beach Park** resembles a sunlit, nostalgic Norman Rockwell painting of young, happy, sun-bronzed people enjoying themselves on the beach. This is the most "fun" beach for all ages, a place where everyone meets and mingles and plays basketball and volleyball, the bikini bunch swims and sunbathes, and towheaded kids soar on the swings.

Drive a few blocks north on Pacific Coast Highway, turning left on Cliff Drive to number 307, the **Laguna Art Museum** (949–494–8971), on a hilltop corner overlooking the ocean and beach. Site of the first gallery built in Laguna Beach, in 1929 for the Laguna Beach Art Association, the museum was extensively expanded and renovated in 1986. Its permanent collection focuses on the 1890–1920 period of California impressionist painters; changing exhibits are offered as well. The

Museum Store sells art books, stationery, and jewelry. (Open daily 11:00 A.M. to 5:00 P.M.; closed Thanksgiving, Christmas, and New Year's Day; admission; kids twelve and under free.)

Drive around to the right past the museum to **Heisler Park,** overlooking the ocean. Its long, narrow, grassy terrace edges the oceanside cliff above two of the city's most popular diving beaches—Bird Rock and Diver's Cove—and luminous turquoise bays. There's no finer spot for picnics, barbecues, sunset-watching, or sitting on a bench looking out at little boats on the horizon. The small, rustic gazebo, frequently used for weddings, offers closer viewing of the ocean and surfers below.

DINNER: Dizz's As Is, 2794 South Coast Highway, Laguna Beach. (949) 494–5250. Tucked in a small wooden cottage, typical Laguna style, this cozy, informal dinner hangout serves first-rate cuisine amid an eclectic 1930s and 1940s art deco style, photos of Marilyn Monroe, antique radios, and the like. International menu spotlights filet mignon with béarnaise sauce, rack of lamb, fresh seafood. Terrace dining. Closed Monday.

LODGING: Surf and Sand Resort, 1555 South Coast Highway, Laguna Beach. (800) 524–8621 (nationwide); (949) 497–4477. At the southerly edge of town away from the hubbub, this favorite getaway has the Aquaterra spa, featuring "couples rituals," and offers 165 luxurious oceanfront rooms, suites, and penthouses with private balconies, minibar, refrigerator, in-room safe, marble bath, whirlpool tub, and hair dryer. Heated swimming pool, Jacuzzi, restaurant, complimentary daily newspaper. Seasonal rates. Overnight parking fee.

Day 2 / Morning

BREAKFAST: Splashes Restaurant, in Surf and Sand Resort, a sophisticated room with glass-topped tables, a cedar-beamed ceiling, and doors opening to the languid surf. Start your day with a power breakfast—order Swedish pancakes, oat bran waffles, *huevos rancheros,* or grilled salmon with poached eggs and spinach.

Drive south about 5 miles along Pacific Coast Highway to historic **Dana Point,** with its boats dancing in the harbor, awesome cliffs, and dreamy beaches. Turn right at Golden Lantern to **Mariner's Village,** where dozens of smart specialty shops and restaurants are connected by dining terraces and dockside walkways.

With 2,500 yachts and a sportfishing and charter fleet residing in two sunny marinas, a slender white forest of masts swaying in the soft briny breeze invites you to linger a while in this delightful romantic setting. Listen to the ships' bells and the water slapping against the docks as trim pleasure boats glide in and out of the harbor.

LUNCH: The Beach House, 25001 Dana Drive, Dana Point. (949) 496–7310. Lunch is refreshing beneath a patio umbrella at the water's edge, with choice of sandwiches, seafood, and salads; Sunday champagne brunch.

Replica of the 1835 brig Pilgrim *in Dana Point Harbor.*

Afternoon

The area is named for author Richard Harding Dana, a young Harvard law student who went to sea to improve his delicate health and wrote a successful book, *Two Years Before the Mast,* exposing the severe hardships of life at sea during the 1800s and also describing the ports he visited. When his two-masted brigantine *Pilgrim* sailed into San Juan Port in 1835, Dana called the sheltered cove and promontory surrounded by tall protective bluffs "the only romantic spot in California." The book was made into a movie starring Alan Ladd.

In 1971 the old anchorage was transformed into a popular recreation-oriented marina with a New England seacoast theme in honor of Dana's birthplace. At **Dana Wharf** watch the sportfishing boats set out mornings and afternoons for adventures at sea, or join a narrated harbor cruise. Or just relax on a bench along cobbled walk ways, where anglers throw lines over the railing and fish, while you settle back to daydream about tall ships drifting into the peaceful harbor.

Follow along Dana Point Harbor Drive past the small park and go over the bridge to **Dana Island** to see the large bronze statue of the author-seaman on a tall pedestal facing the cliffs. Then continue on Dana Point Harbor Drive around the bend of the water, where the 121-foot gleaming replica of Dana's brig, *Pilgrim,* stands tall in the calm water beneath the 400-foot, wind-eroded tawny cliffs mentioned in his book. Tours available.

Alongside, the **Ocean Institute,** at 24200 Dana Point Harbor Drive (949–496–2274), offers tours of the ship and is a unique oceanographic educational facility with many exhibits (open Monday through Friday, 8:00 A.M. to 5:00 P.M.). **Doheny State Beach,** adjacent to the harbor, is California's most popular reserved camping park, with a long, wide beach and great swimming and surfing.

For the 3-mile run to **San Juan Capistrano,** head out Dana Point Drive, which turns into Del Obispo Street, which takes you into San Juan Capistrano; turn left on Camino Capistrano and proceed to the mission.

This quiet, small, sun-filled city was founded when the mission was built in 1776, and their history runs together. San Juan Capistrano was a drowsy little farming pueblo that grew oranges and walnuts. But during the 1930s townspeople began noticing the yearly March 19 return of flocks of tiny swallows that nested in the eaves of the old mission, stayed until October, then flew away.

It didn't take long before crowds of visitors began arriving every spring to witness this yearly phenomenon. The popular song "When the Swallows Come Back to Capistrano" aroused national interest in the small town.

Mission San Juan Capistrano, on Ortega Highway at Camino Capistrano (949–234–1300), is called the "Mission of the Swallows." It was founded by Father Junípero Serra and is the seventh in the chain of California missions. Ask for a map as you enter, and try to allow sufficient time to explore the spacious, ten-acre grounds. The mission survived the 1812 earthquake, though its Great Stone Church was destroyed.

During California's Mexican rule, when all missions and their lands were confiscated, San Juan Capistrano became part of a large rancho. The mission was auctioned off to a family, who lived there for twenty years, until the U.S. government returned it to the Catholic church. Though the town grew, the mission was completely abandoned until 1895, when restoration was begun.

Beyond the entry plaza, gravel paths lead to the broad courtyards and statue of Father Serra and a young Native American boy. Look for swallows' nests up under the eaves. Two nests are visible at the north corridor at the western end of the building. But you'll see many other historic sights and treasures in the old mission: the ancient graceful arches with the smooth worn stones beneath your feet; the rose garden and fountain; the strutting white pigeons; the gnarled, one-hundred-year-old pepper tree beside the padre's quarters; the huge millstone, used for grinding wheat and corn into flour and crushing olives for cooking oil and fuel for lanterns; and the sacred garden with its historic bells.

Three museum rooms and a bookstore contain archaeological finds and ancient artifacts. In Serra Chapel, built in 1777 and restored in the early 1920s, you can feel a strong tug of the past. It is the oldest building still in use in California and the only remaining chapel of the missions where Father Serra said Mass. In the long, narrow chapel, with its 22-foot-high ceiling, paintings depict the Stations of the Cross. The shining reed organ dates from 1892, and the gilded cherrywood altar from Spain is more than 300 years old. The mission is open daily 8:30 A.M. to 5:00 P.M. (closed Thanksgiving and Christmas; open 8:30 A.M. to noon on Christmas Eve and Good Friday). Open later in the summer. (Admission.)

When the swallows return every March 19 to build their nests, the sacred garden bells are rung and a week-long fiesta begins. Weekends are crowded year-round, but far more visitors arrive during spring. The birds remain to care for their young until October 23, when they begin their 6,000-mile journey back to Argentina.

You've still time to browse and shop along **Camino Capistrano,** the city's small main street. Ortega's Capistrano Trading Post, at number 31741, is a large, barn-red corner store selling Native American jewelry, souvenirs, and gifts. Moonrose, at 26715 Verdugo Street, has interesting wind chimes, candles, antiques, jewelry, books, and music.

Every Sunday at 1:00 P.M., the Historical Society provides guided walking tours of the Los Rios Historic District adobes, built in the late 1700s and early 1800s. Tours begin at El Peon Plaza, across from the mission (fee).

Return to Los Angeles via I–5 North.

There's More

Shopping. The Pottery Shack, 1212 South Coast Highway, Laguna Beach. (949) 494–1141. With huge, lifelike deer on its roof, the place has been a "must-see" shopping landmark since 1936 for fine china, glassware, and gifts.

La Rue du Chocolat, 448 South Coast Highway, Laguna Beach. (949) 494–2372. Nestled in a tiny tree-lined alcove, this mouth-watering candy store sells white and dark chocolate delicacies, including turtles, truffles, nuts and chews, and chocolate-dipped strawberries. Souvenir shopping? Buy a chocolate sandal!

Village Faire Shoppes, 1100 South Coast Highway, Laguna Beach. Ethnic restaurants, antiques, galleries, trendy fashions, and more in this large open-air shopping-dining complex.

Surfing. Bird Rock, below Heisler Park, Cliff Drive in Laguna Beach; has the biggest waves.

Bodysurfing. Victoria Beach, West Street Beach, and Crescent Bay, all in Laguna Beach.

Diving. Glen E. Vedder Preserve, at Bird Rock, below Heisler Park in Laguna Beach. Good for reef diving.

Wood's Cove, 1 mile south of Main Beach, in Laguna Beach. Tree-kelp dives; made for scuba divers.

For other locations and diving and surfing conditions, call (949) 494–4573.

Golf. Aliso Creek Golf Club, 31105 South Coast Highway, Laguna Beach. (949) 499–1919. Nine-hole public course, clubhouse, Canyon Lodge American Grill restaurant.

Monarch Beach Golf Course, 33080 Niguel Road, Dana Point. (949) 240–0247. Eighteen-hole public course overlooking the ocean.

Bicycle rentals. Revo Cycles, 34155 Pacific Coast Highway, Dana Point. (949) 496–1995.

Boat cruises. Aventura Sailing Association, Dana Point Harbor. (949) 493–9493. Skipper charters.

Harbor tours. Dana Island Yachts, Dana Point Harbor. (949) 248–7400.

Sportfishing, whale-watching, parasailing. Dana Wharf Sportfishing, Dana Point Harbor. (949) 496–5794.

O'Neill Museum, 31831 Los Rios Street, San Juan Capistrano. (949) 493–8444. This wooden Victorian-era residence, built in the 1880s, has been restored and refurnished as San Juan Capistrano's Historical Society office. On display are old photographs and Native American artifacts. Closed Monday and Saturday.

Special Events

Mid-February, early March, late April, mid-May, and mid-June. Laguna Craft Guild art festivals, Laguna Beach.

Mid-February–early March. Street Fair, Dana Point Plaza, Dana Point. (800) 290–DANA; (949) 496–1556.

Early March. Annual Patriot's Day Parade, Laguna Beach downtown village area. 11:00 A.M. to 1:00 P.M. (949) 494–1018.

Mid-March. Annual Festival of Whales, Street Faire, Ocean Awareness Day, Dana Point. (888) 440–4309.

The Kids Pet Parade, Fiesta Association. (949) 493–1976.

Return of the Swallows and Heritage Fair Fiesta, San Juan Capistrano. (949) 234–1322.

Swallows Day/St. Joseph's Day, annual Swallows Day Parade and Mercado, San Juan Capistrano. (949) 234–1300.

Beginning of April. Artwalk Studio Tours, Laguna Beach. (949) 494–3030. Tour the private studios of more than sixty artists and enjoy a reception at Sawdust Festival grounds.

Mid-April. Monthly Laguna Beach Film Society film screenings, open to the public. (949) 494–8971.

Annual Laguna Beach Music Festival. (949) 376–6000.

May. Heritage Month, guided walks of historical areas, Laguna Beach. (949) 497–0320.

Mid-May. Annual Laguna Charm House Tour, Laguna Beach. Buses leave from the Festival of Arts grounds, 650 Laguna Canyon, (800) 877–1115. Blues Festival, Dana Point, noon to 5:30 P.M. at Doheny Beach.

Annual Chili Cook-Off, Swallows Inn, San Juan Capistrano. (949) 493–3188.

Beginning of June. In-Water Boat Show, Dana Point. Viewing of new and used boats for enthusiasts of all ages. Entertainment, seminars, and food. (949) 496–1094.

Mid-June. Men's Volleyball Open, Laguna Beach.

June–September. Art-a-Fair, Laguna Beach. Juried show open to artists from everywhere. Sculpture, stained glass, and paintings featured. (949) 494–4514.

July. Fourth of July Fireworks Extravaganza, Dana Point.

Laguna Plein Air Painters Association (LPAPA) Annual Plain Air Painting Competition Invitational, Laguna Beach. Watch fifty top American outdoor painters interpret the beauty of Laguna Beach. Contact art museum for date and location (949–376–3635).

July–September. Eight-week art celebration, from Fourth of July weekend through end of August, at Laguna Beach; admission varies. Events include the Festival of Arts, a juried art show featuring the area's finest artists and craftspeople; the Pageant of the Masters, a nightly event wherein live models re-create great works of art in paintings, sculpture, tapestries, and porcelain (800–487–3378; 949–494–1145); the Sawdust Festival, an unjuried show of local artists and craftspeople (949–494–3030); and Art-a-Fair (see separate listing above).

Mid-July, mid-August, and mid-September. Capistrano Valley Symphony Orchestra concert, Marriott Laguna Cliffs Resort, Dana Point.

Mid-July. Women's Volleyball Open, Laguna Beach.

July–October. Music Under the Stars, Mission San Juan Capistrano. (949) 234–1321.

Early September. Tall Ships Festival, Dana Point. Doheny Days Music Festival, Dana Point at Doheny Beach.

Early October. Laguna Beach Annual Film Festival at Festival of Arts grounds, 650 Laguna Canyon Road.

Late October. Farewell to the Swallows, San Juan Capistrano.

Thanksgiving Day. Annual Turkey Trot, 5 and 10K Fun Run, Dana Point.

Early December. Santa's Arrival and Hospitality Night, Laguna Beach. For specific dates call the Laguna Beach Chamber of Commerce at (800) 877–1115.

Other Recommended Restaurants and Lodgings

Laguna Beach

Las Brisas, 361 Cliff Drive. (949) 497–4955. The blue-umbrella'd dining terrace above Main Beach is a popular luncheon and late-afternoon rendezvous, bubbly with that chic French Riviera look. Mexican cuisine emphasizes fresh seafood but also grilled New York steak with borracho beans. Stay for the sunsets. More formal dining inside. Sunday brunch.

Cedar Creek Inn, 384 Forest Avenue. (949) 497–8696. Great-looking French country atmosphere with fireplace and busy bar. From lunch salads, sandwiches, and pastas to dinner steak, prime rib, chicken, and pasta entrees. Free on-site garage parking.

Hotel Laguna, 425 Coast Highway. (800) 524–2927 (in California); (949) 494–1151. Ideally located in the center of town on its private beach, adjacent to Main Beach Park; sixty-five rooms, most of which have been upgraded in this century-old hotel. Two restaurants; lounge; continental breakfast is included in the room rate and served in a hospitality suite on your floor. Valet parking (fee) and complimentary newspaper. Seasonal rates.

Inn at Laguna Beach, 211 North Pacific Coast Highway. (800) 544–4479 (reservations); (949) 497–9722. Opened in 1990 on the hillside just below the museum, overlooking Main Beach. Seventy deluxe rooms, private balconies, TV, VCR, honor bar, minirefrigerator, hair dryer, coffeemaker, bathrobes, ceiling fans, CD player; most rooms include microwave ovens. Heated swimming pool and spa. Complimentary continental breakfast served in your room with daily newspaper. Seasonal rates.

Dana Point

Cannon's Restaurant & Terrace, 34344 Green Lantern. (949) 496–6146. That romantic view over the harbor just doesn't quit. The lunch bunch goes for Cajun chicken sandwiches, excellent Cobb salad; the dinner bunch, for the grilled salmon with lobster tails. Sunday brunch.

Laguna Cliffs Marriott Resort and Spa, 25135 Park Lantern. (800) 533–9748 (United States and Canada); (949) 661–5000. Rambling, Cape Cod–style resort on forty-two acres of lawn and flowers; 377 rooms; seventeen suites with TV, minibar, hair dryer, robes; two heated swimming pools, spa, health club; one lighted tennis court; restaurant and lounge. Two- and three-night packages offer various complimentary amenities.

The Montage Resort & Spa, 30801 Coast Highway. (888) 715–6700; (949) 715–6000. New in 2003, this resort's luxurious accommodations and spectacular views reflect Laguna's Craftsman-inspired architecture. The 262 rooms, including fifty-one suites, have marble bath, ocean view, private patio, robes, hair dryer, French bath amenities, flat-screen TV, DVD, and CD player. Also a 20,000-square-foot indoor/outdoor oceanfront spa, three restaurants, three pools, fitness center. Various packages available.

The St. Regis Monarch Beach Resort & Spa, 1 Monarch Beach Resort. (800) 722–1543; (949) 234–3200. Opened in 2001 along 172 oceanfront acres; 400 guest rooms and suites, most with ocean views from spacious balconies. Luxe amenities include marble baths, goose-down comforters, robes and slippers, private safes; four restaurants; luxury spa with salon and fitness center; 18-hole golf course, seven lighted tennis courts, four swimming pools. Outstanding Sunday buffet brunch. Various packages. Overnight parking fee.

The Ritz Carlton, Laguna Niguel, One Ritz Carlton Drive. (800) 241–3333 (reservations); (949) 240–2000. Luxurious, pricey eighteen-acre resort atop a 152-foot ocean bluff; 393 guest rooms, thirty-one suites with private balconies, two bathrooms, hair dryer, bathrobes, TV, honor bar, mini-refrigerator; two heated swimming pools, two Jacuzzis, four lighted tennis courts, fitness center, salon; four restaurants, lounge, library; golf nearby; overnight parking fee.

San Juan Capistrano

Sarducci's Capistrano Depot, 26701 Verdugo. (949) 493–9593. Besides sandwiches and pastas, special selections include lamb Wellington and blackened halibut with Cajun spices. Large dining patio.

El Adobe de Capistrano, 31891 Camino Capistrano. (949) 493–1163. Noted for good Mexican food; Sunday champagne brunch.

Best Western Capistrano Inn, 27174 Ortega Highway. (800) 441–9438; (949) 493–5661. Features 108 units, in-room coffee, some kitchenettes; heated swimming pool, spa. Laundry room. Daily and seasonal rates.

Mission Inn (motel), 26891 Ortega Highway. (949) 234–0249. Across from the mission; twenty-one rooms, all with microwave oven, refrigerator, in-room coffeemaker, VCR; heated swimming pool, Jacuzzi. On four acres with sixty-five orange trees; picking encouraged.

For More Information

Laguna Beach Visitors Bureau, 252 Broadway, Laguna Beach, CA 92651. (800) 877–1115, ext. 0.

Laguna Beach Chamber of Commerce, 357 Glenneyre, Laguna Beach, CA 92651. (949) 494–1018, ext. 5; www.lagunabeachchamber.org.

Dana Point Chamber of Commerce, P.O. Box 12, Dana Point, CA 92629. (800) 290–3262; (949) 496–1555; www.danapoint-chamber.com.

Dana Point Harbor Association, P.O. Box 548, Dana Point, CA 92629. (949) 496–6040.

San Juan Capistrano Chamber of Commerce, 31781 Camino Capistrano, Suite 306, Franciscan Plaza, San Juan Capistrano, CA 92693. (949) 493–4700.

Mission Visitor Center, 31882 Camino Capistrano, San Juan Capistrano, CA 92693. (949) 234–1300; www.missionsjc.com.

Flower-Filled Seaside

Carlsbad, Encinitas, Del Mar / 1 Night

One of Southern California's greatest assets is its beautiful and inviting coastline, bordered by wide, secluded beaches with gentle surf and small, slower-paced villages with fine restaurants and world-class accommodations. This two-day itinerary covers a little more than 100 miles as it takes you south to a small and charming European-style seaside village with a major amusement park; through the "Flower Capital of the World," where in spring and fall hillsides are ablaze with millions of poinsettias, ranunculas, and gladioli; and to a quiet but posh coastal community noted for its celebrity racetrack and county fair.

☐ Uncrowded beaches

☐ Surfing

☐ Fine dining

☐ Antiques

☐ Legoland

☐ Flowers

☐ Fairs

☐ Horse racing/ horse shows

☐ Hot-air ballooning

Day 1 / Morning

Drive south on I–5, past Anaheim and Santa Ana, and then follow the coastline, continuing through San Clemente, which was Richard Nixon's Western White House, and passing the San Onofre Nuclear Generating Station on the beach. It is then a 20-mile drive alongside **Camp Pendleton,** the largest U.S. amphibious Marine Corps training base in the world. Guided group tours of at least twenty people are available on the first and last Tuesday of each month. Reservations must be made at least sixty days in advance (706–725–4111). As you continue your coastal drive, you'll see drowsy lagoons and farms reaching to the sea. Following Oceanside, take the Carlsbad Village Drive exit, turn right toward the ocean, and turn left on Pacific Coast Highway. Continue about 0.5 mile and you're at the ocean. The heart of Carlsbad Village is just up the road.

Carlsbad, known as the "Village by the Sea," has an Old European style—a friendly small town with the ocean at its front door, clear soft air, and blue skies, a place where visitors come for a day and stay for weeks or months.

You'll want to stroll Carlsbad's uncrowded beaches, swim and surf in its calm water, unwind watching fiery sunsets over the horizon, and discover restaurants and fine lodgings. The small, attractive downtown village area, with sidewalk cafes,

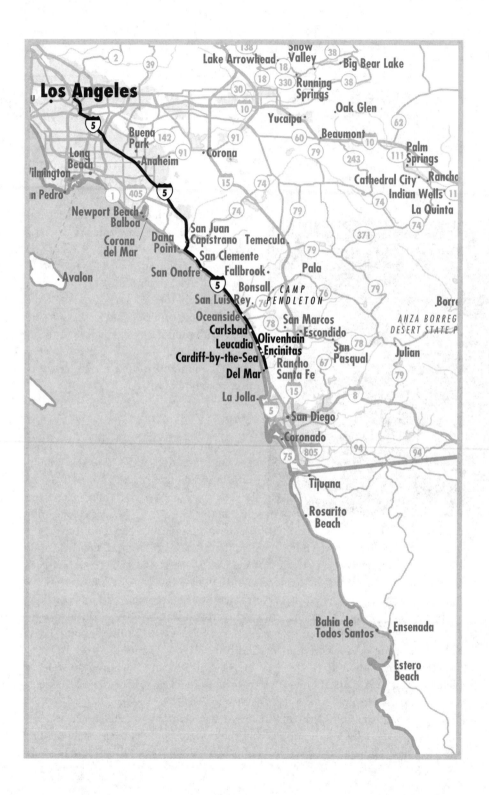

fountains, benches, and flowers, was named for a health spa in Karlsbad, Bohemia. In 1883 a farmer's well tapped both artesian and mineral water, which the farmer then sold to parched railroad passengers, who found it palatable. A hotel was built near the well, and guests indulged in mineral baths. Later, when the water was analyzed and found to contain properties similar to those of the European spa, the spelling was Americanized and the city became Carlsbad.

Among other delights is **Legoland Park,** 1 Lego Drive, Carlsbad. (760) 438–LEGO; www.legoland.com. The popular amusement park sprawled over 128 acres is designed for kids ages two to twelve. Throughout its seven different themed areas—Fun Town, Explorer Village, Knight's Kingdom, Miniland, Dino Island, Imagination Zone, and the Beginning—Legoland uniquely features the small plastic interlocking Lego bricks, the ingenious Danish construction toy we've all tripped over. Legoland's fifty exciting rides, attractions, shops, and restaurants provide daylong fun and action: Kids can ride on three roller coasters, including the Coastersaurus; go on Safari Trek; visit Dig Those Dinos, where junior paleontologists can learn about skeletons and fossils while getting soaked at Raptor Splash; and check out the new attractions, Knight's Tournament, Block of Fame, Fun Town Fire Academy, and Miniland Florida. Crowded on weekends. Admission. Hours and days vary according to season. AAA discounts; also 10 percent discount at Carlsbad Visitors Bureau.

Carlsbad's twice-yearly **Village Faires,** held on the first Sunday in May and November, are California's largest street fairs. Although the railroad doesn't stop here any longer, the old-fashioned, 1887 depot is now home of the Carlsbad Convention & Visitors Bureau. The city is also the home of the plush, internationally known celebrity favorite La Costa Resort and Spa, about 3 miles inland.

A historic reminder of the town's beginning is the site of Frazier's Well, in front of the **Alte Karlsbad Hanse House,** 2802 Carlsbad Boulevard. The three-story, half-timbered, medieval-style building, which resembles part of a foreign-movie set, is now a luxe mineral water spa.

LUNCH: Neimans Restaurant, 300 Carlsbad Village Drive, Carlsbad. (760) 729–4131. The town's centerpiece is this 1802, refurbished three-story gray-and-white landmark mansion, complete with turrets, cupolas, and flags waving from towers. It was formerly the home of a city co-founder and a popular overnight inn during the 1920s. Lunch in the bright American Bar & Cafe lends itself to sandwiches, pastas, and chicken. The Neimanburger is a charbroiled top sirloin served on sourdough. Sunday champagne buffet brunch is outstanding.

Afternoon

Browse through Victorian-style **Village Faire** shops behind the restaurant.

Carlsbad's **State Street** is noted for its antiques and is a magnet for treasure hunters and decorators. The 3 blocks between Oak Street and Laguna Drive have about twenty-five antiques shops along both sides of the street, with some outdoor galleries as well. Among those starting north from Oak Street are the Lion & the Lamb Cottage of Dolls and Bears (3060) and the Carlsbad Village Art & Antique Mall (2752), in the 15,000-square-foot Mural Building, featuring more than one hundred artists and dealers, open 10:30 A.M. to 5:00 P.M.

Take time to stroll around this sparkling, compact village area packed with a variety of restaurants, shops, and streets named for presidents. Then drive or walk back to the ocean just across Carlsbad Boulevard. Its paved seawall or sidewalk above the low ocean bluffs is where you can join joggers, walkers, runners, and those pushing baby strollers. Or find a bench, sit, and watch people on the beach, surfers riding the waves, pelicans doing their daredevil dives, and the magical sunsets. The beautiful beaches are uncrowded, clean, and irresistible. Follow the broad staircase leading down to the warm sand and relax as you watch the slow, easy surf rolling in.

DINNER: Coyote Bar & Grill, 300 Carlsbad Village Drive, Carlsbad. (760) 729–4695. In the Village Faire shops. With its striking decor, it's a steady favorite for tasty Southwestern cuisine. Rotisserie chicken is served with tortillas, beans, rice, *salsa fresca,* and cheddar cheese. Enjoy dinner or lunch in the good-looking dining room with cozy fireplaces or on the patio around inviting fire pits. Happy hour and nightly entertainment Monday, Thursday, and Friday.

LODGING: Tamarack Beach Resort, 3200 Carlsbad Boulevard, Carlsbad. (800) 334–2199 (United States and Canada); (760) 729–3500. Just across from the ocean; sprawling, Spanish-style architecture. Features twenty-three large hotel rooms and fifty-four one- and two-bedroom condominium suites rentable nightly or weekly. Private balconies, honor bar/minirefrigerator, TV, VCR. Gym, heated pool, two spas; barbecues, restaurant. Seasonal rates. Hotel/guest activities include day trips to nearby attractions—Tijuana, Catalina, and so on—plus complimentary wine-and-cheese parties and reduced dining rates to select village restaurants.

Day 2 / Morning

BREAKFAST: Mariah's West Wind Restaurant, 377 Carlsbad Village Drive, Carlsbad. (760) 729–6040. Pancake specialties, breakfast combinations, and 150 omelette suggestions. Patio dining. Open daily 7:00 A.M. to 2:00 P.M.

With its mild climate, Carlsbad has been a major flower-growing center since the 1920s, when its flower and bulb industry of gladioli, ranunculas, and irises began and was commercially successful. From mid-March through April, the fifty-acre Flower Fields on the hillsides behind windmill-shaped Andersen's Inn and Restaurant are an explosion of multicolored ranunculas. The city became a prime avocado-growing center after a nurseryman planted the first avocado groves in 1916 and developed different varieties. Other avocado growers followed and prospered through 1948. But when water shortages arose, growers began selling their land to developers for better profit than farming offered. The first bird of paradise flowers were grown here after seeds planted in greenhouses were transferred to an old avocado grove; the exotic bird of paradise is now Carlsbad's official city flower, appearing in colorful sidewalk and building murals.

The drive south on Carlsbad Boulevard to Encinitas and Del Mar is more pleasant along the ocean than on the freeway, despite the San Diego Gas and Electric Power station that intrudes on the lovely coastal vistas. At times it seems that everyone is on holiday. The bike path has plenty of pedalers, anglers fish at the water's edge, and other people swim and wade in the calm frothy surf or relax on the uncrowded beach and watch large brown pelicans dive-bomb like arrows into the water. **South Carlsbad State Beach,** where colorful umbrellas dot the beach, is popular with campers.

Seasonally, this coastal highway explodes with dazzling yellow, orange, and purple ranunculas and other multicolored flowers grown in the area. A roadside grove of tall, noble eucalyptus trees ushers you into **Leucadia, Encinitas, Cardiff-by-the-Sea,** and **Olivenhain.** These four small cities were consolidated in 1986 as the city of Encinitas, though each retains its individual attractions and lifestyle.

In the 1870s Leucadia's early settlers were English spiritualists seeking freedom of worship, and they named their community after a Greek island whose name means "paradise." Many streets have names of Greek gods. The 1881 founder of Encinitas gave his town a Spanish name meaning "little live oaks." When Cardiff was homesteaded in 1875, its developer named it after a large city in Wales. Olivenhain was settled in 1884 by a small group of Germans; their old meeting hall is one of its attractions.

With Encinitas's millions of commercially grown gladioli, ranunculas, and poinsettias, the area has been dubbed "Flower Capital of the World."

Along this lively road are cafes, lodgings, many antiques stores (D Street), and the Self-Realization Fellowship Retreat and Hermitage. First Street has a strip of Italian restaurants and the good-looking Lumberyard Center's restaurants and shops.

The fine beaches along here are known for great surfing and provide scenic views from the bluffs. The train whistles right through Encinitas, where Moonlight Beach is a favorite family picnic area. These are all wonderful little beach towns you will want to revisit and explore.

Continue south on I–5 past acres of greenhouses, and in ten minutes you'll have arrived in **Del Mar.** Take the Via de la Valle exit to Jimmy Durante Drive (the "Schnozz" was a former resident and mayor). Turn left past the Del Mar Race Track and Fairgrounds, then drive along the town's broad main street, Camino del Mar, to 15th Street and the heart of this small, low-key, genteel town, with its old-world atmosphere and architecture.

LUNCH: Bully's, 1404 Camino Del Mar in Del Mar. (858) 755–1660. Small, dimly lighted, with roomy red leather booths and a congenial bar, Bully's is an old-fashioned steak house and the local watering hole, a place known since 1967 for consistently good food. The succulent Barbecue Beef Bones with fiery barbecue sauce and the excellent french fries are worth the trip. Other options include steaks, prime rib, chicken, seafood, burgers, salads, and sandwiches. There's patio dining in the rear.

Afternoon

Del Mar began as a beach resort town in 1885 and evolved as a vacation getaway for Los Angeles's elite. It's still easy to relax in this amiable, well-heeled residential beach city, which follows a scenic 2.5 miles of curving coastline studded with top-notch restaurants, specialty shops, and noteworthy accommodations. Del Marians also invite you to enjoy their broad beaches for great swimming, fine scuba diving, and matchless surfing atop those long tubular waves that keep rolling in from Hawaii. From sea to sky is a thrilling transition for hot-air balloon enthusiasts, who can enjoy panoramic views as they drift quietly over the glittering coastline in sunrise and sunset flights.

To see more of the city, begin your stroll along Camino del Mar at 15th Street, where you'll find **Stratford Square,** a mock-Tudor building encompassing shops and restaurants. Earthsong Bookstore favors best-sellers with celebrity book-signing parties, in addition to stocking a selection of architecture, art, and children's books. Through an archway, Ocean Song Musica Del Mar Gallery, a wonderful, offbeat boutique specializing in world music, has tables piled with fine import pieces, rugs, ethnic records, and cards.

Across the boulevard is the popular **Del Mar Plaza,** an open-air, multilevel, upscale dining and shopping center featuring men's, women's, and children's apparel; fine art; gift ideas; and fine jewelry. The Plaza's fashionable Italian-style indoor/outdoor restaurants boast smashing ocean-view terraces and chic epicurean variety. There's underground parking; an elevator is in the rear.

The city is famous as home of the **Del Mar Race Track** ("where the turf meets the surf") **and Fairgrounds.** Launched in 1937 by actors Bing Crosby and Pat O'Brien, who lived in the area and began its Hollywood glamour and celebrity status, Del Mar was established as a new playground of the stars, notably Lucille Ball and Desi Arnaz, Harry James, Betty Grable, Jimmy Durante, and Bob Hope. Del Mar buzzes in summer with the annual big Fair and Thoroughbred Racing and year-round satellite wagering.

Walk or drive downhill on 15th Street the few short blocks to the ocean, where **Seagrove Park,** with stately palm trees, overlooks the beach just a few steps down the bluff. Side by side at the beach on Coast Boulevard, two of Del Mar's waterfront dining institutions, Jakes and the Poseidon, offer beachfront terrace dining and are generally packed with seafood and steak aficionados.

Del Mar is noted for gentle surf and warm sandy beaches.

Amtrak's small (1882) beachside station, popular since bygone days when Hollywood movie stars such as Mary Pickford, Charlie Chaplin, Rudolph Valentino, Douglas Fairbanks, and other film stars and vacationers arrived from Los Angeles by train, has been moved north to Solana Beach. Passengers can taxi back to Del Mar or arrange for hotel pickup.

The wide beach with gentle waves spilling onto the sand is too hard to resist. To better savor beautiful Del Mar, you need to spend some time strolling barefoot in the sand . . . sit and relax for a while, watch the bathers, and let the sun work its magic.

Return to Los Angeles by heading back inland on Via de la Valle to connect with I–5 north.

There's More

Smith-Shipley-Magee House, 258 Beech Avenue, Carlsbad. The 1887 home of Samuel Church Smith is now headquarters for the Carlsbad Historical Society.

Shipley-Magee Barn, Magee Park, Carlsbad. Collection of old farming implements and a cistern.

St. Michael's Episcopal Church, 2775 Carlsbad Boulevard, Carlsbad. Small redwood chapel, built in 1896.

Golf production plant tour. Step-by-step tour shows how pro golf clubs are built with state-of-the-art technology and skill.

Taylor Made-Adidas, 5545 Fermi Court, Carlsbad. (760) 918–6000. Free, forty-five- to sixty-minute tours. No retail shop. Twenty-four-hour advance reservation required. Tours are held Tuesday and Thursday at 10:00 A.M.

Water sports. Snug Harbor Marina, in Agua Hedionda Lagoon, 4215 Harrison Street, Carlsbad. (760) 434–3089. Water-ski, Jet Ski, Waverunner rentals. Open daily, 9:00 A.M. to 7:00 P.M.

Golf. Rancho Carlsbad Golf Course, 5200 El Camino Real, Carlsbad. (760) 438–1772. Executive, 18-hole public course.

Museum of Making Music, 5790 Armada Drive, Carlsbad. (877) 551–9976. Unique interactive museum spans one hundred years of the music industry. Extensive exhibit of more than 450 instruments; histories of many different musical eras from classical, jazz, ragtime, the Beatles, and many more. Open Tuesday through Sunday, 10:00 A.M. to 5:00 P.M.

Leo Carrillo Ranch, 6260 Flying L Centre Lane, Carlsbad. (760) 476–1042; www .carrillo-ranch.org. Once a working ranch belonging to actor Leo Carrillo, this historic and educational resource has been preserved and restored for recreational use. Open for tours Tuesday through Saturday, 9:00 A.M. to 5:00 P.M. and Sunday, 11:00 A.M. to 5:00 P.M., later in summer.

Hot-air ballooning. Skysurfer Balloon Company Inc., 2658 Del Mar Heights, Del Mar. (858) 481–6800. Sunset flights over the scenic canyons and coastline.

Farmers' markets. Public parking lot on Roosevelt Avenue between Carlsbad Village Drive and Grand Avenue, Carlsbad Village. Call the Carlsbad Convention and Visitors Bureau (800–227–5722; 760–434–6093) for days and hours. Farmfresh and organically grown fruits and vegetables, herbs, spices, flowers.

City Hall parking lot, 1050 Camino del Mar, Del Mar. Every Saturday, 1:00 to 4:00 P.M. Fresh produce, beautiful fresh flowers, plants, honey, avocados, and eggs. Rain or shine.

Barnstorming Adventures, Ltd., 2160 Palomar Airport Road, Carlsbad. (800) 759–5667; (760) 438–7680. Don helmet and goggles and thrill to open-cockpit biplane rides with certified pilots in daily flights over the beautiful coastline.

Quail Botanical Gardens, 230 Quail Drive, Encinitas. (760) 436–3036. A thirty-acre year-round blossoming showcase of one of the world's most diverse and botanically important plant collections. Scenic walks and trails, tours. Open daily 9:00 A.M. to 5:00 P.M.; gift shop and nursery open 10:00 A.M. to 4:00 P.M. Admission.

Coast Express Rail Line. The Coaster runs daily from Oceanside to San Diego with two stops in Carlsbad. (800) 262–7837.

Carlsbad Premium Outlets. Off I–5 next to the famous Ecke Flower Fields on Paseo del Norte between Palomar Airport Road and Cannon Road, Carlsbad. (760) 804–9000. More than ninety outlets for popular designer name brands offer up to 70 percent off retail prices; restaurant and winery, fast-food eateries, and more in a charming Mediterranean village with swaying palm trees. Open daily 10:00 A.M. to 8:00 P.M.

Witch Creek Winery, 2906 Carlsbad Boulevard, Carlsbad. (760) 720–7499. In the village. The Tasting Room features handsome gift items and gourmet foods. Open daily 11:00 A.M. to 5:00 P.M.

Special Events

Late January. San Diego Marathon & Half Marathon Course, Carlsbad.

World Golf Championships: Accenture Match Play, La Costa Resort and Spa. (800) 854–5000; (858) 438–9111.

Late March and April. Flower fields in bloom.

Early April. Carlsbad Strawberry Festival.

Mid-April. Annual Encinitas Street Faire.

Late April. North San Diego Rockhoppers Volksmarch (10K walk), Carlsbad.

April to May. Del Mar National Horse Show, Del Mar Fairgrounds, Del Mar. (858) 296–1441.

First Sunday in May. Carlsbad Village Street Faire. Largest one-day street fair in California. Cinco de Mayo, Encinitas.

Late June through August. Friday evening jazz concerts in the park, Carlsbad.

Mid-June through early July. Del Mar Fair, Del Mar Fairgrounds.

Mid-July. Carlsbad Triathlon, Carlsbad.

End of July through mid-September. Thoroughbred racing, Del Mar. Closed Tuesday.

August. Annual Arts and Crafts Show, Art-in-the-Village, Carlsbad. (760) 945–9288.

September. Arts Flash. Celebration of art, music, and food. (760) 434–6093.

Early to late October. Oktoberfest, Carlsbad. Oktoberfest, Encinitas.

First Sunday in November. Carlsbad Village Street Faire. Largest one-day street fair in California.

Early December. Christmas Tree Lighting, Carlsbad. Encinitas Holiday Parade.

Other Recommended Restaurants and Lodgings

Carlsbad

The Armenian Cafe, 3126 Carlsbad Boulevard. (760) 720–2233. Small cottage features Belgian and other waffles for breakfast, plus Armenian specialties—pita bread, lamb, and so on. Closed Monday.

Daily News Cafe, 3001 Carlsbad Boulevard. (760) 729–1023. Cute menu. Omelettes, buttermilk pancakes, salads, sandwiches, freshly made croissants, cinnamon rolls, Belly Bombers (burgers). Breakfast and lunch only. Dine inside or on the busy patio. Closes at 4:00 P.M.

Jay's Gourmet Restaurant, 2975 Carlsbad Boulevard. (760) 720–9688. Opposite Neimans. Prepare to stand in line at this small, checkered-tablecloth beehive for its seafood, pizza, calzones, pastas, and veal dishes, with homemade sauces.

The Alley, 401 Grand Avenue. (760) 434–1173. By the railroad tracks. Congenial after-hours cocktails and dancing nightly.

Carlsbad Inn, 3075 Carlsbad Boulevard. (800) 235–3939 (United States and Canada); (760) 434–7020. Across from the beach in the center of town; sixty-two hotel rooms, half with kitchenettes, and 132 condominiums. In-room coffeemakers, TV, video players, cable TV; heated swimming pool, Jacuzzi, health club gym-sauna. Picnic cabana on the beach.

La Costa Resort and Spa, Costa del Mar Road. (800) 854–5000; (760) 438–9111. Internationally known luxury celebrity resort of 511 guest rooms and suites on 400 beautifully landscaped acres, starring an elegant new 43,000-square-foot indoor and outdoor spa, new clubhouse, a boutique, spa cafe, new conference facility, and ballroom. Guest rooms feature minibar-refrigerators, wall safes, hair dryers, coffeemakers, TVs, clock radios, lush terry robes/slippers, and superior service. Buffet breakfast, two restaurants, two championship golf courses, seventeen lighted tennis courts. Brand new as of June 2006 is Kidtopia, a 6,000-square-foot children's activity center and "kid's" club available to children six months to twelve years. Additionally, there is a new separate teen club, "VIBZ," for ages ten and up that features a pool table, video games, a mini-bowling alley, and a wide-screen television. Gift cards and packages are available. La Costa recently completed a $140 million renovation.

Grand Pacific Palisades Resort & Hotel, 5805 Armada Drive. (800) 725–4723 (reservations); (760) 827–3200. Adjacent to Legoland. There's not a more convenient, satisfying place to overnight while visiting Legoland than this spiffy, ocean-view, three-story, ninety-room luxury hotel with 200 time-share units. Spacious attractive rooms feature private balconies, hair dryers, clock radios, coffeemakers, irons/ironing boards, TVs, and VCRs; Olympic-size pool, water park for kids, fitness center, full-service Karl Strauss Grill and Microbrewery; arcade and activity center. Ten percent Legoland discount, various packages.

Encinitas

Pino's Cucina Italiano, 967 South Coast Highway 101. (760) 632–1901. Pizzas, pastas, and salads abound at this Italian eatery. Popular menu items include chicken, veal, seafood, and salads. Open Monday through Friday 11:30 A.M. to 9:30 P.M., Saturday 4:00 P.M. to 10:00 P.M., and Sunday 4:00 P.M. to 9:30 P.M.

Moonlight Beach Motel, 233 2nd Street. (760) 753–0623. One block from Moonlight Beach; the four-story, ocean-view, family-style atmosphere with full kitchens and private decks is great for an extended family stay.

Best Western Encinitas Inn & Suites, 85 Encinitas Boulevard. (800) 333–3333 (worldwide); (760) 942–7455. Dramatically situated atop a bluff overlooking the ocean. Ninety-four rooms and suites, some with kitchenettes, all with balconies, cable TV. Heated swimming pool, whirlpool; coffee shop and restaurant. Complimentary continental breakfast, plus daily newspaper.

Del Mar

En Fuego, 1342 Camino del Mar. (858) 792–6551. Patio diners enjoy the south-of-the-border-style cuisine.

Clarion Del Mar Inn, 720 Camino del Mar (at 9th Street). (800) 453–4411 (in California); (800) 451–4515 (elsewhere); (858) 755–9765. Warm, English-style architecture and country decor; eighty-one good-size rooms, half with kitchenettes, overlook ocean or garden. Cable TV; heated swimming pool, spa; complimentary continental breakfast served in your room; complimentary afternoon English Tea and Cakes in the cozy library every day except Saturday.

L'Auberge Del Mar, 1540 Camino del Mar. (800) 553–1336; (858) 259–1515. Located on the site of the landmark old Hotel Del Mar. Luxurious amenities in French country decor in 120 rooms and suites, many with coastal views, large balconies, minibar and refrigerator, marble baths. Pool, outdoor fitness center, spa; two tennis courts; restaurant. Sunday brunch. Special getaway packages.

For More Information

Carlsbad Convention and Visitors Bureau, 400 Carlsbad Village Drive, Carlsbad, CA 92008. (Visitors Information Center, Old Santa Fe Train Depot, Carlsbad Village Drive.) (800) 227–5722; (760) 434–6093; www.carlsbadca.org.

Encinitas North Coast Chamber of Commerce & Visitor Center, 138 Encinitas Boulevard, Encinitas, CA 92024. (800) 953–6041; (760) 753–6041.

Self-Realization Fellowship Retreat and Hermitage, 215 K Street, Encinitas, CA 92024. (760) 753–1181.

Greater Del Mar Chamber of Commerce, 1104 Camino del Mar, Del Mar, CA 92014. (858) 755–4844; www.delmarchamber.org.

North County Transit District, Administration–Customer Services, Carlsbad, CA 92008; (760) 967–2828. Open Monday through Friday, 8:00 A.M. to 5:00 P.M.

SOUTHERN ESCAPE FOUR

Coves and Caves

La Jolla / 1 Night

- ☐ Beaches
- ☐ Water sports
- ☐ Dining
- ☐ Shopping
- ☐ Museums
- ☐ Parks
- ☐ Galleries
- ☐ Hang gliding
- ☐ Aquarium

Here's a two-day itinerary south to an energetic little seaside resort perched atop the edge of the Pacific Ocean. In addition to all manner of water sports, golf, tennis, and hang gliding, you'll have a tantalizing choice of good dining, visit an ocean-view museum and a delightful aquarium, picnic in the park, prowl upscale galleries, poke around chic boutiques, relax, sun and swim in a protected cove, and pedal a bike on a scenic path along the ever-present ocean.

Day 1 / Morning

Drive south on I–5 about 115 miles to La Jolla. Exit at La Jolla Shores Drive, continue to Torrey Pines Road, turn left, and stay on it to Girard Avenue, in the heart of downtown.

Though La Jolla (pronounced "La Hoya") is probably best known for its variety of summer activities, any season is perfect for a visit. In an exuberance of natural beauty, its 7 miles of sandy beaches are wrapped around a spectacular coastline of towering cliffs, scraggy coves, and hilly terrain. Often referred to as a quaint little village, La Jolla is about as quaint as Clint Eastwood.

Creative people have long been attracted to the scenic locale. The first group of artists and actors seduced by the windswept coast and long, lonely stretches of beach settled here in the 1930s. They created the legendary **Green Dragon Colony** on Prospect Street, with homes and studios overlooking the peaceful cove. Art is still a major part of village life, with dozens of galleries tucked throughout the city.

Additionally, La Jolla is a renowned think-tank hub, framed by the prestigious Salk Institute for Biological Studies, with its Nobel laureates; the University of California at San Diego campus; and Scripps Institution of Oceanography, whose enchanting aquarium attracts some 300,000 visitors yearly.

With its rolling hills, lush, tropical planting, palms and tall aromatic eucalyptus trees, winding streets, posh hotels, dazzling ocean vistas, world-class shopping, and

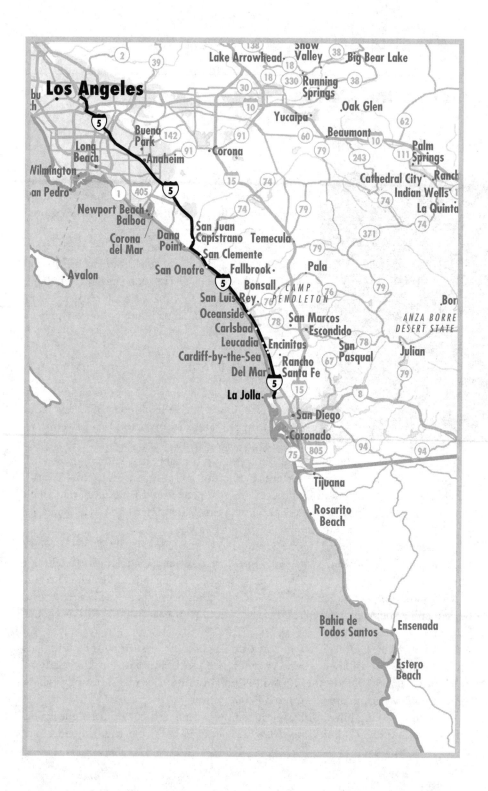

cheery sidewalk cafes, the effervescent city just 15 miles north of San Diego has a decidedly Mediterranean flavor and is frequently compared with the French Riviera.

LUNCH: The Nine-Ten Restaurant, 910 Prospect Street, La Jolla. (858) 454–2181. In the Grande Colonial. A classy, popular pub with marble floors and a warm setting. You'll find friendly service, good, hearty food, and fresh market cuisine. Moderately priced; valet parking.

Afternoon

The best thing about La Jolla is that its small downtown area is so compact you can explore the city by foot, thus avoiding the busy traffic and hard-to-find parking spaces. Even the beaches are an easy stroll from downtown.

Begin with stately **Girard Avenue,** the city's main thoroughfare. This lovely, broad street, lined with tall palms and eucalyptus trees, is vaguely reminiscent of Santa Barbara, with its landscaped areas and wrought-iron benches. Shoppers' favorites along this stretch include Polo Ralph Lauren; Gallery Alexander, with ever-creative exhibits and collections; a preponderance of fine jewelry shops; and Banana Republic.

Girard leads into lively, attractive **Prospect Street,** a sweeping terrace atop the cliffs that overlooks the ocean and offers a complete change of ambience. You won't find many streets quite like this one, where shops and restaurants facing the water present spectacular views of the cove and the famous **La Jolla Caves.** It's a bustling, pedestrian-oriented street for shopping, dining, and browsing, filled with sleek boutiques, galleries, sidewalk cafes and posh restaurants, people, and traffic.

On the ocean side the pink-domed landmark La Valencia Hotel is flanked by cafes and shops. The Chart House Restaurant, 1270 Prospect Street, leads into **Coast Walk,** where boutiques and galleries housed in small cottages set far back from the sidewalk on wide expanses of lawn and brick-paved courtyards, pretty gazebos, and wide shade trees are the legacies of the famed Green Dragon Art Colony. The Gallery of Two Sisters shows a pleasing selection of oil paintings, watercolors, stoneware, and ironwood sculpture by California artists, at good prices.

Shoppers and adventurers won't want to miss the Cave Store, 1325 Coast Walk (858–459–0746), ensconced atop the cliffs. The shop features historical photos of caves in the area, works of local artists, antique furniture, and a coffee cart dispensing drinks. From the shop you can descend the 145 steps built into a man-made, lighted tunnel built in 1902 to **Sunny Jim Cave,** the largest of La Jolla's original seven sea-level smugglers' caves and the only one that can be entered (fee charged for the adventure). Open 9:00 A.M. to 5:00 P.M. daily.

At the end of Coast Walk, follow bikers, joggers, and strollers along the curving and scenic Cliff Walk atop the bluffs overlooking **La Jolla Cove,** the center of attraction for residents and visitors alike. The small protected beach, with its calm and crystalline water, is the favorite area for swimming, scuba diving, snorkeling, sunbathing, and socializing. Cliff Walk also overlooks La Jolla's notorious smugglers' caves in the shallow water below, and from here you can watch people clambering all over them, especially Sunny Jim Cave.

Wander farther down to the **Ellen Browning Scripps Park** at the foot of Coast Walk bordering the cove. Here you're apt to find an old-fashioned tableau of people picnicking or lazily sprawling on the warm grass in the dappled shade of slender palms and the lofty Torrey pines, evoking a feeling of having stumbled into an impressionist painting. La Jolla's balmy climate nurtures the rare, prehistoric, sea-loving Torrey pines, which exist in only one other place on Earth: Santa Rosa Island off Santa Barbara. Bring your own picnic lunch or snack, stake out a bench or patch of grass, and enjoy the superb ocean view or watch the surfers. Many picnickers arrive as late as 5:00 P.M. with food hampers and blankets to enjoy the blazing sunsets over the ocean.

DINNER: Sammy's Wood Fired Pizza, 702 Pearl (corner of Draper), La Jolla. (858) 456–5222. One of the most popular places in town. They don't take reservations, so feel lucky to find a seat at the counter, where you can watch the chefs make designer pizzas and generous salads; both can be shared.

LODGING: The Empress Hotel, 7766 Fay Avenue, La Jolla. (888) 369–9900 (nationwide); (858) 454–3001. In the heart of the village; seventy-three oversize ocean-view rooms and suites offer complimentary continental breakfast in the hospitality room. In-room coffeemaker, refrigerator, hair dryer, cable TV with in-room movies, daily newspaper; restaurant; sauna, Jacuzzi, exercise room; sundeck. The suites feature glamorous marble Jacuzzi tubs in the bedrooms. Manhattan restaurant on premises.

Day 2 / Morning

BREAKFAST: Enjoy the complimentary continental breakfast in your hotel.

Walk or drive to the **San Diego Museum of Contemporary Art,** 700 Prospect Street (858–454–3541). The long, low structure with a sculpture garden overlooking the ocean is the former home of heiress Ellen B. Scripps, the city's benefactress. It was built in 1916 and designed by noted architect Irving Gill, who designed many other buildings in La Jolla. The Book Shop features a fine selection of children's books about artists in addition to adult material, and there is a cafe. Open Thursday through Tuesday 11:00 A.M. to 5:00 P.M. (Thursday until 7:00 P.M.). Closed Wednesday. Admission.

LUNCH: The Spot, 1005 Prospect Street, La Jolla. (858) 459–0800. A local favorite, friendly and casual for sandwiches, good Chicago-style pizza, salad, barbecued baby-back ribs, and daily gourmet chef special.

Afternoon

Drive north on Torrey Pines Road to Expedition Way, off La Jolla Village Drive; turn left toward the ocean and south to the **Stephen Birch Aquarium Museum** (858–534–FISH), on the campus of the University of California at San Diego in **Scripps Institution of Oceanography,** one of the oldest, largest, and most important centers for marine science research.

The boulder-decked outdoor tide pool that overlooks the sparkling coastline captivates children looking for starfish, mussels, and other small local sea animals. Inside, the aquarium features thirty-three tanks displaying more than 3,000 colorful fish from tropical waters as well as from the chill waters of the Pacific Northwest.

Among the stunning, shimmering variety of rainbow-colored fish and plants are a giant octopus; elegant vertical seahorses; fast-moving sharks, which always draw considerable interest; spooky moray eels; and venomous yellow and brown lionfish. A dramatic, 16-foot-deep kelp forest in a 50,000-gallon tank is viewed through a 21-by-13-foot acrylic wall.

The museum features the largest oceanographic exhibit in the United States. The bookshop offers more than 1,500 gifts, as well as extensive science and oceanographic literature. Open daily except Thanksgiving, Christmas Day, and New Year's Day, from 9:00 A.M. to 5:00 P.M. Admission.

Salk Institute for Biological Studies, 10010 North Torrey Pines Road (858–453–4100), on a promontory adjacent to the University of California at San Diego, is renowned for medical research, and foremost biologists come here to study. The powerful building was designed by the late architect Louis Kahn specifically for Dr. Jonas Salk, its founding director. The sprawling complex is a dramatic masterwork of poured concrete, glass, and travertine and is visited by many architects. Tours available Monday, Wednesday, and Friday at noon by reservation only.

For those interested in **hang gliding,** Torrey Pines Gliderport, La Jolla Village Farms Road (858–452–9858)—a popular, expert-rated launching site for hang gliders—is just up the road from the Salk Institute. Drive up the coastal hilltop and park on the towering bluff 300 feet above the ocean (overlooking Black's Nude Beach). Walk up to the knoll and watch the hang gliders assemble their craft, which they bring rolled up like tall masts in long zippered cases. Then watch them take flight in their fragile, multicolored craft like giant butterflies, as the wind off the sea lifts them from cliff's edge and they ride the updrafts to altitudes up to 1,500 feet, soaring over the cliffs and sand out to sea. Weekends are the best time to watch. In spring, when winds are strong, many hang gliders are in the air at once. Whatever the season, the best hours are between 9:00 A.M. and 5:00 P.M., when the updrafts are strongest.

From here retrace your way back to Los Angeles on I–5 north.

There's More

Golf. Try the 9-hole Pitch & Putt course at Spindrift Golf Course, 2000 Spindrift Drive (858–454–7126). Torrey Pines Municipal Course, 11480 Torrey Pines Road (858–570–1234), will remind you of Pebble Beach, where cliffside fairways on two 18-hole championship courses overlook the blue Pacific.

Swimming/tennis. La Jolla Beach and Tennis Club at Spindrift Golf Course, 2000 Spindrift Drive. (858) 454–7126. Registered hotel guests and members only.

Bike riding. Follow the marked scenic route along the coast or through town.

Skin and scuba diving. The craggy coves of Bird Rock, La Jolla Underwater Park, and underwater Scripps Canyon are the best areas for skin and scuba diving.

Surfing. Windansea Beach, considered one of the best surfing beaches along the West Coast, is at the end of Nautilus Street, between the village and Bird Rock to the south. For gear contact San Diego Diver's Supply, 7522 La Jolla Boulevard (858–459–2691).

Snorkeling/swimming. Can't beat La Jolla Cove.

Tennis. La Jolla Recreation Center, 615 Prospect Street (858–552–1658); La Jolla YMCA, 8355 Cliffridge Drive (858–453–3483); La Jolla High School, 750 Nautilus Street (858–454–3081).

Special Events

January. La Jolla Stage Company season, at the Firehouse. Ongoing productions. (858) 459–7773.

Beginning of February. Buick International Open PGA Golf Tournament, Torrey Pines Golf Course. (800) 888–BUICK.

Beginning of March. Pacific Coast Men's Doubles Tennis. La Jolla Beach and Tennis Club. (858) 454–7126.

Mid-April. La Jolla Park and Rec. Egg Hunt, 615 Prospect Street.

End of April. La Jolla Half Marathon and 5K Run. La Jolla Kiwanis, (858) 454–1262.

Mid-May. La Jolla Junior Olympics, La Jolla High School Field (Fay Avenue). (858) 334–4270. Mardi Gras in May. La Jolla High School Foundation, (858) 551–1250.

End of May. La Jolla Garden Tour. La Jolla Historical Society, (858) 726–0227.

First week in June. La Jolla Festival of the Arts. Torrey Pines Kiwanis, (858) 456–1268.

June through August. Sunday concerts by the Sea, in Scripps Park series.

End of June beginning of July. Annual La Jolla Tennis Tournament. La Jolla Tennis Club at L. J. Recreation Center. (858) 454–4434.

July 4. Independence Day Concert and Fireworks, La Jolla Cove.

First week of August. Jewel Ball, La Jolla Beach and Tennis Club.

Second Sunday in September. Annual Rough Waterswim, La Jolla Cove.

October. Annual Underwater Pumpkin-Carving Contest. (858) 270–3103.

First Sunday in December. Holiday Festival, Christmas Parade.

Other Recommended Restaurants and Lodgings

La Jolla

Alphonso's of La Jolla, 1251 Prospect Street. (858) 454–2232. A lively, crowded hangout for Mexican specialties, but it's hard to get in the door or find a seat at a patio table.

George's at the Cove, 1250 Prospect Street. (858) 454–4244. A longtime convivial favorite for creative regional cuisine amid romantic candlelit tables overlooking the cove. Fine dining, patio or inside. Casual bistro menu. Call for hours. Valet service.

Harry's Coffee Shop, 7545 Girard Avenue. (858) 454–7381. Where late risers go for breakfast. Sometimes everyone in town shows up when you do. Admire the wall paintings while waiting for your eggs or hamburgers. Daily specials, children's menu. Park in the rear; open Monday through Saturday, 6:00 A.M. to 3:00 P.M.

Top O' the Cove, 1216 Prospect Street. (858) 454–7779. Set high on the bluffs in an ocean-view bungalow with candlelit tables; expensive but a consistent winner for fine continental cuisine. Sunday brunch.

Crab Catcher, 1298 Prospect Street. (858) 454–9587. Overlooking the coastline, featuring a variety of chicken and fresh crab and seafood entrees. Pleasant service. Lunch and dinner. Sunday brunch.

Manhattan of La Jolla, 7766 Fay Avenue. (858) 459–0700. In the Empress Hotel. Sleekly sophisticated northern Italian cuisine in a New York setting. Sink into an upholstered booth and watch the tropical fish drift by. Pasta, seafood, steaks, and chicken in generous portions; attentive waiters.

La Valencia Hotel, 1132 Prospect Street. (800) 451–0772; (858) 454–0771. The choice of distinguished visitors since Garbo and other stars used to hide out here in the 1930s. There are 115 rooms and suites, including fifteen luxurious Ocean Villas. Amenities include TV, VCR, room safe, clock radio, hair dryer, coffeemaker, minibar, refrigerator, daily newspaper, nightly turndown service; twenty-four-hour room service; swimming pool, three restaurants, lounge. Overnight parking fee. The Mediterranean Room's tropical, palm-fringed patio is a lively rendezvous for breakfast, lunch, dinner, and Sunday champagne buffet brunch.

The Lodge at Torrey Pines, 11480 North Torrey Pines Road. (800) 656–0087; (858) 453–4420. Overlooking the Pacific, many of the lodge's 170 guest rooms and suites have balconies and fireplaces and are well decorated with distinctive furnishings, granite counters, deep soaking tub, robes, slippers, minibar, coffeemaker, and in-room safe. Sparkling 9,000-square-foot spa with fourteen treatment rooms; fitness center; extensive conference facility; two restaurants; golf course; and swimming pool with underwater music. Various packages available. Complimentary transportation provided for hotel guests within 5-mile radius.

The Grande Colonial, 910 Prospect Street. (800) 826–1278 (nationwide); (858) 454–2181. Fully restored and renovated historic 1913 landmark in Victorian-style hotel, 1 block from the beach. Seventy-five elegantly appointed rooms, including three suites; TV, clock radio, refrigerator on request, daily newspaper, turndown service. Heated swimming pool. Valet parking fee.

Inn by the Sea (Best Western), 7830 Fay Avenue. (800) 526–4545; (858) 459–4461. In the heart of the village. Private balconies for 129 rooms and two suites; TV with movie channels, clock radio, minirefrigerator available on request (no charge), hair dryer, room service, complimentary continental breakfast poolside. Heated swimming pool, conference facilities; complimentary valet and self-parking.

For More Information

Official Visitor's Bureau, La Jolla Town Council, 7734 Herschel Avenue, Suite F, La Jolla, CA 92037. (858) 454–1444. Open Monday through Friday, noon to 5:00 P.M.

La Jolla Historical Society, 7846 Eads Avenue, La Jolla, CA 92037. (858) 459–5335. Open Tuesday and Thursday, 2:00 to 4:00 P.M., or write to Box 2085, La Jolla, CA 92038.

SOUTHERN ESCAPE FIVE

Lively Seafront Holiday

San Diego, Coronado / 2 Nights

- ☐ Zoo
- ☐ Parks
- ☐ Old Town
- ☐ Trolley tours
- ☐ History
- ☐ Historic hotels
- ☐ Museums
- ☐ Harbor cruise
- ☐ SeaWorld

In this two-night, three-day excursion, you'll barely get to sample all the highlights of this versatile seaport city where California was born in 1769. Cheer a performing killer whale; ride a ferry across the sparkling bay to a tony Victorian resort enclave. Historic San Diego has been host to Franciscan Father Junípero Serra, Wyatt Earp, Charles Lindbergh, the Prince of Wales, Clint Eastwood, and Marilyn Monroe.

Day 1 / Morning

Drive south on I–5, the Santa Ana Freeway, for this 120-mile excursion, which should take about two and a half to three hours, depending on freeway traffic. The scenic drive passes through orange groves, farms, little beach cities, and rolling countryside of low, cinnamon-colored foothills and sweet, soft air.

At the northern edge of San Diego, adjacent to I–5, that gleaming, elaborate, white Gothic-style structure with 190-foot-tall twin spires is the landmark San Diego Mormon Temple. As you near San Diego, you can see the skyline high-rise beyond the water-skiers and sailboats. Your first stop is the world-famous **zoo** in Balboa Park.

Take the Civic Center/10th Avenue exit to A Street, turn left, and turn left again at 12th/Park. Follow signs to the zoo and parking area along President's Way. The zoo, spread over one hundred well-landscaped acres, is the city's most popular attraction, noted for its exotic and rare wildlife. Cuddly teddy-bear koalas and playful pygmy chimpanzees are among its collection of 3,900 animals of 800 different species, including a pair of rare giant pandas. Most are in barless, moated enclosures resembling their natural habitats.

You can wander about on your own or pay a bit more for admission that includes the forty-minute, narrated, 3-mile double-deck bus tour (better view from the upper deck) that roams through 60 percent of the zoo.

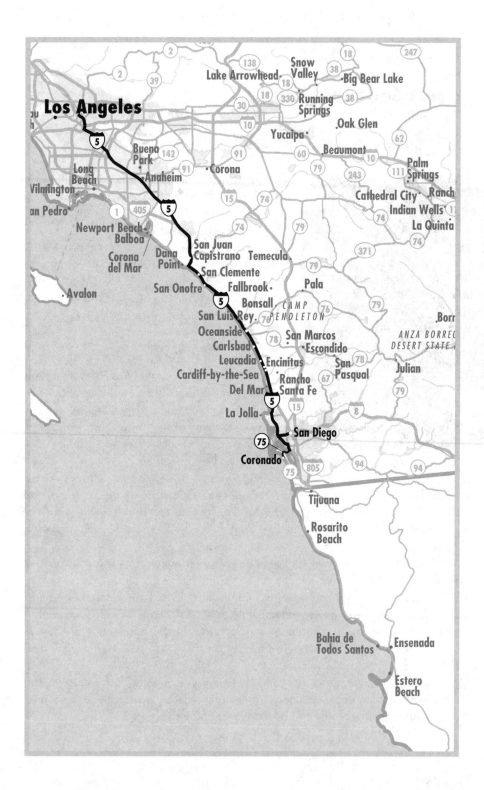

Besides the galaxy of graceful flamingos poised for photos near the entrance, among animals you'll see on the bus tour are the 500-pound pygmy hippos, California sea lions working on their suntans, the elusive Chinese leopard, Alaskan brown bears, zebras, 17-foot-tall giraffes, and the slinky jaguar. Roosters and chickens strut and fly freely throughout.

Though the bus tour covers a lot, by taking it you'll miss the world's largest collection of monkeys and apes, the children's petting zoo, the birds, and the Skyfari Aerial Tram. The bus tour also makes it difficult to see many animals that aren't out front and center, or to see above or through groups of people along the paths. Though walking may become tiring, you can stop, watch animals of interest, and take photos. (Open daily from 9:00 A.M. to 4:00 P.M.; closing hours are extended in summer. Admission; free parking. Public information, 619–234–3153.)

To see more of the park's attractions, drive out Park Boulevard, turn right on President's Way, and turn right again at the first boulevard; park behind the Spreckels Organ Pavilion.

LUNCH: The Prado, 1450 El Prado Way. (619) 557–9441. At the San Diego Museum of Art. Have lunch with the sculptors—Henry Moore, Joan Miró, Barbara Hepworth, and Alexander Calder—indoors or in a charming garden courtyard. It's a popular gathering place for Latin/Italian cuisine. Lunch features skirt-steak tacos, crab cakes, and a pitcher of refreshing sangria. For dinner go for the fourteen-ounce top sirloin or chicken. Open for lunch or dinner daily, but closed Monday for dinner. Closed between lunch and dinner.

Afternoon

Balboa Park is a lush, 1,400-acre visual and cultural treasure one can happily spend several days exploring, with its hub of museums, theaters, and cafes. The ornate Spreckels Organ Pavilion, with curving, colonnaded walks and a large outdoor organ, offers free concerts Sunday at 2:00 P.M. and Monday evenings in summer.

The park's rich, sixteenth-century Spanish-Moorish baroque architecture is enhanced with ornamental gardens and fountains, arched walkways, and a 200-foot bell tower. Ride the free red tram shuttling from one plaza to another, with frequent stops.

The Prado, across the center of the park, is embroidered with a cluster of ten museums and two art galleries winding through plazas, rose gardens, and a lily pond. The **San Diego Museum of Art**'s extensive collection ranges from pre-Columbian to twentieth-century art; it also has a Sculpture Court and Garden and a charming cafe (closed Monday). The Reuben H. Fleet Space Theater and Science Center envelops you in a giant domed screen showing 3-D Omnimax films.

Some museums charge admission; hours vary, but most are open daily from 10:00 A.M. to 5:00 P.M. You can buy a map and guide for 60 cents at the **Balboa Park Visitors Center,** 1549 El Prado (619–239–0512). The renowned **Old**

Globe Theatre, designed in round, sixteenth-century style, is part of a three-theater complex presenting Shakespeare and musicals. Purchase same-day tickets at the box office if they are available (information, 619–239–2255), or buy half-price, day-of-performance tickets at Time's Art Tix downtown at the Horton Plaza ticket booth (619–497–5000). With Balboa Park's evening theater performances, plus many cafes and snack bars, you can spend a pleasurable, stimulating day and evening here.

DINNER: Fifth and Hawthorn, 515 Hawthorn (corner of 5th Avenue), San Diego. (619) 544–0940. Convenient uptown location close to the park. Smart looking, with white napery on candlelit tables. The menu favors California cuisine of fresh seafood, innovative salads, and light summer or smaller-portion (also lower-priced) entrees like filet mignon and pasta.

After dinner head south to Coronado Island on I–5 to Highway 75, which comes up very soon; take 75 over the San Diego–Coronado Bridge. Stay to the right for the carpool lane as you approach the toll gates at the exit to avoid paying the toll. (There's no toll returning to San Diego.)

LODGING: Coronado Island Marriott Resort, 2000 2nd Street, Coronado. (800) 228–9290; (619) 435–3000. French elegance throughout this waterfront, sixteen-acre, four-star, four-diamond, world-class hotel. Features 300 deluxe spacious rooms with sitting area, and twenty-eight villas in country French decor; terraces, TV, minibar/refrigerator, coffeemaker, in-room safe, hair dryer, terry robes, marble bathroom with tub and stall shower, excellent lighting, concierge service. Three heated swimming pools and whirlpools, six lighted tennis courts, full-service spa. Three restaurants and a cocktail lounge. Overnight parking fee. Sunday brunch.

Day 2 / Morning

BREAKFAST: At the resort. Or, if it's Sunday, investigate the buffet brunch at the noted **Hotel Del Coronado,** 1500 Orange Avenue, Coronado (800–HOTEL–DEL; 619–435–6611). Each brunch features a different international theme menu, served in the famed, enormous (156-by-66-foot) Crown Room. Brunch is a lavish array of hot and cold dishes, including salad bar, omelette station, hand-carved prime rib, sizzling pasta station, and incomparable desserts. Purchase your brunch tickets in the lobby. (Brunch served Sunday from 9:00 A.M. to 2:00 P.M.; reservations suggested; free validated parking.)

Following brunch explore this rambling, 1888 Victorian hotel, whose famous guests have included Edward, the Prince of Wales (said to have met Wallis Simpson, the future Duchess of Windsor, here in 1920); Charles Lindbergh; fourteen presidents; and Thomas Edison, who reportedly supervised the incandescent light installation. This is also the locale of *Some Like It Hot* and other films. The "Del" is a grand old showpiece, with its red cone-shaped roof, gleaming white trim, cupolas, and turrets (see "Other Recommended Restaurants and Lodgings"). Take the bird-cage elevator to the lower-lobby level and browse the Galleria shops. Wander through the hotel's public rooms, beautiful gardens, and wide beach.

To see more of Coronado's downtown area, from 8th Street to the "Del," stay on Orange Avenue, the main street of the village and Coronado's noted "restaurant row." In this stretch of sixty-eight restaurants, you'll find Chameleon Cafe (1301) for Southwestern cuisine with Pacific Rim flavors and the intimate Primavera Ristorante (932), popular for its consistently fine northern Italian cuisine.

Coronado is San Diego's resort community, graced by lovely parks and tree-lined streets; it has a relaxed, small-town flavor and offers luxury hotels, golf, tennis, bike paths, and boating. It also has a history of famous guests and residents, such as millionaire John D. Spreckels, whose former mansion is now the vintage Glorietta Bay Inn, and L. Frank Baum, who wrote the classic *Wizard of Oz*. In 1927 Charles Lindbergh, the "Lone Eagle," took off from Coronado's North Island for his famous solo New York to Paris flight and was feted at the Hotel Del Coronado on his tri-umphant return.

Continue along Orange Avenue until it ends and then turn right, continuing 2.5 blocks to **Ferry Landing Marketplace,** 1201 1st Street at B Avenue, with its bayfront Victorian-style white buildings with red roofs. This lively shopping-dining complex and fishing/ferry pier has a grassy park and a small swimming beach fronting along San Diego Bay. Sailboats crisscross the water; there's a great view of the downtown San Diego skyline, as well as of the sweeping San Diego–Coronado Bridge.

But the best part is watching the passenger ferry arrive at the pier hourly from San Diego. Before the San Diego–Coronado Bridge was built in 1969, Coronado could be reached only by ferry. The service was discontinued for almost twenty years, but now the popular ferry again carries pedestrians and bikes across the bay.

Drive back to San Diego over the 2-mile-long San Diego–Coronado Bridge; go north on I–5 to **Seaport Village,** 849 West Harbor Drive at Kettner Boulevard (619–235–4014).

LUNCH: Harbor House, 831 West Harbor Drive, Seaport Village, on the board-walk. (619) 232–1141. Along with its stunning harbor view, the restaurant is noted for seafood, fresh salads, prime ribs, and steaks.

Afternoon

Enjoy Seaport Village's waterfront shopping and dining complex. It is in a fourteen-acre old-style harbor setting, with a Victorian clock tower and a lighthouse. Landscaped cobbled walks lead around restaurants; shoppers are in heaven with about seventy-five stores to browse for gourmet cookware, Scandinavian imports, and souvenirs. Saddle up on the century-old Looff carousel, then stroll the wooden boardwalk along the water.

See the highlights of San Diego aboard **Old Town Trolley Tours,** which includes Seaport Village among its ten different stops, for a stimulating, informative ninety-minute city tour encompassing Balboa Park, the zoo, Old Town, and Coronado. You can get off at any place of interest, then reboard another trolley to complete your tour. Knowledgeable drivers sprinkle entertaining commentary with anecdotes, chitchat, and history. Clint Eastwood made his day in *Dirty Harry* at Seaport Village; Wyatt Earp lived in the Gaslamp Quarter in 1850 and owned the most popular bordello in the West. Note where Charles Lindbergh stayed while his plane *Spirit of St. Louis* was being built nearby (619–298–8687). Other tours include "**City Sight Seeing San Diego**," a one-and-a-half-hour, "hop on hop off" tour aboard a red double-decker bus. Cruise Ship Terminal Departure, (619) 231–3040. You can also take the fully narrated, ninety-minute **Seal Tours**, San Diego's only amphibious tour, combining both a land and a water segment in one tour by riding a "water bus" through town and then splashing right into the ocean. Departs from Seaport Village. (619) 298–8687.

Take Harbor Drive to the Embarcadero at the Cruise Ship Terminal, where the **Maritime Museum**'s trio of historic ships are permanently anchored along the waterfront, showcasing the city's rich maritime past. The magnificent tall ship windjammer *Star of India,* built in 1863, is the oldest iron-hulled merchant ship afloat. Alongside are the 1890 steam ferryboat *Berkeley* and the 1904 steam yacht *Medea.* Looking out to sea, you'll find the busy tuna fleet as well as the dramatic sight of destroyers, cruisers, and other large vessels of the U.S. Navy's Pacific Fleet.

Downtown's dynamic **Horton Plaza** dominates a 7-block stretch between Broadway and G Street. This shopping-dining hub houses three department stores and some 150 shops, as well as restaurants, theaters, and a multilingual International Visitors Information Center.

You're within a few blocks of the historic and lively **Gaslamp Quarter,** bounded by Broadway to Harbor Drive, 4th Avenue to 6th. This historic district dates from the end of the Civil War. After a neglected period it has been restored— its Victorian 1880 buildings now house trendy shops and ethnic restaurants, galleries, and bistros—and is one of the most popular areas in the city. Come for lunch or dinner and stay to hear the jazz the quarter is noted for. Along 5th Avenue the 700 and 800 blocks appear to have more attractive restaurants. Parking is a problem, though many have valet parking, and the one-way streets make it difficult for hungry visitors.

DINNER: **Ostario Panevino,** 732 5th Avenue, San Diego. (619) 595–7959. In the lively Gaslamp Quarter, small and inviting, with a warm decor of brick walls and small, granite-topped tables. Veal specialties, ravioli, rigatoni. Delicious bread is served with your salad, and you can watch the chef bake your pizza in the brick oven.

LODGING: Coronado Island Marriott Resort.

Day 3 / Morning

BREAKFAST: Bay Beach Cafe, at Ferry Landing Marketplace, Coronado. (619) 435–4900. Just north of your hotel. Dine indoors or enjoy the balmy breeze on the cheery deck overlooking San Diego Bay as sailboats drift past your morning coffee or mimosa.

Leave for **Old Town.** Cross the San Diego–Coronado Bridge, take I–5 north to the Old Town Avenue exit, turn right, follow the signs, and turn left on San Diego Avenue. As you cross the bridge, the air is so clear you can see far across to the mountains framing the city.

San Diego began in Old Town in 1769, when Father Junípero Serra established California's first mission, Mission San Diego de Alcala, and the Presidio, a military installation on a hilltop overlooking San Diego Bay. Soldiers' families and early settlers gradually moved down to the flatland, and the old pueblo is the 6-block area of Old Town. The **old central plaza** along San Diego Avenue, the main street, is lined with restaurants, shops, and history. Pick up a free copy of the *Old Town Gazette* with handy map and history at any merchant. Along here are several cafes, including the Old Town Mexican Cafe, where former President Clinton has eaten and where you can watch the tortilla ladies in the window making fresh tortillas, patting them between their hands. Shopping variety includes several Mexican import shops and the Apache Indian Art Store. Free walking tours of Old Town are given daily at 11:00 A.M. and 7:00 P.M. from the Old Town State Park Information Center, in front of Seely Stables on Calhoun. For more information call the Old Town State Park at (619) 220–5422 and ask for one of the park rangers.

Around the corner, **Heritage Park** is a delightful cluster of multistory, restored Victorian-era mansions of bright colors, ivory trim, cupolas, balconies, verandas, and old-fashioned gardens. They house antiques and dolls and offer romantic overnighting at Heritage Park Bed and Breakfast (800–995–2470; 619–299–6832). From here turn right on Twiggs and left on Juan Street in Old Town to reach Bazaar del Mundo.

LUNCH: Casa De Bandini, 2660 Calhoun Street, Old Town San Diego. (619) 297–8211. Dine in the courtyard of Juan Bandini's restored 1823 adobe mansion, a State Historic Site. Relax beneath a shady umbrella as you sip a cool margarita in this pretty place near a splashing fountain. Gourmet Mexican and seafood specialties.

Afternoon

Bazaar del Mundo, next door at 2754 Calhoun Street, is a festive south-of-the-border-style dining-shopping garden marketplace of sixteen international shops for handcrafted gifts, Guatemalan fashions, jewelry, pottery, and folk art. Restaurants here include Casa de Pico, Lino's Italian Cuisine, and Rancho El Nopal Restaurant & Cantina for Mexican/American specialties. Shops are open Tuesday through Saturday from 10:00 A.M. to 5:00 P.M. (619) 296–3161.

To get to **SeaWorld,** take I–5 north to the SeaWorld Drive exit and turn left. The 150-acre marine park is located on Mission Bay. Plan to stay several hours to see the six major shows staged during the day, featuring performing killer whales, seals, otters, sea lions, dolphins, and penguins. Shamu, the three-ton terpsichorean killer whale, is the pride of SeaWorld. Read your guide map and review the show schedule so you'll know which way to go in this spread-out park. Between show-times you can visit twenty marine animal exhibits and three aquariums.

Spend the rest of the day in SeaWorld. Browse the pleasant shops, snack in the cafes, and cool off with ice cream or frozen yogurt. Open year-round; hours vary by season. Admission; free parking. (800) SEA–WORLD; (619) 226–3901. www.seaworld.com.

There's More

San Diego Harbor Excursions, 1050 North Harbor Drive at Broadway, San Diego. (800) 442–7847; (619) 234–4111. Take in a one- or two-hour narrated cruise of San Diego Bay; food and drink aboard. Fee.

Cabrillo National Monument and Visitor Center, on the tip of Point Loma, San Diego. (619) 557–5450. The statue of Juan Rodriguez Cabrillo commemorates his 1542 discovery of California. The old Point Loma lighthouse provides an unbeatable panoramic view out to sea and is a prime spot for whale-watching. Open daily, 9:00 A.M. to 5:15 P.M.

Mission San Diego de Alcala, 10818 San Diego Mission Road, San Diego. (619) 281–8449. The first of California's twenty-one Franciscan missions, established by Father Junípero Serra on Presidio Hill in 1769. The mission houses Father Serra's original records and an ecclesiastical art museum. Self-guided tour; services daily; admission. Open daily, 9:00 A.M. to 4:45 P.M.

San Diego Trolley, Santa Fe Depot. Broadway and Kettner Boulevard, San Diego. (619) 234–5005 or (619) 233–3004. The red trolley takes you on a 20-mile trip from downtown to the border, where you can walk across to Mexico. Every quarter-hour daily, from 5:00 A.M. to 1:00 A.M.; fare each way. www.sdcommute.com.

San Diego Factory Outlet Center at the International Border, 4498 Camino de la Plaza, San Ysidro. (619) 690–2999. Thirty-five well-known manufacturers offer factory-outlet prices for designer clothing, housewares, toys, shoes, leather goods, and more. Open daily. Exit I–5 at the sign LAST U.S. EXIT and turn right; proceed 1 block.

Spreckels Park, Orange Avenue between 6th and 7th Streets, Coronado. Donated by John D. Spreckels, a charming park with children's playground and nostalgic bandstand for Sunday-evening summer concerts.

Tidelands Park. Twenty-two acres of shoreline below the San Diego–Coronado Bridge in Coronado. A lively sandy beach spot to swim, picnic, walk, and bicycle; children's playground.

Farmers' market, Ferry Landing Marketplace, 1st and B Street, Coronado. Every Tuesday 2:30 to 6:00 P.M.; fresh fruits and vegetables.

Casino resorts. The San Diego area has one of the largest collections of Indian gaming casinos in the country. Highlights include:

Sycuan Resort & Casino, 5469 Casino Way, El Cajon. (800) 2–SYCUAN; (619) 445–6002; www.sycuancasino.com. Boasts a spectacular 1,200-seat bingo palace, poker, pai gow, and the popular slot machines. Fine restaurants; live entertainment at the Showcase Theatre.

Sycuan Resort, 3007 Dehesa Road, El Cajon. (619) 442–3425. Located 3 miles from the casino; features 103 rooms, including suites. Eleven lighted tennis courts, golf at the Singing Hills Country Club, two swimming pools and Jacuzzi, lounge and restaurant.

Barona Valley Ranch Resort & Casino, 1932 Wildcat Canyon Road, Lakeside. (619) 443–2300; www.barona.com. Enjoy fifty-two gaming tables and more than 2,000 slots. Resort features swimming pool, three restaurants, fitness center and spa, and the championship Barona Creek Golf Club. Various packages available. Breakfast, lunch, and dinner buffet daily.

Golden Acorn Casino, 1800 Golden Acorn Way, Campo. (619) 928–6000. Great card games; delicious dinners at the casino's twenty-four-hour restaurant. Enjoy the blackjack table and the 750 slot machines.

Viejas Casino, 5000 Willows Road, Alpine. (619) 445–5400. Try your luck at table games and more than 2,000 slot machines and have dinner at one of the five restaurants. Across the street is the Viejas Outlet Center, featuring fifty-seven stores.

Special Events

Early to mid-January. Annual four-day San Diego Boat Show, international exhibitors. San Diego Convention Center and adjacent marina. (858) 274–9924.

Mid-January. Annual Nations of San Diego International Dance Festival. Largest dance festival in Southern California. (619) 557–2889.

San Diego Marathon.

Mid-January to mid-May. San Diego Opera season. (619) 232–7636.

Mid-February. Annual Heritage Day Parade, San Diego. Vendors, entertainment. (619) 286–9989.

First week of March. Mardi Gras in the Gaslamp Quarter. Celebration with participating restaurants and bars; exciting Mardi Gras Parade.

Mid-March. Annual St Patrick's Day Parade, San Diego. (858) 268–9111.

Early April. Annual San Diego Crew Classic, Mission Bay. (858) 488–0700.

Mid-April. Annual Coronado Flower Show weekend. Plant sales, exhibits, entertainment, and gorgeous flowers. Spreckels Park. (619) 437–8788.

Early May. Annual Fiesta Cinco de Mayo, three-day celebration throughout Old Town San Diego State Park.

June–September. San Diego Symphony Summer Pops Series. Performances under the stars, Friday and Saturday at 7:00 P.M.

SeaWorld's Summer Nights. Entertainment and fireworks nightly; extended evening hours.

Mid-June to beginning of July. San Diego County Fair.

July 4. Annual Coronado Independence Day Celebration. Parade, concert, floats, marching bands at Spreckels Park, fireworks over Glorietta Bay.

Old Town State Park Fourth of July celebration; flag raising, entertainment.

Mid-July. Bastille Day Celebration, Civic Center, San Diego.

August–December. San Diego Chargers football home games. (619) 280–2121.

Mid-September. San Diego Thunderboat Regatta/Bayfair/Thunderboats Unlimited.

Early October. Oktoberfest, Zoo Founders Day, free day at the zoo, 9:00 A.M. to 4:00 P.M., San Diego. (619) 234–3153.

October. Fleet Week. Tribute to the military with parades, ship tours, and the Miramar Air Show.

Mum Festival at San Diego Wild Animal Park. Largest chrysanthemum festival on the West Coast.

Month of October. Children's Month at the San Diego Zoo. Children ages eleven and younger admitted free.

End of November. Annual Mother Goose Parade. Features floats, clowns, a band, and equestrians. (619) 444–8712.

Annual San Diego Thanksgiving Dixieland Jazz Festival. (619) 297–5277.

Early December. Coronado Christmas Open House and Parade, Annual Christmas on the Prado, Balboa Park, San Diego. (619) 437–8788.

Mid-December. Annual Port of San Diego Bay Parade of Lights.

San Diego Wild Animal Park Festival of Lights.

Mid-December to mid-March. Whale-watching, Point Loma, San Diego. Annual migration to Baja, California.

Other Recommended Restaurants and Lodgings

Gaslamp Quarter

La Strada, 701 5th Avenue. (619) 239–3400. Chic trattoria, large room, white table-cloths, open kitchen to pizza oven and grill, northern Italian cuisine.

Gaslamp Strip Club, 340 5th Avenue. (619) 231–3140. Grill your own steak at one of three grills. Menu also includes tasty seafood and chicken. Dinner only.

Croce's Restaurants and Jazz Bars, 802 5th Avenue at F Street. (619) 233–4355. Two restaurants, three bars offer both American and Southwestern cuisine. Live jazz and R&B nightly.

The Horton Grand Hotel, 311 Island Avenue. (800) 542–1886; (619) 544–1886. Belle of the lively Gaslamp Quarter. Guests favor the cozy intimacy of this 1886 Victorian hotel. All 108 rooms, including twenty-four suites, have antique decor, cozy fireplaces, and TV (but rather small bathrooms). Suites feature microwave ovens, wet bar, two TVs. Restaurant, lounge, bar, Saturday afternoon tea, Sunday champagne buffet brunch. Overnight parking fee.

Downtown

Napa Valley Grill, 502 Horton Plaza. (619) 238–5440. Great view over the harbor from the top of Horton Plaza. Napa Valley cuisine; pasta, fish, steak, chicken; Sunday brunch.

Omni Hotel, 675 L Street. (619) 231–6664. Across a pedestrian sky bridge from the home of the San Diego Padres, Petco Park. The 511 rooms, including thirty-six condominiums, feature minibar, makeup mirror, CD clock radio, DVD player, coffeemaker, and bathrobes. The Terrace Grill is perfect for sandwiches and snacks; espresso bar, fitness center, and large meeting facilities.

Coronado

Coronado Brewing Company, 170 Orange Avenue. (619) 437–4452. Dine alongside the open-pit fireplace while enjoying wood-fired pizzas, pastas, burgers, buffalo strips, sandwiches, and salads. Fresh fish, steaks, and chicken are other favorites.

Hotel Del Coronado, 1500 Orange Avenue. (619) 435–6611. Landmark 1888 Victorian charmer sprawled along thirty-three beachfront acres; 688 renovated, air-conditioned rooms with TV, minibar, some with hair dryers and balconies. Beautiful gardens, two heated swimming pools, spas. Terrific Sunday buffet brunch. One restaurant and a deli. Overnight parking fee.

Loews Coronado Bay Resort, 4000 Coronado Bay Road. (800) 235–6357; (619) 424–4000. Four-diamond AAA and four-star *Mobil Travel Guide* awards for this luxury waterfront resort spread on a private fifteen-acre peninsula. Its 438 rooms, including thirty-eight suites with private balconies, are custom furnished with minibar and refrigerator, two telephones, TV, spacious bathroom with oversize tub and separate shower; twenty-four-hour room service. Enjoy the good life around three heated swimming pools, spas, a fitness center, three bayside tennis courts, and an eighty-slip marina. Cafe and deli; Sunday brunch. Children's activities; getaway packages; overnight parking fee.

Glorietta Bay Inn, 1630 Glorietta Boulevard. (800) 283–9383; (619) 453–3101. Built in 1908 as residence for "Sugar Baron" John D. Spreckels, San Diego's greatest benefactor, this Edwardian mansion has been beautifully restored and is a designated Historic Landmark. Just a block from the ocean, the inn features one hundred rooms and suites, some with kitchenettes, patios, or balconies overlooking Glorietta Bay. Complimentary continental breakfast is served daily in the veranda room; heated swimming pool, spa pool, music room, and business center.

For More Information

San Diego Convention and Visitors Bureau, International Visitor Information Center, 11 Horton Plaza, San Diego, CA 92101. (619) 236–1212; www.san diego.org.

Old Town Chamber of Commerce, 3965 Artista, San Diego, CA 92110. (619) 291–4903.

Coronado Visitors Bureau, 1047 B Avenue, Coronado, CA 92118. (935) 437–8788.

South of the Border Serenade

Tijuana, Ensenada / 3 Nights

This three-night, four-day adventure south of the border from San Diego to sunny, friendly Mexico affords an interesting change in culture, language, currency, food, drink, and scenery. You don't have to take a plane to get to a foreign country when Mexico is within a few hours' drive of Los Angeles. In teeming Tijuana, the internationally famous U.S.-Mexican border town, and in Ensenada, a smaller resort town 70 miles farther south, in Baja, California, you experience a different lifestyle as you are serenaded by mariachis; shop for duty-free bargains in perfume, cosmetics, and Mexican-made liquor, jewelry, pottery, and other imports; and tour a century-old winery. (*NOTE:* Each U.S. citizen may bring back $400 worth of purchases, duty-free; adults may each bring back one liter of alcohol. At this writing the dollar is worth about eleven pesos.)

☐ Duty-free shopping

☐ Authentic Mexican cuisine

☐ Beaches

☐ Winery

☐ Mariachis

☐ Fishing

☐ Discos

These aren't two sleepy, dusty little Mexican villages. Tijuana is a gaudy, vibrant jumble of noise, traffic, and people. Ensenada, though more laid-back, is a vital, upbeat, friendly port that never wants to sleep.

For a more enjoyable Mexican sojourn, bring along a gallon of drinking water to have on hand. The best way to avoid stomach upsets or traveler's diarrhea is to not drink the tap water. Stick to sealed bottles or cans of beer or soda. (Mexican beers are great.) Drink these beverages right out of the bottle. Never use ice in your drinks. Avoid salads, raw fish, raw meat, and raw vegetables; eat only fruits you can peel. Coffee and tea are safe when made with boiled water. Brush your teeth with mouthwash or bottled water. Tuck some Pepto-Bismol, Imodium, and/or Lomotil in your travel med-kit in the event of any stomach upsets.

Tank up before you cross the border into Mexico. Be certain to purchase Mexican auto insurance as your U.S. insurance does not cover you for liability or property damage in Mexico.

Due to tightened border security, you will need proof of citizenship—passport or birth certificate (a driver's license is not sufficient)—upon return to the United States.

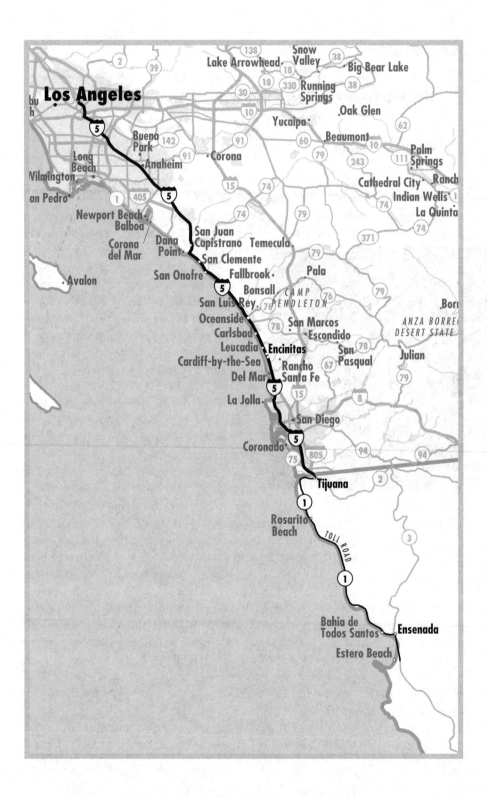

NOTE: To phone Mexico from the United States, dial 011–52 plus the city prefix number, unless otherwise noted.

Day 1 / Morning

From Los Angeles drive south on I–5, the Santa Ana Freeway, to San Diego—about 120 miles—and then drive 15 to 20 miles farther to cross the Mexican border, skirting Tijuana now and visiting it on your return from Ensenada, when you can allow whatever amount of time you'd like to spend there. Ensenada can be reached via a free road and also a toll (*cuota*) road. This escape is via the well-maintained, less crowded toll road from Tijuana.

On I–5 south just past Carlsbad, take the Encinitas Boulevard exit to Coast Highway 1 and have lunch in charming Encinitas, an easy freeway exit and return.

LUNCH: Pino's Cucina Italiana, 967 South Coast Highway 101, Encinitas. (760) 632–1901. This popular favorite for fresh pasta dishes, antipasto, and delicious lasagna is a fine place to relax and enjoy good Italian specialties en route to your Mexican adventures.

Afternoon

Return to I–5 and continue south through San Diego and to the Mexican border. They wave you right through, but on your return to the United States you must stop for customs inspection, though not every car is inspected. Have your passport or birth certificate handy. Be prepared for a long wait at that time. Congestion at the border can take more than two hours during the week and longer on week-ends and holidays. Try to avoid crossing the border at those times. Although it is not mandatory, you should purchase Mexican auto insurance, since your U.S. insurance does not cover you for liability and property damage in Mexico. You can obtain it through your auto club in advance of your trip or on both sides of the border. It is easiest to buy it on the U.S. side. You'll see many signs along the way; most are near fast-food eateries and convenient to the freeway. Have your auto registration slip in hand, since if you have to trot back to the car for it you'll lose your place in line. This insurance typically costs about $10 a day for a three-day visit.

At the border leaving the United States, you want to be in the Rosarito/Ensenada lane; stay to the right. You also want the *cuota* (toll) road. If at any time you need to verify directions, do so at the toll booth as you pay your $2.25 for each toll (three times each way). Ask your question quickly, before you pay, as they hustle you right through.

Speed limits and distances are posted in kilometers and are easy to convert into miles. Just multiply the kilometers by six and move the decimal point one space to the left. Watch all road signs carefully for directions or you may wind up in Mexicali or Tecate.

The scenic, well-kept transpeninsular highway curving along the blue-green ocean skims above lonesome sandy beaches. There is a turnoff to Rosarito Beach, about 17 miles south of Tijuana. If you want to drive through to see this popular beach city, the road intersects back to the Ensenada toll road. Magnificent vistas accompany you all the way down the coast on this uncrowded highway. You pay your last *cuota* at **Ensenada,** 7 miles from town, as you catch a glimpse of beautiful Bahia de Todos Santos (Bay of All Saints).

Check into your hotel to get your bearings, then go on out to explore downtown Ensenada. When driving, you'll soon note that not all streets have names, but some are identified at major intersections on the horizontal light bars in the center of the street. Remember that Avenida Lopez Mateos is 1st Street, and Ruiz Street and Castillo are the north and south downtown boundaries. Boulevard Costero, also known as Lazaro Cardenas, is the divided highway along the ocean.

Ensenada's vitality is contagious, marked by the town's liveliness; friendly, hospitable people; and endless shopping and dining attractions. Stores and restaurants all accept U.S. dollars. (*NOTE:* An easy way to figure the conversion is to divide the peso by eleven for an approximate amount and add a bit.) There is a good deal of traffic and few parking spaces, so you might prefer wandering about on foot along Avenida Lopez Mateos, the city's main drag. This busy street has redbrick sidewalks, handsome wooden benches, large planters, and inviting street-side dining areas.

DINNER: Casamar Restaurant-Bar, 987 Boulevard Lazaro Cardenas (Boulevard Costero). Easy to find in the tourist area on the busy bayfront boulevard, Casamar has been considered the area's finest for steak and fresh seafood for more than twenty years. The large dining room has lighted candles, tablecloths, and attentive service. The house specialty is Abalone Casamar (in season), a pricey entree of sautéed abalone topped with crabmeat, chopped shrimp, and wine sauce. Popular Lobster a la Veracruzana heads an extensive menu of fish, shrimp, and lobster selections; steaks are New York cut and filet mignon with mushroom sauce. Treat yourself to a flaming dessert of luscious peach Melba—vanilla ice cream with peaches and whipped cream flambéed tableside. Enjoy music in the adjoining El Galeon Bar from 9:00 P.M. Tuesday through Saturday.

LODGING: Hotel Villa Marina, Avenida Lopez Mateos and Blancarte Street, Ensenada, Baja California, Mexico. 8–33–21, (800) 310–9687. (U.S. mailing address: P.O. Box 727, Bonita, CA 91908.) Attractive, twelve-story hotel is a convenient downtown landmark; 146 rooms, well furnished, nice bathrooms; some private balconies have bay views. Cable TV, air-conditioning, room service, heated swimming pool, Jacuzzi. Shopping gallery; cafeteria coffee shop, and penthouse restaurant; monitored parking lot.

Day 2 / Morning

BREAKFAST: Full breakfast at the hotel's coffee shop. Includes hotcakes, and eggs American or Mexican style.

Avenida Lopez Mateos is alive with little shops and restaurants. There are *farmacias* (pharmacies) where you can buy prescription drugs over-the-counter without prescriptions at substantially lower prices than in the United States. Cosmetics and perfumes are less expensive, too. Mariachis stroll along with guitars and trumpets en route to serenade diners in cantinas and restaurants. *Licores* (liquor) stores offer attractive prices, particularly in Mexican-made Kahlúa; corner food carts feature local specialties for hungry patrons. Merchandise is not as inexpensive as it used to be, though prices are said to be lower than those in Tijuana. You'll find good values in ironwood sculpture, pottery, T-shirts, sterling-silver jewelry (stamped 925), Mexican handicrafts, and leather apparel. Sidewalk vendors offer wind chimes, jewelry, and novelty items. Guess?, at the corner of Avenida Lopez Mateos and Avenida Ruiz, is a cool place to shop. Across the street in **Plaza Hussong**—an attractive multistory shopping center—you can explore the beautiful Mango Mango Restaurant, serving Mexican and American specialties, and then relax on wide, shady wooden benches and watch the traffic stream by.

You'll probably hear the noise coming from **Hussong's Cantina,** a few doors away, at Ruiz 113, before you see it. Just as in the movie *Casablanca* in which "everybody goes to Rick's," everyone who visits Ensenada goes to the legendary swinging Hussong's. This plain-looking saloon with a long bar, sawdust on the floor, and mariachi entertainment caters to a boisterous young crowd; it has been the town's number-one watering hole and hangout since it opened in 1892 and still shatters records for crowds and noise.

Across Ruiz from Hussong's, **Papas and Beer** is where all that loud rhythmic music pours from. Visit its busy upstairs bar and disco, where you can join congenial locals munching on the cafe's tasty signature french fries (*papas*), washed down with cool Mexican beer. The **Oxidos Cafe** at street level serves American dishes, seafood, and sushi. A few doors away, **Dorian's Department Store** has long been an upscale choice for cosmetics, jewelry, and clothing.

LUNCH: Las Brasas Restaurant (Pollos Rostizado), Avenida Lopez Mateos 486, between Avenida Gastelum and Avenida Ruiz, Ensenada. Here's where they roast 220 chickens a day, and from the sidewalk you can watch the golden birds spinning on the rotisserie (sixty at a time), while tortilla ladies deftly pat and shape dough into perfectly round thin tortillas, using something similar to a hamburger press. Dine inside or on the sunny patio. One-half roast chicken is served with fries, tortillas, and beans. Other selections include seafood and Mexican specialties. (Closed Tuesday.)

Afternoon

Ensenada has delicious bread, *bollilos* (rolls), and pastries to snack on or buy to take home and stash in the freezer. Look for the PANADERIA (bakery) sign. Among others are Panaderia La Mexican, on Castillo Street; Panaderia el Nuevo Cristal, just off Benito Juarez at Calle Sexta (6th Street), next to the cathedral; and the Tea Salon next to El Rey Sol, a charming bakery and gourmet coffee, espresso, and cappuccino spot.

Tour **Bodegas de Santo Tomas,** Avenida Miramar 666 (8–25–09), Baja California's oldest winery, established in 1888. Take Lopez Mateos to Miramar and turn right, proceeding about 6 blocks to the sprawling winery. There are forty-five-minute guided, narrated tours. For small fees, visitors enjoy wine tastings and samplings of assorted breads and cheeses, all available for purchase. The Gift Shop and Wine Stores are stocked with wine, logo T-shirts, glasses, and other attractive souvenirs. (Open daily from 10:00 A.M. to 4:00 P.M., with tours on the hour from 10:00 A.M. to 1:00 P.M., and one at 3:00 P.M.)

In this festive, lighthearted city, the better shopping area on Lopez Mateos is from Blancarte around the Hotel Villa Marina to Castillo Street. **Sara's** elegant, cool shop features cosmetics, perfumes (including Ralph Lauren, Calvin Klein, and Chanel), charming Lladro figurines; boutique clothing is downstairs. In this stretch you'll also find Casa Crystal's sleek silver jewelry and art objects. Mario's Silver Shop gleams with lovely gold and silver jewelry, handbags, and fine guitars. Explore Asin's large selection of Lladro figurines from Spain as well as Mexican wood carvings at good prices. Across the street, Old Pier Block is reliable for T-shirts, straw hats, and handbags. Shoppers should also look for open-air markets and vendor stands on some of the side streets. Many stores offer discounts or are open to negotiation.

DINNER: Las Cazuelas restaurant/bar, Boulevard Costero and Sangines (next to La Casa del Abulon), Ensenada. 6–54–60. Drive to Costero Boulevard, turn left, and continue about 1 mile. This is another favorite, with excellent cuisine and service that spoils you. Moderately priced menu features Mexican dishes—delicate burritos, shrimp ranchero, *chipotle,* and so on—and also prime rib, filet mignon, lobster, fresh seafood, and New York steak. Live rhythmic lounge music enhances your dinner, as will a dessert of peach Melba prepared and flambéed tableside.

LODGING: Hotel Villa Marina.

Day 3 / Morning

BREAKFAST: Sorrento Restaurant, on Avenida Lopez Mateos next to the Cortez Motor Hotel, Ensenada. Regular American breakfast fare of bacon and eggs can be recharged with *chiliquiles,* hot red sauce, chorizo, and Salsa Ketchup. But the pancakes are delicious—light and fluffy.

After breakfast browse around this exciting part of downtown. If you're driving, note that parking meters are not in effect on Saturday and Sunday; the green zones are free to park in while shopping in the nearby stores. The busy sidewalks and roads are clean, and along Avenida Lopez Mateos arcades protect shops and shoppers from the sun. For cold drinks and snacks, Blanco, a large supermarket, is on Gastelum off Lopez Mateos.

Follow Boulevard Lazaro Cardenas along the blue crescent-shaped bay to Estero Beach, 6 miles south of Ensenada, for lunch at tony **Estero Beach Resort.** You'll pass a military base, groves of olive trees, roadside stores, and vendors selling baskets and pottery. Turn right at the sign for Estero Beach and then left to the resort.

Built in 1937, the resort is a sprawling, cushy complex of villas, elegant shops, a restaurant, and a museum. Drive down the long, impressive entrance road lined with tall palm trees and tropical plantings, and park toward the rear near the restaurant.

LUNCH: Las Terrazas Restaurant, Estero Beach Hotel and Resort, Ensenada. Dine on the beachfront cafe's charming patio beneath crisp white parasols. Try the shrimp or lobster cocktail or sample other menu specialties of fried chicken, fish, hamburgers, and Mexican dishes; Mexican buffet Saturday and Sunday.

Afternoon

Walk past the restaurant, villas, and cottages for a glimpse of the ocean and the stunning blue lagoon. Follow the broad terrace that edges the private bay to its curved viewpoint beneath a large thatched umbrella encircled by stone benches. Relax a while in this idyllic tropical setting and watch the swimmers in the bay and the small boats in the ocean beyond.

Your next stop is the museum, or **Exhibition Center,** to see the outstanding Mexican Cultural Exhibit, an extensive collection of pre-Columbian sculpture and ancient art. Then take time to explore the hotel's two elegant shops, offering fine merchandise totally unexpected in this semi-remote beach area.

Bazaar Mexicano is a treasure house of a large variety of select merchandise from all over Mexico, including handicrafts, iron-wood sculpture, art objects, hand-embroidered clothing, silver, and jewelry. Most notable is the beautiful hand-painted pottery from Tonala, Tlaquepaque, and elsewhere in Mexico—pitchers, vases, birds, and other designs in soft, luminous colors and glazes. An adjoining room displays more pottery, enormous paper flowers, and other handicrafts beneath a huge skylight. Prices seem good throughout, but you may do better in the roadside shops en route back to Ensenada.

Near the resort entrance, the striking Mayan-style **Import Shop,** framed by huge stone pillars, showcases exquisite and expensive merchandise, including fine crystal, Rolex watches, silver and gold jewelry, designer clothing, and other imports from Brazil, Portugal, Israel, Italy, Sweden, and India, among other countries, as well as Mexican glassware. Both shops are open daily from 9:00 A.M. to 6:00 P.M.

On the way back to Ensenada, look for roadside shops offering lower-priced baskets, pottery, and other native handicrafts. Here's the place to employ your bargaining skills. **Galeria Mexicana** has a large selection of well-priced vases and other pottery. Across the road, **Bazaar de Mexico** offers clothing, jewelry, and pottery. Additionally, several small roadside markets also sell reasonably priced Mexican art, pottery, and clothing. Look for **Ramon's** sign for HIELO (ice—and cold drinks), where shelves are stacked with pottery at very good prices.

DINNER: El Rey Sol, Avenida Lopez Mateos No. 1000 (corner of Blancarte), Ensenada. Blue awnings highlight this 1947 landmark French restaurant, long considered Ensenada's finest. Rather expensive gourmet entrees include chicken mole, filet mignon, and New York steak. Service can be indifferent, but—ole!—mariachis serenade diners, and the steaks are tender.

On your last evening in Ensenada, stroll along effervescent Avenida Lopez Mateos, which has considerably more car traffic at night than during the daytime. The air is balmy, and lilting music filters from the cantinas and from the radios in the uninterrupted lines of cars. The sidewalk is crowded with people out for an evening promenade. It's a very upbeat scene that will leave you with a warm memory of Ensenada.

LODGING: Hotel Villa Marina.

Day 4 / Morning

BREAKFAST: At the hotel.

Leave Ensenada early, taking the toll road north to **Tijuana.** Allow sufficient time to spend in Tijuana, plus a good couple of hours crossing the border back into the United States. It's a magnificent drive on the divided highway that rolls gently between the tawny cliffs and the peaceful ocean.

As you drive into Tijuana, look for **Avenida Revolución,** the well-known main tourist street. You'll know when you've reached it because of the crush of cars and people; the restaurants, bars, liquor stores, shopping plazas, and sidewalk vendors; and the nonstop movement.

Dynamic Tijuana claims that more Americans visit it than any other foreign city, and, like you, they're all looking for somewhere to park. This vibrant town with twenty-two million border crossings annually is a shopper's best friend, offering lower, duty-free prices in French perfume, cosmetics, liquor, designer clothing, and other imports. As in Ensenada, *farmacias* (pharmacies) sell prescription drugs over-the-counter at lower-than-U.S. prices. The city is further noted for sizzling nightlife and lively spectator sports, such as horse and dog racing and bullfights.

Exciting, tawdry, and raucous Tijuana gained notoriety and glamour during the 1920s Prohibition era, when excitement-loving, thirsty Hollywood stars flocked to its bars and gambling casinos. The city was expensively renovated in the 1970s—streets were widened, potholes filled, and street vendors deposited in indoor malls and arcades. Tune up your bargaining skills—this is the major league.

Sara's tony store on Avenida Revolución, at 4th, is known for discounted cosmetics, perfume, crystal, and Lladro figurines. Take the elevator upstairs for designer fashions and ongoing sales. A parking structure is just up 4th Street.

Trendy **Le Drug Store,** with a sidewalk cafe at Revolución and 4th, is a good source for souvenirs and postcards. Near the corner you can have your photo taken astride a festively clad donkey, for a fee. Ever-popular Caesar's Restaurant, at 4th Street, the originator of the Caesar salad, serves continental cuisine.

Bargain hunters will find outlet stores located in the large plazas away from the crowded city center. But there are familiar, prestigious names to shop along Avenida Revolución. Note that in all outlet stores, you should examine your selections carefully before purchase to be sure they're in new condition. Further, be aware that some designer names may be bogus or rip-offs.

Guess? has an attractive outlet store at 540 Avenida Revolución between 1st and 2nd Streets diagonally across from the Hard Rock Cafe. Although this store is fun to browse, it doesn't seem to offer any substantial bargains, as prices are fairly close to those in Los Angeles.

Ralph Lauren Outlet Store, in a miniplaza on 7th Street between Avenida Revolución, Madero, and Negrete, offers deep discounts on its popular Polo shirts, cologne, neckties, shirts, and men's suits. Look for women's sweaters, cotton knit dresses, and other items at the rear of the shop.

Ellesse Outlet Shop is in the same miniplaza as Ralph Lauren, on 7th Street between Avenida Revolución, Madero, and Negrete. It features some Calvin Klein merchandise along with other designer labels, though not all may be the real thing.

LUNCH: Hard Rock Cafe, Avenida Revolución at 2nd Street. 85–02–06. This addition to the popular chain has its distinctive signature red car halfway through its roof as in other locations. You'll find the typically long lines of patrons waiting for a table, hamburgers, and fries, as well as familiar Hard Rock decor and noise.

Afternoon

To visit the striking **Tijuana Cultural Center,** at Paseo de los Héroes and Avenida Mina in the Tijuana Rio Zone, turn right on 2nd Street to Paseo de los Héroes, go around the circle, go back 1 block, and then turn right on Mina. Easily recognized by its monumental dome and powerful architecture, the center houses Omnimax theater films, exhibit halls, a performing arts theater, a restaurant, and shops. (Open Tuesday through Sunday from 10:00 A.M. to 8:00 P.M.)

Across the street, modern **Plaza Rio's** greatly enlarged shopping mall has a diversity of restaurants, department and specialty stores, a supermarket, and the popular Suzett Bakery. The unusual, expanded **Plaza del Zapata** across the way features only shoes, of all types, from many outlets.

To get to the San Ysidro border, make a right on Paseo de los Héroes and go straight until you see the sign for San Diego, which leads to the crowded border, where you'll find about six lanes of cars crossing to the U.S. side. Watch for signs above the individual gateways indicating the lanes for cars with two passengers or carpools of four people, and get in the correct lane. Otherwise, as you near the gate you'll have to edge your way in line ahead of other drivers, who may not be too gracious about letting you get in front of them. Keep your proof of citizenship readily available in case customs wants to see it.

When you've crossed the border, you are on I–5 north. Stay on it until you reach Los Angeles, or cut over to 405.

There's More

Riviera del Pacifico, Boulevard Costero, Ensenada. (800) 526–6676. The sprawling building with graceful arches was a famous 1930s plush gambling casino patronized by Hollywood film stars and is now a social and cultural center. Enjoy a drink to yesteryear on Patio Bugambilia and stroll the lushly landscaped grounds.

La Bufadora, Ensenada's most famous attraction, is 20 miles south, to the tip of Punta Banda Peninsula. At this dramatic and natural "blowhole" carved into the cliffs, when the tides are high the ocean crashing into the rocks spouts a geyser of foam and water almost 100 feet high.

Flea markets and swap meets, Ensenada. Los Globos is the largest, outdoors on Calle 9, 3 blocks east of Reforma. Open weekends. Additional outdoor weekend swap meet at Riveroll and Calle 6.

Export Free, 841 Avenida Revolución between 2nd and 3rd Streets, Tijuana. Great place for perfumes, liquors, gifts, and cigars.

La Casa del Tobacco, 1115 Avenido Revolución at 6th Street, Tijuana. A don't-miss for Cuban cigars and a cup of espresso.

Bullfights are a rich part of Mexico's heritage. Tijuana has two major bullrings, at 100 Caliente Boulevard and at the Bullring-by-the-Sea. Season runs May through September; open Sunday at 4:30 P.M.; closed in June. For specific dates call 80–18–08; for tickets and transportation call (888) 775–2417.

Foxploration, just five minutes from Rosarito Beach. (866) FOX–BAJA. This working movie studio is where the box-office hit *Titanic* and other films were made. See the props used and experience the actual movie sets. Tours Monday, Thursday, and Friday, 9:30 A.M. to 5:30 P.M. and Saturday and Sunday 10:00 A.M. to 6:30 P.M.

Racetrack. Just south of Paseo de Los Héroes, Tijuana. Agua Caliente racetrack offers year-round greyhound racing, nightly except Tuesday, at 7:45 P.M. Admission.

Bingo daily at 6:30 P.M. The U.S. information and hot line number is (800) 998–9668.

Plaza Cívica, downtown, on Boulevard Costero, Ensenada. In attractively land-scaped Three Heads Park, a broad terrace displays giant (12-foot) sculptured busts of Mexico's greatest heroes: Benito Juárez, Miguel Hidalgo, and Venustiano Carranza.

Special Events

End of January. Annual Caesar Salad Festival, Tijuana.

January, February, and early March. Whale-watching trips, Ensenada.

Mid-February. Hussong's Fishing Tournament, two days, Ensenada.

Late February to early March. National Surfing Championship, Caribbean Mardi Gras, Ensenada.

Mid-March. Benito Juárez Birthday, Ensenada.

End of March. Tijuana-Rosarito-Ensenada Bicycle Race, Tijuana.

Early May. Annual Regatta Newport–Ensenada, Mountain Bike Ride. Batalla de Puebla, Ensenada.

Late June to early July. Expo Ensenada, eighteen days, Ensenada.

Mid-July. First Half Marathon by Cross Country, Ensenada. 100K Race–Tijuana-Rosarito-Ensenada.

Middle to end of August. Fair of the Californias, Tijuana.

Early September. Congress of Investigation Sea of Cortez, four days; annual seafood festival; annual three-day Fiesta Viva Expo, Ensenada.

Mid-September. Mexican Food Fair, Ensenada.

Independence Day, Ensenada Discovery, annual Chili Cook-Off, Ensenada.

Early October. Southwestern Yacht Regatta, three days. Mountain Bike Ride, Sordomudo Ranch, Ensenada.

Mid-October. Chili Cook-Off, Octoberfest, three days; Ensenada Gran Prix, Ensenada.

Mid-November. Annual Score Ford/Tecate Baja 1000, Ensenada; Revolution Day, Ensenada.

Mid-December. Christmas Posadas, Tijuana.

Other Recommended Restaurants and Lodgings

Ensenada

Baja Inn Hotel, Boulevard Costero 1536. (888) 226–1033. Sunday Mexican-American Buffet Brunch includes fresh fruit platter, egg specialties, chilaquiles, refried beans, French toast; 7:00 A.M. to 1:00 P.M. Fifty-one nicely furnished rooms, three suites, satellite TV, heated swimming pool, restaurant, bar, underground garage, twenty-four-hour security guard.

Corona Hotel, Boulevard Costero 1442 (U.S. mailing address: 482 West San Ysidro Boulevard, Suite 303, San Ysidro, CA 92173). 6–09–01. Sweeping four-story modern hotel; heated swimming pool, lobby bar, room service, restaurant.

Cortez Motor Hotel, Avenida Lopez Mateos 1089. 8–23–07; (800) 528–1284 (reservations). Excellent location, spacious guest rooms and bathrooms, cable TV, heated swimming pool, restaurant, cocktail lounge, underground monitored parking.

Estero Beach Hotel Resort, P.O. Box 86, Ensenada, B.C. Mexico. 176–6225; www.hotelesterobeach.com. Luxury beachfront resort; 107 rooms, cottages, villas, and suites, with private terraces overlooking Estero Bay. Museum, shops, tennis courts, lagoon, restaurant, exclusive RV park.

Tijuana

Guadalajara Grill, 19 Paseos de Los Héroes in the Zona Rio. Good variety of tasty Mexican dishes and a popular steak house.

La Leña, 4560 Agua Caliente Boulevard. 86–29–20. Near the golf club. It's busy because everybody goes for the tender, tasty New York and T-bone steaks.

Grand Hotel Tijuana, 4500 Agua Caliente Boulevard. (800) 472–6385. Sophisticated, modern, twenty-five-story five-star hotel; 422 deluxe rooms and suites. Heated swimming pool, Jacuzzi, tennis courts; three restaurants, bars; conference center.

For More Information

Ensenada State Secretary of Tourism, corner of Calle las Rocas and Costero Boulevard, Ensenada. 53–667–6–22–22.

Tijuana Tourism and Convention Bureau, Paseo de Los Héroes, 9365–201 (U.S. mailing address: P.O. Box 434523, San Diego, CA 92143–4523). (888) 775–2417 or 011–52–66/84–05–37.

Tijuana Information Booth at the San Ysidro border is open daily from 8:00 A.M. to 7:00 P.M. The information booth for pedestrians is 1 block past the border, on the right-hand side.

Tijuana Information Center Downtown, Avenida Revolución and 1st Street. 52–66–85–84–72. Open daily from 9:00 A.M. to 7:00 P.M.

USA Office of Information for Baja California (International Marketing/Promotions Associates, Inc.), 7860 Mission Center Court (#202), San Diego, CA 92108; (619) 298–4105 or (800) 522–1516 (in California); (800) 225–2786 (in the rest of the United States).

Fondo Mixto de Ensenada, P.O. Box 4492, Camino de la Plaza, Suite 1191, San Ysidro, CA 92173. (800) 310–9687. In Ensenada: Boulevard Costero and Miramar Streets. (800) 310–9687.

Amusement Park Heaven

Disneyland, Anaheim, Knott's Berry Farm, Buena Park / 1 Night

Though Southern California has many super attractions, this lighthearted escape to two world-famous amusement parks is the ultimate in fun, fantasy, and entertainment. Let the years roll back as you soar on a rocket jet, ride roller coasters upside down, watch parades, and amble through a lively Old West mining town. One visit is never enough, especially for children. You and your family will want to return again and again to experience exciting new attractions and revisit old favorites.

☐ Amusement parks

☐ Theme parks

☐ Shopping

☐ Parades

Day 1 / Morning

From Los Angeles take I–5, the Santa Ana Freeway, south for the short (27-mile) drive to **Buena Park** for Knott's Berry Farm and down the road to Anaheim for Disneyland. This area is generally slightly warmer than Los Angeles, so dress accordingly. Allow about an hour and a half in travel time, depending on traffic.

To reach Knott's Berry Farm, take the Beach Boulevard exit, turn right, and stay on Beach Boulevard, passing the Medieval Times Dinner and Tournament and the Ripley's Believe It or Not Museum. You'll soon see some of Knott's high-flying amusement rides. Stay to the right, drive beneath the large Knott's Berry Farm banner, and pull into the parking lot on the left. (Free three-hour parking for customers of Mrs. Knott's Chicken Dinner Restaurant and California Marketplace; fee for theme-park parking.)

Knott's Berry Farm, at 8039 Beach Boulevard in Buena Park (714–220–5200), grew from a mom-and-pop roadside berry stand and small farm in the 1920s to a mega-million-dollar roller-coaster-thriller attraction. Knott's Berry Farm is a story with a happy ending that began when Walter Knott started gathering a few abandoned derelict buildings from deserted western towns and moved them to the farm around 1940, as a diversion for diners waiting in line for his wife Cordelia's fried chicken dinners and delectable boysenberry pie. Ghost Town, a California mining town, gradually took shape as more rustic buildings were added and the theme further embroidered. Other entertainment areas followed. Visitors

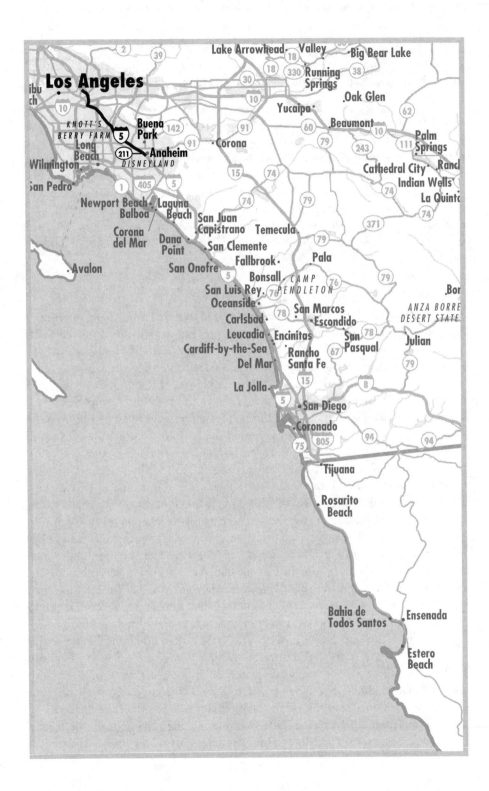

still stand in line for the fried chicken, and the berry farm is one of Southern California's leading attractions. You can extend your visit by overnighting at Knott's deluxe hotel (see "Other Recommended Restaurants and Lodgings" at the end of the chapter).

LUNCH: Mrs. Knott's Chicken Dinner Restaurant, Knott's Berry Farm, Buena Park. (714) 220–5080. You may have to wait for a table (reservations are for parties of twelve or more). One and a half million chicken dinners a year are served, so go with the favorite: Mrs. Knott's Traditional Chicken Dinner, served from 11:00 A.M. A basket of hot buttermilk biscuits is followed by chunky chicken noodle soup or cherry rhubarb appetizer, next is a mixed green salad, and then the large, thick-crusted, golden pieces of fried chicken with mashed potatoes, country gravy, and vegetable. For dessert it's boysenberry or apple pie, vanilla ice cream, or boysenberry sherbet.

Afternoon

The country's oldest theme park is actively geared to family enjoyment, offering six distinctive entertainment areas: Camp Snoopy, Fiesta Village, the Boardwalk, Old West Ghost Town, Wild Water Wilderness, and Indian Trails. Each features its own restaurants, specialty shops, exciting rides, shows, and ever-new attractions.

Pick up a map at the entrance to help guide you through the 150-acre park and to check the daily showtime schedule. Go to the right for **Camp Snoopy,** a special wonderland with more than thirty rides, attractions, and a petting farm for small children. Then work your way around the park. In **Fiesta Village,** with its bright Marketplace and mariachis, zoom on Montezooma's Revenge, a thrilling upside-down-and-backward ride. Jaguar!—the 2,700-foot-long big cat of roller coasters—soars 60 feet into the air, then dives, twists, circles, and swoops high above the ground. The Boardwalk, a thrilling attraction, transforms the Roaring 20s area into a beach-themed roller coaster featuring HammerHead, a rousing high-intensity water-oriented ride that spins riders from a shark grotto to a height of 80 feet, at times riding upside down and sideways. The soaring Windjammer roller coasters race side-by-side in 60-foot plunges and soaring vertical loops, and the high-speed Boomerang roller coaster turns you upside down six times in a minute. If you crave more excitement, strap yourself into the Parachute Sky Jump. Before you can say "Geronimo," you're in a daring, twenty-story parachute fall.

Supreme Scream is one of the world's tallest descending thrill rides, raising riders thirty stories into the air before blasting them back to earth. **Perilous Plunge,** the tallest, steepest, and wettest water ride, sends boat riders up a 121-foot-tall lift before plummeting them down a scary water chute. **GhostRider,** the longest wooden coaster in the western United States, is a spectacular thriller.

Introduced in 2004, the **RipTide** is a spinning, high-flying thrill ride located in the Boardwalk area. The **Silver Bullet** is a western-themed roller coaster sus-

pended high in the air that turns upside down six times and completes one vertical loop. It climbs 146 feet and has an initial drop of 109 feet. It also spirals and
corkscrews.

Move on to **Old West Ghost Town,** where lively country music fills the air
and where rural Main Street, with its covered wagons, Old West saloon, and blacksmith at the forge, evokes a sense of history. Browse for knickknacks at the General
Store. Tall, leafy eucalyptus trees provide generous shade, and masses of bright flowers soften the hundred-year-old weathered wooden buildings, with their wide
verandas and sagging doorways, moved here from forgotten towns. Though there
may be hundreds of people about, somehow you don't feel crowded in this low-
key, comfortable ambience.

Just beyond Old West Ghost Town, **Indian Trails** explores the heritage of
Native American tribes as artisans demonstrate handicrafts, including canoe carving, mask and totem-pole making, beadwork, weaving, and pottery. While storytellers spin legends, kids can have their faces painted. The Native American food is
good here, particularly the Indian fry bread and the Navajo tacos.

It's wise to visit **Wild Water Wilderness** last, as you do get wet in this century-
old California river wilderness park. The high spot is Bigfoot Rapids, a wet and wild
ride where passengers are bounced and splashed as they ride down a long, turbu-
lent man-made river, spinning in fast-moving currents and shooting under waterfalls. The Mystery Lodge attraction takes you on a mystical, magical journey deep
into the Native American West. The park hours vary and are seasonal. For information call (714) 220–5200. There's an admission fee and senior discount.

Adjacent to the theme park, **Soak City, U.S.A.,** at 8039 Beach Boulevard, is
Knott's separately gated thirteen-acre colorful water-adventure park geared primarily
to preteens and families. Packed with twenty-one intense water rides and attractions,
the park is elaborately themed to vintage Southern California beach towns of the
1950s and 1960s.

Leave Knott's Berry Farm and drive to Disneyland Park and the Disneyland
Hotel, about 10 miles away. The easiest route to the Disneyland Hotel is to get back
on I–5 south and take the Ball Road exit. Turn right to West Street, then turn left;
the Disneyland Hotel is on your right, at the corner of Cerritos and West (check-in
is after 3:00 P.M.). Stop in the main lobby to purchase your tickets/passports to
Disneyland and then board the tram, which drops you at the Main Gate, or ride the
monorail, which deposits you in Tomorrowland. Both go round-trip all day until the
park closes.

Disneyland is the most popular attraction in the world—a must-see, ever
since it opened in 1955, for statesmen, royalty, celebrities, and just about everyone
else who visits or resides in Southern California. It offers more than sixty adventures in eight different themed lands. Wandering through its eighty-five acres is not
just another stroll in the park; in *this* park you take your imagination along to visit
Tomorrowland, Fantasyland, Adventureland, Critter Country, Frontierland, New

Orleans Square, Mickey's Toontown, and Main Street U.S.A., a nostalgic prototype of a circa 1900 small town, where the streetlamps are more than 150 years old.

The folks at Disneyland recommend that no matter the season, the best times to see the most popular attractions are before noon and after dinner. Restaurants are busiest at lunch and dinner hours—same as at home—so try to eat early or late. You'll also find weekdays less crowded than Saturday and Sunday. Disney's free FASTPASS, offered on selected attractions, is a great time-saver. Guests receive a computer-assigned boarding time as an alternative to standing in line.

Enter the park and receive your free *Disneyland Today* schedule of daily enter-tainment and a handy map showing attractions plus dining and shopping in each area. Board a double-decker minibus or a horse-drawn trolley or else stroll up Main Street to romantic Sleeping Beauty Castle, the entrance to **Fantasyland.** As you cross the drawbridge over the moat where swans elegantly glide, keep looking for Mickey and Minnie Mouse, Goofy, Pluto, and Chip 'n' Dale, Disneyland's official greeters, who love to have their picture taken with visitors.

Along Main Street stop at the inviting plaza, with benches, flowers, and trees, to relax, people-watch, and listen to the ragtime pianist expertly playing old tunes in toe-tapping rhythm. You'll find musicians throughout the park, playing various instruments to entertain visitors.

There's certainly no place like Disneyland—big, sunny, clean, and busy, where people of all ages amble in different directions to browse, eat, shop, snack, board another ride, and greet a new adventure. There are flowers, happy music, and lots of smiling children. If you feel lines are too long at your favorite ride, you can soon find another and return later. Listen and watch for the parade of elaborate floats down Main Street, with Mickey and other Disney figures singing and swaying to rollicking music.

DINNER: At **Disneyland Park,** Anaheim. There are satisfying, healthful eating places throughout the park. Consult your guidebook if you don't spot someplace you'd like to try. At Cafe Orleans in New Orleans Square, the dinner menu features beef Bourguignon, Seafood Parisienne served over rice, or spicy chicken with pasta.

LODGING: The **Disneyland Hotel,** 1150 West Cerritos Avenue, Anaheim. (714) 778–6600. This sixty-acre tropical gardens family resort features 990 guest rooms and sixty-two suites with balconies, in-room safes, iron, ironing board, snack/beverage bar, room service, closed-circuit TV channel and Disney Channel; two swimming pools, water slide, spa, sandy beach, several restaurants, nightly enter-tainment, shops, lobby lounge, fitness center, meeting space. No charge for children seventeen years old and younger who stay with a parent. Disneyland Passports and packages, complimentary tram to Disneyland Park. Resort fee includes parking.

Day 2 / Morning

BREAKFAST: In hotel, at **Goofy's Kitchen,** a colorful and fun place where children enjoy meeting Minnie Mouse, Goofy, and other Disney favorites who visit at tables. All-you-can-eat buffet features waffles, egg specialties, cereals, and fruits with interactive food stations. Kids receive a special memento.

Take the tram or the futuristic monorail back to Disneyland Park to enjoy a full day of fun and adventure. Just past the entrance, walk up the wide staircase to ride the **Disneyland Railroad,** pulled by a genuine steam locomotive. The train visits all the different lands in a restful, fifteen-minute narrated ride during which you can see the cars ahead as you round a curve and hear the nostalgic train whistle. You can get off at any stop or stay aboard until you're back at your station.

LUNCH: Plaza Inn on Main Street, Disneyland Park, Anaheim. This busy buffeteria has a Victorian decor of pink umbrellas and white furniture. Attractive, wholesome-looking foods include baked chicken, spaghetti, salads, and meat-and-cheese sandwiches with pasta salad; children's menu. It's pleasantly cool inside, but you can also tote your tray out to the terrace.

Afternoon

Spend the rest of the day and evening or as long as you like visiting other themed areas. Ride the Matterhorn bobsled that zips in and around the tall mountain in a fast roller-coaster ride. Tuck into It's a Small World, a delightful child-oriented ride, and sail around a glitzy ornamental world while festively costumed figures sing a happy tune. Embark on Star Tours, a thrilling flight-simulated spaceship journey into space. Then follow the Indiana Jones adventure in an intriguing expedition through the Fabled Temple of the Forbidden Eye. Look for Tarzan's Tree House to climb in Adventureland. When you're ready for a break from the rides, head to Downtown Disney, a public esplanade of innovative restaurants, shops, and entertainment venues that leads to the entrances of Disneyland and Disney's California Adventure. Here you'll find Build-a-Bear Workshop, ESPN Zone, House of Blues, Rainforest Cafe, Monster's Inc., Turtle Talk, Lego Imagination Center, and other colorful and fun-filled stores.

After dark go to Frontierland, to experience Fantasmic, Mickey Mouse's imaginative musical spectacular of fire-breathing dragons, laser storms, heroes, and villains.

Disneyland's California Adventure, the resort's 2001 centerpiece adjacent to the original Disneyland Park, offers fifty-five acres of themed attractions that celebrate the magic of the California dream. It is comprised of an entertainment center with rides, restaurants, retail shops, theaters, and **Disney's Grand Californian**

Hotel, a luxurious hotel of 750 rooms and suites with many amenities, plus restaurants, swimming pools, children's pool, spas, meeting facilities, and a fitness/health center. One of the newest rides here is Twilight Zone: Tower of Terror. This supernatural thriller, with its thirteen-story free-fall drop, has amazing special effects and is based on the old television series.

Disney's Paradise Pier Hotel, 1717 South Disneyland Drive (714–999–0990), is a fifteen-story high-rise with 502 guest rooms, including fourteen suites and poolside cabanas. Concierge-level rooms have many amenities, and the hotel, decorated in a California beachfront theme, offers a swimming pool and whirlpool, fitness center, two restaurants, lobby bar and coffeehouse, poolside bar, gift shops, and game arcade. You can enter Disneyland from an exclusive entrance that's just steps away from the hotel.

Disneyland Park's days and hours vary year-round. To verify park operating hours, call (714) 781–4565 or (213) 626–8605, ext. 4565. Information is also available on the park's Web site, www.disneyland.com. Seasonal passports/ticket admission. Parking fee.

Return to Los Angeles via I–5 north.

There's More

Medieval Times Dinner and Tournament, 7662 Beach Boulevard, Buena Park. (714) 521–4740; (800) 899–6600 (nationwide). Enjoy a hearty four-course feast in a huge (1,134-seat) indoor ceremonial arena of an eleventh-century–style castle. Dine while watching a lively two-hour pageant of knights in colorful raiment, astride costumed horses, competing in daring equestrian tournaments, sword fights, and jousting. Dinner is served by friendly "serfs" and "wenches." No silverware was used in A.D. 1539, so drink your fresh vegetable soup from its small metal bowl and tear your hot and tasty whole roast chicken, spare ribs, and potato apart with your fingers, just like Henry VIII. Dinner includes two rounds of beer, wine cocktail, or soft drinks and pastry dessert. There are lots of encouraging shouts and cheers for favorite knights as they gallop heroically through the arena. Performances seven nights; seasonal matinees Sunday. Phone for showtimes; reservations are required. Free parking; ask your hotel about bus service.

Pirate's Dinner Adventure. 7600 Beach Boulevard, Buena Park. (714) 690–1497, (866) 439–2469. Interactive dinner theatre, opened in March 2006, featuring a one-of-a-kind show with excitement, food, special effects, and good energy. You are transported to the 1800s, when pirates ruled the high seas. Enjoy adventure and the entertainment of 150 actors, stunt performers, and singers. Audience members sit in one of six ships and feast on a scrumptious three-course meal. Look for an 18th-century replica of a Spanish galleon floating in a 250,000-gallon indoor lagoon. Call for days and hours.

Ripley's Believe It or Not Museum, 7850 Beach Boulevard, Buena Park. (714) 522–1155. One block north of Knott's Berry Farm, you'll see an amazing, entertaining collection of curiosities that are true, strange, and bizarre, from Ubangi women whose lips are pierced to have saucers inserted into them to a Chinese shrunken head about the size of a lemon. These and many other oddities displayed in glass showcases were accumulated by Robert Ripley, TV and radio pioneer and syndicated newspaper columnist, during his world travels. Open Monday through Friday from 11:00 A.M. to 5:00 P.M. and Saturday and Sunday from 10:00 A.M. to 6:00 P.M. Admission, senior discount.

Angel Stadium of Anaheim, 2000 State College Boulevard, Anaheim. (714) 634–2000. This 70,000-seat stadium hosts events year-round. Two miles east of Disneyland, the stadium is home to the Anaheim Angels major-league baseball team.

Baseball. The Anaheim Angels season runs from April through September. Tickets are usually available before each game. (714) 634–2000.

Anaheim Indoor Marketplace, 1440 South Anaheim Boulevard, Anaheim. (714) 999–0888. Largest swap meet in the area, with some 200 variety shops that sell name-brand merchandise at 50 to 70 percent below retail prices. Entertainment, family fun. Open daily 10:00 A.M. to 7:00 P.M. Free shuttle service from Anaheim hotels.

Special Events

Mid-March. St. Patrick's Day Celebration, Downtown Anaheim Farmer's Market. (714) 956–3586.

May. Cinco de Mayo Festival, La Palma Park. (714) 765–5274. Carnival, ethnic foods, and soccer tournament.

June. Taste of Anaheim, Arrowhead Pond. (714) 758–0222.

June to September. Disneyland opens summer season with Light Magic Parade and Fantasy in the Sky, Anaheim.

July 4 festival. Peralta Park, Anaheim. Fireworks, food, entertainment, games. (714) 765–5274.

August. Entertainment Under the Stars, Pearson Park Amphitheater. (714) 765–5274.

August 5–6. America's Best Food Show, Anaheim. Festival with music and great cuisine. (949) 366–6488.

August 19–27. Southern California Home and Garden Show, Anaheim Convention Center. Features the newest home and garden products and services. (714) 765–8900.

October. Camp Spooky, Knott's Berry Farm, Buena Park. (714) 220–5200. Traditional non-scare Halloween celebration for kids eleven and younger, trick or treat, costume contests.

October 4–8. California International Auto Show, Anaheim Convention Center. More than 300 imported and domestic model cars are on display. (714) 765–8900.

October through April. NHL Hockey, Mighty Ducks of Anaheim, Arrowhead Pond of Anaheim. (714) 704–2400.

Middle through late October (selected dates). Annual Halloween Haunt, Knott's Berry Farm, Buena Park. (Not recommended for children younger than twelve.) World's biggest, scariest, most famous Halloween party. (714) 220–5200.

October 28. Anaheim Fall Festival, downtown Anaheim. Pancake breakfast and carnival welcoming the fall season. (714) 991–8745.

End of November through end of December. Thanksgiving Day, New Year's Week, Very Merry Christmas Parade, Disneyland, Anaheim. (714) 999–4565.

December. Christmas at Knott's Berry Farm. (714) 220–5200. Features sledding, strolling carolers, and a variety of performances and holiday activities.

Nutcracker Holiday, downtown. (714) 765–5274. Traditional Christmas celebration with candy canes and all the trimmings.

Other Recommended Restaurants and Lodgings

Anaheim

Hilton Anaheim, 777 Convention Way. (800) HILTONS; (714) 750–4321. Two blocks from Disneyland, AAA four-diamond rating, has 1,573 deluxe guest rooms and suites, cable TV, three rooftop recreation gardens, sundecks, heated swimming pool, four spas, pool bar, 25,000-square-foot sports and fitness center with indoor pool and basketball court, golf center, pitching range. Concierge service. Three restaurants and lounges. Daily breakfast buffet. Free shuttle to Disneyland Park. Various packages. Overnight parking fee.

Anaheim Marriott, 700 West Convention Way, Anaheim. (800) 228–9290 (reservations); (714) 750–8000. Two blocks from Disneyland, AAA three-diamond rating. Has 1,033 guest rooms, including seventy-two suites, two concierge levels. AM/FM radio, cable TV, in-room pay movies. Heated indoor and outdoor swimming pools, two spas, fitness facility and sunning decks, video-game room. Gift shop, four restaurants, lounge. Daily breakfast buffet. Family vacation and other packages. Overnight parking fee.

Knott's Berry Farm Resort and Hotel, 7675 Crescent Boulevard, Buena Park. (800) 333–3333 (reservations); (714) 995–1111. Just steps from the park, it combines 360 guest rooms and suites with exclusive resort amenities, including coffeemakers, hair dryers, wall safes, cable TV with pay-per-view movies, iron/ironing board, twenty-four-hour room service, pool, spa, one lighted tennis court, pro shop, fitness center, two restaurants, daily breakfast buffet, large meeting space, and charming Snoopy-themed guest rooms/suites. Various packages.

For More Information

Anaheim/Orange County Visitor and Convention Bureau, 800 West Katella Avenue, Anaheim, CA 92802. (714) 765–8888; www.anaheimoc.org.

Visitor Information Line. (714) 991–INFO, ext. 9888.

Anaheim Convention Center, 800 West Katella Avenue, P.O. Box 4270, Anaheim, CA 92803. (714) 765–8950.

The Old West and the Wine Road

Temecula and Wineries / 2 Nights

In this two-night itinerary, you wander through a restored 1890 cowboy town with a colorful past of Native Americans and the Butterfield Overland Stage, walk through historic buildings and visit museums filled with mementos of the city's beginnings and Old West lifestyle, hunt for antiques and collectibles, have lunch in a bank vault, taste-tour thirteen wineries and learn the romance of the grape, play golf and tennis, and spend the night in a casual/luxe resort.

☐ Antiques

☐ Dining

☐ Golf resort

☐ Tennis

☐ Wineries

☐ Museum

☐ History

☐ Hot-air ballooning

Day 1 / Morning

From Los Angeles take I–5 south to Riverside Freeway 91 (before Fullerton). Head east on 91 (past Corona) and pick up I–15 south to **Temecula,** about 90 miles. Take the Rancho California Road exit to Old Town Temecula/Front Street and turn right.

Park your car and then amble down **Front Street,** the main thoroughfare of rambling wooden buildings with thick wood-plank verandas out front. The new buildings are skillfully designed to blend in well with the old 1890s structures. Temecula is curb-to-curb antiques shops and a collector's mecca, with all manner of memorabilia. In addition to many individually run stores, groups of dealers are housed together in various antiques malls. Even if you're not an antiques maven, you will enjoy the stores. Each has something different and appealing to offer, and the furniture, in particular, gleams in richly polished woods and is nicely displayed.

Old Town Temecula has been dedicated as the Old Town Temecula Historical Preservation District and is a pleasant, relaxing, happy place to browse; walk around and poke into its shops. The small, 6-block-long area along Front Street and some side streets retains its flavor of the Old West between the 1800s and the 1900s. The city is often called Southern California's "New Frontier"; its first inhabitants, the Shoshonean Indian tribe, christened it "Land Where the Sun Shines through the Mist," or Temecula.

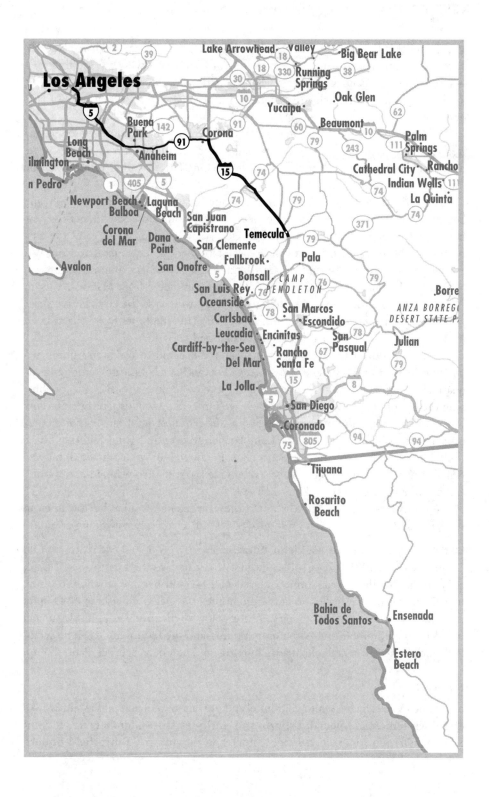

Temecula's history began in 1797, when its Native American village was discovered by Father Juan Santiago from San Juan Capistrano, who was looking for a new mission site. Santiago wrote to King Charles IV describing the village. The king named the area Rancho Temecula, and it became one of several Spanish land grants.

In 1845, during the Mexican-American War when the missions were secularized, Rancho Temecula was given to Felix Valdez, and the great ranches were divided into smaller parcels with private ownership. This was the beginning of the romantic era of the rancheros and vaqueros of early California.

After the first Butterfield Overland Stage arrived in September 1858 and became a regular stop on the route between St. Louis and San Francisco, new homesteaders began settling in. Mail service began, and in April 1859 the first inland Southern California post office was established in Temecula. The Civil War brought an end to the Butterfield Overland Stage service, and transportation was limited until January 1882, when a rail line was completed from National City to Temecula. As large numbers of people began migrating west, the city's business and population increased, but a series of floods in the late 1880s destroyed the railroad tracks, and the old Temecula depot was abandoned.

Temecula dozed until 1904, when Walter Vail came to town and purchased most of the land in the valley (87,500 acres) for Vail Ranch, his cattle empire headquarters. The great cattle drives began, and the city became a focal point for shipping cattle and grain. For the next sixty years, Temecula was a lusty, prosperous cow town with a population of about 200 and a western lifestyle of ranchers and cowboys hanging out at the Swing Inn, Long Branch Saloon, and other watering holes. In 1964, when the Los Angeles–San Diego Freeway, I–5, was completed, the Vail Ranch was sold to developers. It was subdivided as a master-planned community and became incorporated as a city in 1989.

With its fertile soil and mild climate, the vast grazing land has been planted in vineyards and in citrus and avocado groves. It's still a noted horse-raising area.

LUNCH: The Bank of Mexican Food, corner of Front and Main Streets, Old Town, Temecula. (951) 676–6160. Built in 1914, it housed the First National Bank of Temecula for thirty years until it closed in 1941 and became an antiques shop. In 1978 it was refurbished as an authentic home-style Mexican restaurant. Despite the building's rather hideous green exterior color, it's pleasantly cool inside the tall wood-beamed dining room with comfy booths, and the food is good. Menu selections include tostadas, crab enchiladas, burritos, and luncheon specials. Patio dining.

Afternoon

After lunch you can check into your hotel and play a round of golf or stay and browse Old Town Temecula's **specialty shops and antiques stores.** Strolling down Front Street, you'll soon come to a favorite visitors' stop, the attractive **Butterfield Square** complex of shops and dining, marked by its red lamppost and flagpole. Continuing along Front Street, you'll find Rocky Mountain House, featuring crystal, Native American art, and jewelry. The Welty Building, between 3rd and Main Streets, was a former store and saloon built by the Welty family in 1902. It later became the Ramona Inn, then a prizefighters' gym where Sharkey, Dempsey, and other heavyweights worked out. Now it's an antiques store and deli. More antiques are around each corner and in the malls. ABC Trading Company features bottles and other collectibles, Far East Collection shows Oriental imports, and A to Z Antiques and Country Seller-Friends highlights country curtains, antiques, and furniture. The large, impressive Welty Temecula Hotel, on Main Street, was built in 1882 by the Welty family. It is now a private residence.

Between Main and 4th Streets, Calico Coffee Company is the place for fine gourmet coffees, teas, kitchen gifts, candy, aprons, and well-priced wines from local wineries. Old Town Antique Faire houses thirty antiques dealers, whose wares include collectibles and vintage oak furniture. Chapparal Antique Mall, at 28645 Front Street, distinguished by a large wooden wagon out front, is a complex of more than seventy dealers, offering pottery, china, folk art, toys, quilts, and many more old-time collectibles.

Stroll both sides of Front Street. The Machados store is another historic site, built by the owner in 1892 as a general store. It later became the local post office, with the owner as postmaster; had a good life as the Long Branch Saloon for many years; and now is a mall of about eighteen antiques dealers.

Stop by the **Temecula Valley Museum,** at Moreno Road and Mercedes Street (951–694–6450), at the north end of town in Sam Hicks Park. Like a visit to great-grandmother's attic, this is a gem to visit, with artifacts dating from the days of the Old West and old-fashioned household and farm items of the 1800s and early 1900s, collected locally. Wall shelves display fascinating early-twentieth-century items, including an old telephone, grand old typewriters and cameras, irons, a treadle sewing machine, buckets, pottery, branding irons, and old saddles. Tables display large scrapbooks to browse, filled with photographs that show the town as it looks today as well as way back when. Nearby, an impressive diorama features Temecula in about 1914. Temecula's favorite son was Erle Stanley Gardner, author of the famous Perry Mason stories popularized on television, who lived in Temecula from 1937 until his death in 1970. The museum exhibits a sampling of Gardner's 185 mystery novels and a collection of memorabilia about the prolific author. (Open Tuesday through Saturday from 10:00 A.M. to 5:00 P.M. and Sunday 1:00 to 5:00 P.M.; donations accepted.)

DINNER: Temet Grill, Temecula Creek Inn, 44501 Rainbow Canyon Road, Temecula. (800) 962–7335; (951) 676–5631. Intimate dining room with cathedral ceiling overlooks the golf course and features wine country cuisine. Varied appetizers highlight Dungeness crab cakes, and entrees feature delicious seafood, chicken, and steaks. The wines are from local vineyards and elsewhere.

LODGING: Temecula Creek Inn, 44501 Rainbow Canyon Road, Temecula. (800) 962–7335; (951) 676–5631. Centered atop 300 acres, 129 large, well-furnished rooms in soft colors, each with sitting area and all with fairway views, are tucked into low-rise lodges. Honor bar, minirefrigerator, coffeemaker with fresh coffee beans and grinder, iron and ironing board, hair dryer, cable TV, compartmented bathroom, two phones; three 9-hole championship golf courses, putting green, driving range, two tennis courts, heated swimming pool with hydro spa; dining room, lounge with weekend entertainment; conference facilities. Outstanding Sunday champagne buffet brunch.

Day 2 / Morning

BREAKFAST: At Temecula Creek Inn. Full breakfast is included in the golf package and is served in the sunny dining room overlooking green fairways and energetic golfers. Try the scrambled eggs with smoked salmon and toasted bagel with cream cheese or the avocado-and-green-chili burrito with scrambled eggs and salsa, covered with melted cheese and served with refried black beans and excellent coffee.

After breakfast golfers will want to get out on any of Temecula Creek Inn's three challenging 9-hole **golf courses:** the Creek, the Oaks, or the Stone House. Wine lovers will want to visit the nearby wineries, about 4 miles east of the city.

Temecula Valley is a prime Southern California wine-growing area. Its soil and climate, in addition to the vintners' skill, produce award-winning wines served in the White House as well as to the Queen of England and the rest of us. **Temecula wine country** was first discovered in the 1840s by the legendary wine master Jean Louis Vignes and was rediscovered in the 1960s. The first vines were planted in 1967.

Obtain a "Wine Country Tour Map" from the hotel. Take I–5 north to the first exit and follow the circular wine trail along Rancho California Road (about 4 miles east of the city). Continue past Palomar Village, follow the sign TEMECULA WINE COUNTRY straight ahead, pass a golf course on the left, and you'll soon see the vineyards and hilly terrain on both sides of the highway.

The thirteen wineries and vineyards that cover about 4,000 acres in the rolling hills of the valley's eastern region are close together on a scenic road and easily visited in a day or half-day outing. Most offer complimentary daily or weekend tasting and tours; hours and days vary. Some charge a small tasting fee.

Be sure to check the winery guide and map for the days and hours each winery is open to avoid disappointment after long uphill drives (some wineries are on dirt roads). Frequently, fast traffic behind you may not allow you sufficient time to slow down and turn into the narrow winery driveways. In that case, it may be better to continue along the road and catch that one as you circle back. Learn to speak Chardonnay as you sample the wines and talk to the proprietors or winemakers about the various wines. Attractive gift shops and delis feature mementos and

Vineyards flourish in fertile Temecula Valley.

choice edibles to purchase for an impromptu picnic beneath fragrant grape arbors.

Your first stop on the left side of the road is **Callaway Vineyard and Winery** (32720 Rancho California Road; 800–472–2377, ext. 399; 951–676–4001). Atop 750 acres, it's the largest premium Southern California winery. Red and white wines are popular here—Queen Elizabeth favors the White Riesling. Visitor center, picnic area/gift shop; informative, complimentary hourly tours given Monday through Friday at 11:00 A.M., 1:00 and 3:00 P.M.; Saturday and Sunday 11:00 A.M. to 4:00 P.M. on the hour. Large tasting room open daily 10:00 A.M. to 5:00 P.M. Tasting fee. Open daily 10:00 A.M. to 5:00 P.M.

Continue on the same side of the road to **Mount Palomar Winery** (33820 Rancho California Road; 800–854–5177; 951–676–5047). Daily tasting, 10:00 A.M. to 4:45 P.M.; tasting bar charges fee for samples. Riesling and Meritage are the most popular wines. This is the only winery in Temecula that makes Cream Sherry. Gift shop. Purchase bread, cheese, and gourmet deli fare and enjoy a picnic under the grape arbor.

Farther on is **Falkner Winery,** at 40620 Calle Contento, a small road to the left (951–676–8231). In a spectacular hilltop setting with a waterfall and panoramic vistas, its high-quality wines include Syrah, Riesling, and "Reserve" Chardonnay.

Amante is their signature wine. The tasting room is open daily from 10:00 A.M. to 5:00 P.M. Tours are available weekends. Unique gift shop, Sunday jazz concerts, and picnic area.

Go back and across the road to **Thornton Winery** (32575 Rancho California Road; 951–699–0099). Attractive Mediterranean-style buildings with a wide court-yard and a large fountain overlook the sweet valley of vineyards. Six award-winning sparkling wines are produced in the *methode champenoise*. Weekend tours only. Tasting fee. Champagne lounge; exclusive gift shop. Call for hours.

LUNCH: Cafe Champagne, in the courtyard of the Thornton Winery. Intimate, with open kitchen; overlooks vineyards. A popular luncheon destination, offering California cuisine of mesquite-grilled steaks, salads, and sandwiches enhanced with Thornton's sparkling wines and fresh herbs grown in the herb garden. (Reservations, 951–699–0088.)

Afternoon

Continue along the *route de vin* to **Maurice Car'rie Winery** (34225 Rancho California Road; 951–676–1711). The large white Victorian-style tasting building set back on a broad lawn is bordered with roses. Patio tables and chairs and a little gazebo are inviting for picnics. Good-looking interior has a large chandelier and a ceiling skylight. Tasting 10:00 A.M. to 5:00 P.M. daily. The most popular wine of their seventeen varietals is Sara Bella Cabernet. Gift shop, deli items, picnic area.

Continue along the quiet road to the white windmill that marks the entrance to **Van Roekel Vineyards & Winery** (34567 Rancho California Road; 951–699–6961). It has an attractive tasting bar. A showroom features Merlot, among many other premium wines. Raspberry champagne is their biggest seller. There's a gourmet deli, picnic area, spacious gift shop displaying glassware, aprons, logo cups, and small split bottles of wine that are perfect gifts or souvenirs. Tasting daily 10:00 A.M. to 5:00 P.M.

Back down the road again is **Baily Vineyard and Winery** (33440 La Serena; 951–676–WINE). A wonderfully scenic hilltop location for wine sampling, with a panoramic view of vineyards and Mount Palomar from the veranda. Tasting daily 11:00 A.M. to 5:00 P.M.; fee includes winery logo glass. Cabernet Blanc is the most popular wine here. Gift shop; Carol's Restaurant & Deli, a favorite for freshly pre-pared foods. Closed Monday and Tuesday.

DINNER: Temecula Creek Inn. If you enjoy music with dinner, the lounge presents weekend entertainment and jazz Thursday nights, and the food service is good. The filet mignon is delicious, with green peppercorn béarnaise and gratin potatoes. Linger over brandy and dessert—a surprisingly good bread pudding or ice cream sundaes.

LODGING: Temecula Creek Inn.

Day 3 / Morning

BREAKFAST: Temecula Creek Inn starts the day just right with a breakfast crois-sant of scrambled eggs, Canadian bacon, and Gruyère cheese garnished with fresh fruit.

After breakfast lounge around the pool, play another round of golf on the uncrowded courses, hit some tennis balls, visit more wineries, or return to Old Town Temecula.

To visit more of the valley's fine wineries, start with **Hart Winery** (41300 Avenida Biona; 951–676–6300). This hospitable winery offers daily tastings of red and white wines from 9:00 A.M. to 4:30 P.M.; the tasting fee gets you another win-ery logo glass.

Continue to **Cilurzo Vineyard and Winery** (41220 Calle Contento; 951–676–5250). This family-run operation was the first vineyard in Temecula and specializes in red wines, with Petite Syrah heading the list. Tasting daily from 10:00 A.M. to 5:00 P.M.; tours weekends (call ahead). Tasting fee is refunded with wine purchase. Gift items; lakeside picnic area.

Drop in at **Filsinger Vineyard and Winery** (39050 De Portola Road; 951–302–6363). The white stucco building with red-tile cupola is adorned with a colorful flower-bordered gazebo. The vineyard consists of twenty-five acres planted in varietals producing seven wines and three champagnes. Most popular are the Gewürztraminer and Blanc de Blanc champagne. Tasting and tours Friday from 11:00 A.M. to 4:00 P.M., weekends from 10:00 A.M. to 5:00 P.M.; Monday through Thursday call for appointment; fee to taste wines is refunded on purchase. Gift items, picnic area.

LUNCH: Pick up some lunch fixings along the way and snack on Filsinger's pretty picnic patio.

Afternoon

Retrace your route from Old Town Temecula back to Los Angeles.

There's More

Lake Skinner, off Rancho California Road, 10 miles northeast of Temecula. (951) 926–1541. For year-round family fun, this beautiful recreation area offers fishing, boating, hiking (about 300 campsites, many with full hookups), cafe, equestrian trails. Site of the annual Balloon and Wine Festival. Campground reservations: (800) 234–7275.

Pala Casino Resort and Spa, 11154 Highway 76, Pala. (760) 510–5100; www.pala casino.com. Country-style resort features 507 rooms, 82 suites, pool beneath the beautiful Palomar mountains, Jacuzzi, cabanas, luxe spa, fitness center. Casino has

2,250 Las Vegas–style slot machines, 60 game tables, restaurants, and nightly entertainment.

Temecula Stampede, 28721 Front Street, between 1st and 2nd Streets, Old Town Temecula. (951) 695–1760. Temecula's country-western nightclub features 4,000 square feet of dance floor, plus mechanical bull. After 6:00 P.M. Friday and Saturday, here's where the action is. Live bands, special concerts, dance lessons. Admission Friday and Saturday nights.

Sam Hicks Park, Mercedes and Moreno Streets, at the north end of Old Town. This small, historic park features Temecula's Monument Rock, a massive (twenty-ton) granite marker with fifty-six names of pioneers sandblasted on its surface, in tribute to former settlers.

Pechanga Resort & Casino, 45000 Pechanga Parkway, Temecula. (877) 711–2WIN; www.pechanga.com. Located in beautiful wine country, this gleaming $262-million, thirteen-story casino has 522 rooms and suites, an 88,000-square-foot casino, food court, entertainment, five themed bars and lounges, and five network boxing events. With a 1,200-seat theater, 2,000 slot machines, and 40,000-square-foot meeting space, Pechanga claims to be the largest Indian-owned casino west of the Mississippi, giving Las Vegas new competition.

Hot-air balloon rides. A Grape Escape Balloon Adventure, 39525 Los Alamos Road, Suite A–104, Murrieta. (800) 695–2122. Soar over the beautiful valley in a colorful seven-story giant. Daily one-hour sunrise champagne flights with a FAA-certified commercial balloon pilot leave from the wineries. After the flight, each passenger receives a First Flight certificate. Don't forget the camera. Phone for reservations. Prices vary.

Imagination Workshop Temecula Children's Museum, 42081 Main Street, Temecula. (951) 308–6370. This innovative and creative hands-on workshop allows children to play with "gizmos and whatnots," and to follow blueprints or design their own plan while inventing their own creations. There are secret passageways and puzzles in this exciting museum of fun and discovery. Call for hours.

Wilson Creek Winery, 35960 Rancho California Road. (951) 699–9463. Its broad selection of premium wines includes popular almond champagne. The beautiful grounds include picnic areas, a charming wedding gazebo, gift shop, and tasting room. Tasting daily from 10:00 A.M. to 5:00 P.M.

Stuart Cellars, 33515 Rancho California Road. (951) 676-6414. Vintage varietals barrel-aged and beautifully crafted; specializes in red wines. Hospitality Center is open for tasting daily 10:00 A.M. to 5:00 P.M. Spectacular panoramic picnic area.

Golf. There are now different golf courses to choose from. Highlights include: Bear Creek Golf Club, 22640 Bear Creek Drive North, Murrietta (951–677–8621);

Rancho del Cielo Golf Course, Las Caballos Road at Santa Rita Road (951–302–0712).

Special Events

Farmers' markets. Every Saturday from 8:00 A.M. to noon in Old Town, 6th and Front Streets. Wednesday, Promenade Mall parking lot, 9:00 A.M. to 1:00 P.M.

Beginning of February. Annual Winegrowers Winter Barrel Tasting, fifteen wineries. Sample wines, festive foods; meet the winemakers.

Mid-March Annual Rod Run, Vintage Car Show. Old Town Temecula.

Old Town Temecula Bluegrass Festival, Front Street.

April. Temecula Wine and Music Festival, Southcoast Winery.

May. Annual Western Days in Old Town Temecula. (951) 694–6412.

Beginning of June. Temecula Valley Annual Three-Day Balloon and Wine Festival. (951) 676–4713. Daily liftoff, entertainment, wine tasting, children's fair at beautiful Lake Skinner.

Fourth of July. Parade, Old Town Temecula.

September. Annual International Film Festival. (951) 699–6267.

First weekend in October. Annual Great Temecula Tractor Race. (951) 676–4718. Temecula Showgrounds. Three days; mudboggin' obstacle course, country fair, country-western music, and food, craft vendors.

Mid-November. Winegrowers Harvest wine celebration; sample new wines and wine country cuisine at all thirteen wineries.

Last weekend in November until Christmas. Dickens Christmas in Old Town. Holiday Lights and Festive Sights.

Other Recommended Restaurants and Lodgings

Baily's Fine Dining & Catering, 27644 Ynez Road, Temecula. (951) 676–9567. Located in the bustling, commercial shopping-dining center of the town. Enjoy dinner on the pretty patio or inside this upscale, busy cafe where bins of wine are stacked in the entrance foyer. California/continental cuisine; dinner is served nightly. Knowledgeable wine staff helps you select from a large variety of Temecula valley wines, including those from Baily Vineyard and Winery.

Rosa's Cantina Restaurant, 28636 Front Street, corner of Main, Old Town. (951) 695–2428. Popular for good Mexican food; serve-yourself, casual dining inside or on patio. Moderate-priced specialties include tacos, burritos, chimichanga, nachos, tostados, and *combinaciones.*

Texas Lil's Mesquite Grill, 28495 Front Street, Old Town. (951) 699–5457. A lively local favorite for big steaks, ribs, hefty sandwiches, and the hottest Texas chili this side of the Alamo. Kids eat free.

Swing Inn Cafe, 28676 Front Street, Old Town. (951) 676–2321. Popular since the cowboys and ranch days; cozy and busy. Home-style cooking—spaghetti, soups, sandwiches, and daily lunch and dinner specials. Breakfast served all day.

Inn at Churon Winery, 33233 Rancho California Road. (951) 694–9070. A new chateau winery and twenty-two-room bed-and-breakfast combination atop a hillside with marvelous views, fireplace, Jacuzzi, and private balcony offers full breakfast and evening reception. The winery's premium and estate wines include Syrah, Chardonnay, Merlot, and Sauvignon Blanc. Tasting daily 10:00 A.M. to 5:00 P.M.; the fee includes souvenir glass. Deli and gift shop. Enjoy a picnic in the beautiful gardens.

Embassy Suites Hotel, 29345 Rancho California Road and I–15. (800) 362–2779; (951) 676–5656. Lake setting of 176 two-room suites with wet bar, refrigerator, microwave, TV, VCR, stereo, heated swimming pool, Jacuzzi, fitness center, restaurant, lounge. Complimentary full, cooked-to-order breakfast; complimentary evening beverage.

Loma Vista Bed and Breakfast, 33350 La Serena Way, Temecula. (951) 676–7047. Set high on a hilltop, the B&B overlooks citrus groves and vineyards. Six guest rooms with air-conditioning and private baths with tubs/showers. Rates include a champagne breakfast, served in the spacious dining room, and wine and cheese in the afternoon. Guest rooms are named after wines—champagne, Chardonnay, and so forth—and individually furnished. Packages offered with hot-air balloon companies Monday through Thursday.

For More Information

Weekend Visitor Information Center at Temecula Stage Shop, Front Street across from Chapparel.

Temecula Valley Chamber of Commerce, 27450 Ynez Road, Suite 10, Temecula, CA 92391. (951) 676–5090.

Temecula Valley Convention & Visitors Bureau, 26790 Ynez Court, Suite A, Temecula, CA 92591. (866) 676–5090; (951) 676–5090.

Temecula Valley Vintners Association, P.O. Box 1601, Temecula, CA 92390. (951) 699–3626.

SOUTHERN ESCAPE NINE

Wine, Pontoons, and Safari

Escondido, Lake San Marcos / 1 Night

This varied two-day itinerary takes you on new adventures, with plenty of change of pace and scene. Using **Escondido** as a convenient hub to explore the rural area, you visit and taste-tour local wineries, go on a safari through an 1,800-acre wildlife preserve, view a historic battlefield, and go boating on a peaceful, secluded lake.

☐ Wild-animal park

☐ Wineries

☐ Lake

☐ Ethnic and gourmet dining

☐ Resorts

☐ Boating

Day 1 / Morning

Drive south from Los Angeles on I–5 to Oceanside. Take Highway 78 east to I–15 north. Exit at Mountain Meadow Road; turn right to the stop sign and left on the frontage road, Champagne Boulevard, proceeding for about 2.5 miles to the Welk Resort.

LUNCH: Welk Resort, 8860 Lawrence Welk Drive, Escondido. (800) 932–9355; (760) 749–3000; www.welkresort.com. The enticing Buffet du Chef in the resort's large dining room overlooking the inviting golf fairways features carved-to-order roast beef, roast chicken, or fish fillets, plus another entree as well as an extensive salad bar assortment. The buffet is served Saturday, Sunday, Tuesday, Wednesday, and Thursday from 11:15 A.M. to 2:30 P.M. Regular popular luncheon menu is also available daily.

Afternoon

From the Welk Resort take I–15 south to the Via Rancho Parkway exit. Turn right at the signal as the street turns into Bear Valley Parkway and continue on this road to Kit Carson Park and **Queen Califia's Magical Circle,** a unique sculpture garden. (Note that the entrance to the garden is not visible from the main road, so visitors must enter the park and head north.)

Queen Califia's Magical Circle, the only American sculpture garden created by French artist Niki de Saint Phalle, is comprised of nine large-scale sculptures, a circular "snake wall," and a maze entryway. The key architectural feature is a 400-foot-long circular wall surrounding the garden, and the focal point is an enormous mosaic

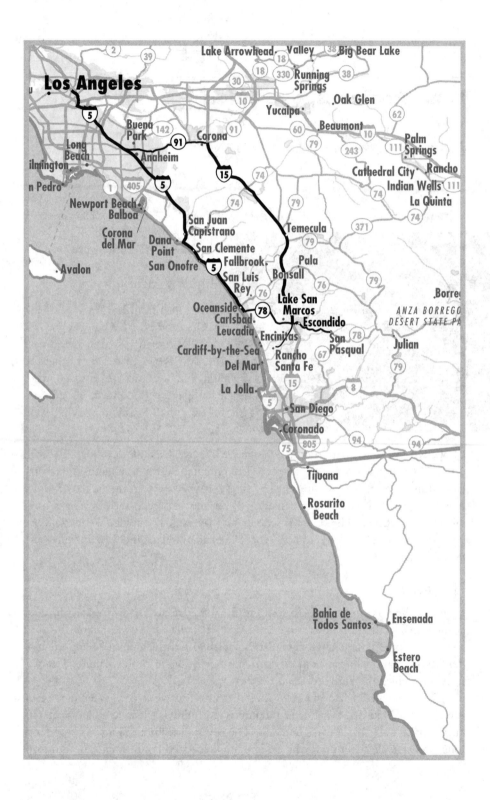

sculpture of Queen Califia standing on the back of a five-legged eagle, surrounded by eight large totemic sculptures. The garden took nearly four years to complete.

Exit the park and take I–15 to Highway 78 west to the San Marcos Boulevard exit. Turn left onto San Marcos Boulevard, make a slight right onto Knoll Road, and then turn left onto Rancho Santa Fe Road. Turn left onto Lake San Marcos Drive and follow the signs to the Quails Inn Hotel in **Lake San Marcos,** a small, exclusive, nontouristy city in a rural resort setting.

After checking into your lakefront hotel, you'll have time for a refreshing **boat ride** on Lake San Marcos. Ask the desk clerk to arrange a ride for you, and walk or drive to the boathouse, just past Quails Inn Dinnerhouse. Here a small lawn tapers down to the lovely lake, where swans pose elegantly and ducks quack as they paddle around close to shore. After receiving easy instructions to operate the canoes or open-air pontoon boat, you'll soon be out on the cool, secluded, 1.25-mile-long lake, gliding around the little inlets to the dam and back. (Hourly boat fee.)

DINNER: Quails Inn Dinnerhouse, Lake San Marcos Resort, Lake San Marcos. (760) 744–2445. Overlooking the lake, the restaurant is a town favorite for the spectacular seafood/salad bar and other entrees. For faster service take the stairway down to the convivial Lakeside Lounge, which also overlooks the water. Tuesday through Sunday the dinner menu offers fish-and-chips, cheeseburgers, prime rib, salmon, and different nightly specials. Dancing and entertainment. Happy hour Thursday through Sunday 4:00 to 6:00 P.M.

LODGING: The Quails Inn Hotel at Lake San Marcos Resort, 1025 La Bonita Drive, Lake San Marcos. Reservations: (800) 447–6556; (760) 744–0120. You'll appreciate this quiet and romantic lakeside setting of 139 large, nicely appointed rooms, including suites and cottages, some with patio overlooking the private lake. In-room coffeemaker, hair dryer, cable TV, room service, separate bathroom vanity counters with roomy storage, bathtub and stall shower, and daily newspaper. Three restaurants; cocktail lounge with entertainment nightly. Boating on the lake; 18-hole Championship Country Club golf course and access to 18-hole executive course; four tennis courts, four paddle-tennis courts; two sparkling swimming pools; spa, well-equipped exercise room; large conference center. Sunday champagne brunch. Children and pets are always welcome. Golf getaway packages, Legoland guest packages and ticket discounts. Seasonal rates.

Day 2 / Morning

BREAKFAST: Gordon's on the Green at Lake San Marcos Country Club, 1950 San Pablo Drive, Lake San Marcos. (760) 744–9385. Cross the bridge where the pretty dining rooms overlook the lush fairways. You don't have to be Jack Nicklaus to enjoy the Golfer's Tee-Off breakfast of eggs with ham or bacon, potatoes, and muffins; other options include waffles and buttermilk pancakes. Also open to the public for lunch and dinner.

Investigate the good-looking **Village Center** across from the hotel, with coffee shop, small market, liquor store, pharmacy, and shops; hotel guests may charge purchases to their rooms. Then walk down to the lake and enjoy a quiet stroll alongside the tranquil water. Relax and watch the ducks, the swans, and the little children who chase the ducks across the lawn and into the water as they offer them food. If you have time, go for another sail around Lake San Marcos—it's a wonderful experience. You may want to have lunch early today as lots of activities are scheduled for the afternoon.

Drive up San Marino Drive to Rancho Santa Fe Road, turn right to San Marcos Boulevard, and turn right again several blocks later to San Marcos's famous **Old California Restaurant Row,** on the left. Here's an exciting variety of eighteen fine restaurants and specialty shops in one convenient location (see "Other Recommended Restaurants and Lodgings").

LUNCH: Bruno's Authentic Italian Restaurant & Pizzeria, 1020 San Marcos Boulevard, San Marcos. (760) 744–7700. Recommended enthusiastically by fussy diners, the lunch buffet, served Monday through Saturday, features ten items, including veal parmigiana, several pizzas, seafood, and pasta. Other menu selections are hearty sandwiches and a salad bar. Sunday champagne buffet brunch.

Afternoon

To visit the San Diego Wild Animal Park, take San Marcos Boulevard past Old California Restaurant Row to Freeway 78; go east to I-15, then south to the Via Rancho Parkway exit. Turn left onto San Pasqual Road, and follow it until it becomes Highway 78, leading to the park (about 6 miles).

San Diego Wild Animal Park, 15600 San Pasqual Valley Road (Highway 78) in Escondido (760–747–8702). It's almost a culture shock on the Wgasa Bush Line Monorail's fifty-minute narrated safari, where you skirt the 5-mile perimeter of Asian and African animal habitats. As your guide describes many of the 2,500 animals living in the 2,200-acre preserve—a haven for vanishing wildlife species— you may feel as though you've been deposited in Africa as you see animals roaming freely in dramatic open plains.

In addition to Asian and African elephants, you'll see giraffes, Persian gazelles, flamingos, zebras, ostriches, Arabian oryx, Sumatran tigers, wild horses, 4,000-pound white rhinos, many species of antelope, and numerous other wild animals and birds. You won't always see the tigers and other animals that sleep throughout the day, and many are too far away. A zoom lens for your camera is useful, as are binoculars. The right-hand side of the monorail affords better viewing.

When your safari ends, visit the seventeen-acre Nairobi African Village, with its restaurants, snack bars, and shops. Check the map you received at entry for schedules of the engaging bird, elephant, and other daily shows. Youngsters adore the Petting Kraal and Animal Care Center, where they can cuddle the koalas and watch nursery feedings. Lush botanical gardens, a wooden bridge, a waterfall cascading down boulders, a tree house, and large, colorful macaws all enhance your exit (if you can find it) from the park. (Open daily from 9:00 A.M. to 4:00 P.M., later in summer; seasonal events and special exhibits; admission and parking fee; entry ticket includes monorail, animal shows, and exhibits.)

To get to the Orfila Vineyards & Winery, turn left on San Pasqual Road; go 3 miles, passing a large produce stand, Old San Pasqual Road, and a Christmas tree farm. Look for vineyards on the low hillside at the left of the road, and continue to the large ORFILA VINEYARDS & WINERY sign, turning left through the gates past a picnic lawn to the wine-tasting room.

In the deliciously cool, flag-decorated tasting room of **Orfila Vineyards & Winery,** 13455 San Pasqual Road, Escondido (760–738–6500), you'll sample a variety of multi-award-winning wines of San Diego's largest premium winery, then enjoy self-guided tours through the vineyard and winery (or you can join a guided tour at 2:00 P.M.). Orfila's seventy acres of vineyards in San Diego County include thirty acres of estate vineyards planted in new varieties of Syrah and Sangiovese, plus forty-five acres in Fallbrook growing Merlot, Chardonnay, and other grapes. Many visitors purchase luncheon snack foods—cheese, crackers, individual pizza, or smoked salmon—and a bottle of wine and then picnic on the patio beneath the shady grape arbor overlooking the vineyards and the beautiful San Pasqual Valley. The Winery Gift Shop is stocked with wine, T-shirts, glasses, corkscrews, coasters, cookbooks, beribboned gift baskets, and fascinating food- and wine-related items you won't find elsewhere. Wine tasting is offered daily from 10:00 A.M. to 6:00 P.M.

To reach I–15 north to Los Angeles, go west on San Pasqual Road to San Pasqual Valley Road/Highway 78. Stay on 78 west for 7 to 10 miles until you come to I–15. From I–15 take the Beach Cities/Riverside 91 exit to the left. Then look for I–5 north just past Anaheim and take it into downtown Los Angeles.

There's More

Ferrara Winery, 1120 West 15th Avenue, Escondido. (760) 745–7632. San Diego County's oldest grape-growing winery is a designated State Historical Point of Interest. If you enjoy the challenge of finding Ferrara, the tasting room offers a selection of premium wine daily from 10:00 A.M. to 5:00 P.M. Enter the winery, with its two redbrick pillars and machinery out front, from the parking lot next to number 1160 in a residential street.

Palomar Observatory, forty-five minutes northeast of Escondido on Palomar Mountain. (760) 742–2119. The home of the 200-inch Hale Telescope offers two kinds of tours. On the third Saturday of each month, four one-hour free tours are given on a reserved basis for groups; call or write for reservation forms.

The observatory is open daily, except Christmas Eve and Christmas Day, from 9:00

A.M. to 4:00 P.M.; admission is free. Visitors can take a free self-guided tour and view the Hale Telescope from the gallery in the dome; there is no viewing through the telescope. The gift shop is open weekends only from 10:00 A.M. to 4:00 P.M. Take Highway 76 to County Road S6 and wind up the mountain to the observatory gate.

San Pasqual State Historic Park and Museum, east of the San Diego Wild Animal Park on Highway 78, 115808 San Pasqual Valley Road, Escondido. (760) 489–0076. For history buffs, the fifty-acre hillside park overlooks the site of the **Battle of San Pasqual,** which took place December 6, 1846, between U.S. forces and Mexico during the Mexican-American War. This battle was a small conflict but the most severe fought in California. You can travel back into California history at the modern Visitor Center and Museum, which presents the story of the battle in a short video, along with maps, displays, and artifacts. Open Saturday and Sunday from 10:00 A.M. to 5:00 P.M. Other exhibits highlight the history of the pastoral San Pasqual Valley. Outdoors, visitors can follow easy pathways and nature trails through the park and perhaps even spot an animal or two roaming through the nearby San Diego Wild Animal Park.

An annual reenactment of the Battle of San Pasqual is presented on the Sunday closest to December 6. In a colorful presentation, dragoons, Californios, Marines, and horsemen dressed in period attire use muskets, cannons, and horse charges to provide a lively, memorable event.

Heritage Walk Museum Complex, Grape Day Park, 321 North Broadway, Escondido. (760) 743–8207; www.ci.escondido.ca.us/visitors/uniquely/historic. For a quick glimpse into Escondido's past, take Highway 78 east, turning left on Washington to Grape Day Park, with tall, beautiful shade trees. Heritage Walk Museum Complex includes buildings preserved from Escondido's beginnings in 1888. Stroll around to see the town's first library, a little yellow 1894 cottage, the 1900s Red Barn with wagon and windmill, a two-story 1790 country house, a blacksmith shop currently used for restoring stagecoaches, and the 1888 Santa Fe Railroad Depot, which ended passenger service in 1945 and is at present used by the local historical society. Buildings are open Thursday through Saturday from 1:00 to 4:00 P.M. but can be viewed anytime.

Bates Nut Farm, 15954 Woods Valley Road, Valley Center. (760) 749–3333. About fifteen minutes northeast of Escondido, here's where to stock up on packages of dried fruits, candies, and fresh-roasted nuts from all over the world. Kids get to feed ducks and geese and pet the sheep and goats. Gift boutique; special festive events during the year. Open daily from 9:00 A.M. to 5:00 P.M.

California Center for the Arts, 340 North Escondido Boulevard, Escondido. (760) 839–4138. This stunning $80-million center is on twelve Village Green acres adjoining Grape Day Park. The 1,500-seat Concert Hall and 400-seat Center

Theatre for Performing Arts present hundreds of performances each season. The Art Museum, with sculpture court, showcases three major exhibitions yearly of contemporary California and international artists. Museum hours: Tuesday through Saturday from 10:00 A.M. to 5:00 P.M. and Sunday from noon to 5:00 P.M. Admission.

Farmers' market, on Grand Avenue between Calmia and Broadway, Escondido. (760) 745–8877. Tuesday from 3:00 to 6:00 P.M.

Special Events

Mid-April, early August, middle to the end of October, mid-November, late November, and mid-December. Bates Nut Farm Fairs and Shows, Valley Center.

April. Street Fair, Lake San Marcos.

Mid-May. Escondido Street Faire, downtown Escondido. Third largest street fair in California; 600 booths, crafts, live entertainment on several stages, farmers' market, pancake breakfast, food from around the world. From 9:00 A.M. to 5:00 P.M.

Early June, mid- to late June, early August, and late December. San Pasqual Battlefield events, Escondido.

End of June, two weekends. Scottish Highland Games, Lake San Marcos.

Mid-July. Street Fair, Lake San Marcos.

Early September. Escondido Historical Society's Grape Day Festival, at Grape Day Park, Escondido. From 9:00 A.M. to 5:00 P.M. (760) 743–8207.

End of October. Escondido Fall Street Faire. Arts, crafts, vendors, children's rides. (760) 945–9288.

First Sunday closest to December 6. Battle Day, San Pasqual State Historic Park. Starts at 10:00 A.M. (760) 737–2201.

First weekend in December. Holiday Luncheon, Christmas Tree Lighting, Lake San Marcos.

Mid-December. Christmas Parade, 1500 North Broadway to Grand Avenue, Escondido. Starts at 10:00 A.M.

Other Recommended Restaurants and Lodgings

San Marcos

Fish House Vera Cruz and Old California Mining Co. In Old California Restaurant Row. (760) 744–8000. The two restaurants share the same building, with separate entrances and dining rooms. The Fish House is popular for tasty, fresh, mesquite-broiled seafood. Old California Mining Co. is equally popular for fine steaks, mesquite burgers, and great desserts.

Acapulco Mexican Restaurant and Cantina. In Old California Restaurant Row. (760) 471–2150. A local hangout for its variety of Mexican dishes, lively happy hour with complimentary hors d'oeuvres, and Sunday brunch.

Escondido

The Brigantine Restaurant, 421 West Felicita Avenue. (760) 743–4718. South of Grape Day Park. A reliable choice for seafood entrees.

Cocina del Charro, 625 North Quince. (760) 745–1382. Serves authentic Mexican specialties, *carne asada* burritos, and enchiladas for lunch and dinner; Sunday brunch.

Welk Resort, 8860 Lawrence Welk Drive. (800) 932–9355; (760) 749–3000; www .welkresort.com. Sprawling, 600-acre resort with two 18-hole golf courses established by the late orchestra leader has 427 spacious rooms, suites, and two-bedroom villas, all with views of the golf course, with patios or balconies. In-room coffeemaker and TV; gift shops, market/deli; five swimming pools with spas. Restaurant and lounge; karaoke. Conference facilities; live theater performances year-round.

Rancho Santa Fe

The Inn at Rancho Santa Fe, 5951 Linea del Cielo, Rancho Santa Fe. (800) 654–2928; (858) 756–1131. American-California cuisine offered in the Vintage Room, a cozy, romantic spot with glowing fireplace, for breakfast, lunch, and dinner.

For More Information

San Diego North Convention and Visitors Bureau, 720 North Broadway, Escondido, CA 92025. (800) 848–3336; (760) 745–4741; www.sandiegonorth.com.

San Marcos Chamber of Commerce, 144 West Mission Road, San Marcos, CA 92069. (760) 744–1270.

Gold Rush and Desert Grandeur

Julian, Anza Borrego, Borrego Springs / 1 Night

☐ Gold-mining town

☐ Apple pie

☐ Apple and pear orchards

☐ Museum

☐ Country shopping

☐ Desert state park

☐ Historic trails and
   nature walks

☐ Wildflowers

☐ Bighorn sheep

There's plenty of variety in this two-day itinerary that gets you off the fast track. It takes you high up in the mountains of north San Diego County to a small, historic gold-mining town still reflecting its aura of the 1870 gold rush days, then down to the mighty Anza Borrego Desert to explore the natural wonders of the nation's second largest state park. You'll also stay overnight in a luxurious, desert-oasis resort and browse a small, upscale resort community surrounded by spring wildflowers.

Day 1 / Morning

Leave Los Angeles via I–5 south through Oceanside, then head east on Highway 78 into Escondido, continuing on 78 up the mountains to Julian, about a three-hour drive. Following Highway 78 on the scenic drive up to Julian, the backcountry road borders a woodsy stream as it climbs and weaves through broad rolling plains where cattle graze in sunny pastures. In fall the open fields tumbled with fat golden pumpkins are bucolic treats for city dwellers. Look for roadside stands selling eggs, cider, pears, and apples (in fall) and buy as you go along. Better yet, wait until the return trip to purchase fresh produce to take home. About 7 miles from Julian, you'll pass **Dudley's Bakery and Restaurant** on the left near Highway 79, noted for baking twenty varieties of bread daily and for its long lines. It's so popular that customers can call in a pickup order: (760) 765–0488, 8:00 A.M. to 5:00 P.M. (Closed Monday and Tuesday.)

Julian, a former gold rush mining town and a National Historic Site, is a sleepy, 4-block-square rural community. At 4,235 feet high in the oak-and-pine hills, Julian's apples and cider lure thousands of visitors to its Fall Harvest Festival in October and November. The town celebrates other seasons, too, with festivals and arts and crafts shows. There's also a resident dinner theater. Cafes and restaurants

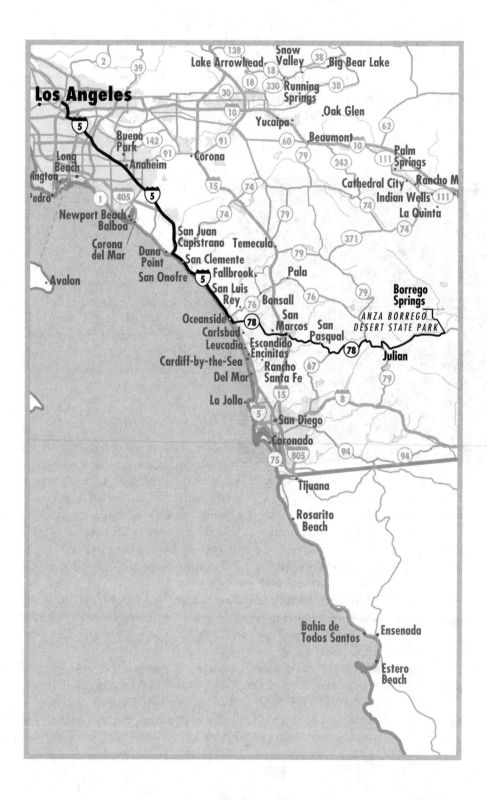

feature fresh apple pie year-round by the slice, or you can lasso a whole pie.

In our harried, computerized age, visitors come to Julian for more than apples. They come for its atmosphere and nostalgic reminders of simpler times and for the romance of an exciting, lusty era they missed.

Julian has about 1,000 residents; adding in the surrounding suburbs, the population hits 2,000. There are no movie houses, glitz, or shopping malls in this rustic, pint-size village that dozes all week and hums with tourists on the weekend. Most stores close between 5:00 and 6:00 P.M., and all are open weekends.

LUNCH: Romano's Dodge House, 2718 B Street, Julian. (760) 765–1003. Around the corner from Julian Lodge. Considered the best Italian food in town; you're treated like one of the family, except you don't have to help with the dishes. Sample the lasagna, pizza, and veal and pasta selections. (Sorry, no apple pie here.) There's a small bar. Closed Tuesday.

Afternoon

Julian is a true success story, one that began in 1869, when miners found placer gold in a nearby stream. Searching farther upstream, they discovered gold ore in 1870. As claims were staked out and mines multiplied, the exciting gold rush began. One of the local residents, Mike Julian, helped record and lay out the town site, and the townspeople named it after him.

In a dizzying boom, gold seekers, prospectors, and miners showed up from all over the West, by sea from Northern California and by stage from San Diego. Within a month nearly 1,000 gold hunters arrived to work the town's mines. Julian expanded rapidly, as buildings sprang up along bustling Main Street. In its prime the town had four general stores, fifteen hotels, a dozen saloons, two livery stables, and two stage lines to San Diego.

The bonanza ended ten years later, when the rich veins of gold in the mines were exhausted after producing millions of dollars worth of gold. The stampede ended when the migrant miners rushed off to a new boom in Tombstone, Arizona, in 1880.

Julian didn't become a ghost town, as did so many others. Farmers found the rich soil and pleasant mountain climate ideal for growing apples and pears. A ragtag bunch stayed on and homesteaded the fertile valley and hills. Julian soon became an active farming-trading community.

Drop in at the **Town Hall,** at the corner of Washington and Main, in a historic 1913 building—it's the center for year-round activities. Take a look at its historic photos and pick up a list of special events. The chamber of commerce is located here (see "For More Information").

Around the corner, **Julian Pioneer Museum,** 2811 Washington Street (760–765–0227), is the city's oldest building. Built in 1875, it was originally the town's brewery and later a blacksmith shop. Restored and enlarged, the museum is

Julian's Town Hall is a center for year-round events.

called "Julian's Attic" by the townsfolk. It's filled with a jumble of old furniture, photos and historical records, mining equipment, a gleaming old square Weber grand piano, a Victorian carriage, and many other items depicting the city's life in the gold rush days of 1869. Open Thursday through Sunday, 10:00 A.M. to 4:00 P.M.

Among the shops and cafes at this historic part of **Main Street** near the site of the Washington Mine around the Fire Station are several antiques stores tucked in small cottages. Mosey down Main Street, with its wooden 1800s buildings, to **Mom's Pie House,** where you can watch the bakers from the streetside windows making hundreds of apple pies daily. Next door, the **Warm Hearth** is a treasure to browse, with its perky country music and old-fashioned but trendy country-style antique items, such as Coca-Cola signs, baskets, and tins of Lipton's tea. Check out the Native American pottery, baskets, kachinas, and jewelry in the rear of the store, all authentic and rather expensive. Near the end of Main Street, **Julian Cider Mill,** a family-owned local institution, offers welcome cups of its hot cider in winter and sips of cold boysenberry-apple cider in summer. From about October through March, you can watch apples being pressed into cider. Additionally, you'll always find a nice assortment of dried fruit, honey, nuts, candy, and popcorn.

Across the way on B Street, take time to browse **KO Corral's rustic court-**

yard shops. To tour Julian's only remaining 1897 operating gold mine, drive up hilly C Street about 6 blocks to the **Eagle and High Peak Gold Mines** (760–765–0036). Take the one-hour guided tour through 1,000 feet of underground tunnels, and relive the gold-fever days. Daily tours start at 10:00 A.M.; the site is closed before 10:00 A.M. and after 4:00 P.M. (Picnic area, closed most holidays; fee.)

Among the two dozen or more remaining historic structures in town, the 1869 **Julian Gold Rush Hotel,** 2032 Main Street (800–734–5854; 760–765–0201), is on the National Register of Historic Places. The sole survivor of the town's fifteen hotels in its heyday, it began as a restaurant owned by a freed Georgia slave whose wife's delectable southern cooking attracted hungry travelers on the Butterfield Stage. They built a successful hotel around it, and it's now a popular, AAA-approved, Victorian B&B with sixteen rooms, most with baths down the hall. The separate Honeymoon House and Patio Cottage have fireplaces.

When you have explored Julian, drive through to the end of Main Street for the 2-mile, one-hour drive down the mountainside to Borrego Springs and Anza Borrego Desert State Park. Be advised to leave in daylight, as this is a very curvy, very dangerous mountain road. The road is cut right through the low mountains, with pure desolation on both sides toward the flat desert plains below. It's a hair-raising ride down Banner Grade, with many curves as the road descends to the desert floor where the vast, 600,000-acre park stretches to the soft, sensuous foothills, as you wind and twist through Yaqui Pass. Just after Rams Hill you arrive at **La Casa del Zorro Desert Resort Hotel,** a welcome oasis of palm trees, lush green grass, and fountains.

Check into your hotel, and if there's time and daylight, get back on S3, Borrego Springs Road, to explore the little town of **Borrego Springs,** and plan to visit the huge state park tomorrow. Follow the green Christmas Circle turnaround along Palm Canyon Drive to the good-looking, smartly landscaped mall of shops and restaurants—Bailey's Cafe; Pot Luck, for specialty gifts; Borrego Goldsmith Jewelers; and others. Across the street, a smaller shopping complex includes the Performing Arts Center, a restaurant, and a gas station. The library and the Borrego Springs Chamber of Commerce are 1 block farther along (see "For More Information"), if you need any information or brochures. All stores close between 5:00 and 6:00 P.M., earlier in summer.

Borrego Springs's population of 3,000 increases in winter to about 8,000. This peaceful community is often compared with Palm Springs of the 1930s. But residents know there is no danger of urban sprawl or crowding as the city is completely surrounded by the magnificent desert park.

Its enviable lifestyle of peace and quiet in the warm, clean desert air includes golf, tennis, swimming, and other good-life amenities. Temperatures can rise in the summer from 107 degrees to around 124 degrees, but evenings are cooler. Accommodations range from luxury resorts to smaller hotels.

DINNER: La Casa del Zorro, 3845 Yaqui Pass Road, Borrego Springs. (800) 824–1884; (760) 767–5323. Two dining rooms feature lamb chops, chicken, steak, fish, and vegetarian dishes.

LODGING: La Casa del Zorro Desert Resort Hotel, 3845 Yaqui Pass Road, Borrego Springs. (800) 824–1884; (760) 767–5323. This luxury desert hideaway, a *Mobil Travel Guide* four-star and a AAA four-diamond resort, offers seventy-nine elegantly decorated rooms, deluxe suites, and casitas on thirty-eight acres of lush desert landscaping. Rooms feature alarm clock, coffeemaker, hair dryer, daily newspaper, terry robes, large fireplaces (in deluxe rooms and casitas), TV, comfortable lounge chairs, and good lighting. Complimentary coffee in the lobby; Olympic lap pool, three swimming pools and spas, six night-lighted tennis courts, putting green, fitness room; salon, gift shop; two restaurants, bar and lounge. Seasonal rates, special events, and conference center. Country club golf nearby.

Day 2 / Morning

BREAKFAST: At the hotel. In two dining rooms, elegantly served continental breakfast includes a generous bowl of fresh fruit or yogurt plus muffins, toast, or croissants, juice, and coffee. Full breakfast features Belgian waffles and egg specialties.

Drive to Borrego Springs and, following the green Christmas Circle turnaround on Palm Canyon Drive, continue on S22 to the state park, past the shopping village, about a 7-mile drive through the vast, serene desert. In spring, after the winter rains, thousands of tourists arrive from early March through mid-April to marvel at the spectacular view of wildflowers carpeting the arid desert floor and hillsides.

Anza Borrego Desert State Park, the largest park in California and in the United States, covering more than a half million acres, attracts close to a million visitors in the winter season, from October through May. These visitors explore and experience the park's open wilderness beauty, taking self-guided auto tours to many points of interest and hiking, camping, mountain biking, and backpacking amid the palm-studded canyons, plains, and desolate badlands. Elevations range from 15 feet to more than 7,000 feet of the towering Santa Rosa Mountains.

The park is named for Spanish explorer Juan Bautista de Anza, who led an expedition for Spain from Mexico through Cahuilla Indian territory in 1774 and discovered the first overland route to California. Markers commemorate the historic event. *Borrego* is the Spanish name for the elusive peninsular bighorn sheep that take refuge here.

The area resembles a surreal desert moonscape and is as natural and rugged as when the Spaniards first arrived hundreds of years ago. Surrounded by the tall cinnamon mountains, it is a scene of desolation and solitude, absolutely haunting in its stark, lonely beauty and grandeur. Park rangers advise visitors to carry plenty of water and to wear a hat and sunblock. It can be very hot.

Drive up to the visitor center and park in the lot. The entrance is not visible from the road, in its underground building sheltered beneath a low hillside with a desert sand roof dotted with low native plants. The 7,000-square-foot center provides slide shows for groups upon request; these explain the desert's history and its variety of more than 600 species of plants and 300 species of reptiles and birds, including the fast little roadrunner. Among native animals are the bobcat, coyote, and kangaroo rat.

The center offers naturalist talks; guided walks, hikes, and tours; and provides brochures and maps of the most scenic places. *NOTE:* The visitor center (760–767–4205) is open daily only from October through May, from 9:00 A.M. to 5:00 P.M., and open only on weekends and holidays from June through September. The Administration Office (760–767–5311) has opposite hours, open weekdays from 8:00 A.M. to 5:00 P.M. and closed weekends and holidays.

The favorite and most scenic hike is the Palm Canyon Nature Trail, a 1.5-mile hike up through the hills to an oasis of a grove of about 1,000 palm trees thriving in the rocky canyon. Other trails cover the historic routes traveled in the 1840s and 1850s by Kit Carson, the Mormon Batallion, adventurers, gold seekers, the first transcontinental mail service, and the famous Butterfield Overland Stage traveling from St. Louis to San Francisco, a twenty-four-day journey of extreme hardships wherein passengers frequently had to get out and help push the stagecoach over steep mountain passes. Today's visitors on self-guided auto tours can follow the deep wagon-wheel ruts along the road, look across the incredible shimmering desert, and reclaim a bit of Old West history for themselves.

To return to Los Angeles, you need to retrace your way, driving back up the mountain and through Julian and down Highway 78. From Anza Borrego Park go back on the road to Casa del Zorro, following the curve to the right on S3. This is the same very winding and curvy road you drove down from Julian, only now it winds sharply up and around the mountains. The spectacular views make up for all the curves, with the mountains covered in various shades of green.

Afternoon

You can spend time browsing again in Julian, have lunch or more apple pie, or continue through town on Main Street, turning left on Washington and onto Highway 78, a rolling, pleasant road. You'll pass many fruit orchards on the way (see "There's More"). Continue on Highway 78 to I–5 north to Los Angeles.

There's More

Country Carriages, available in front of Julian Drug. (760) 765–1471. Offers narrated, romantic, old-fashioned buggy rides through downtown Julian and the scenic countryside. Fee.

If you like to buy fresh fruit, look for apple and pear orchards located throughout Julian. Pears are available in different seasons, with a good crop in September; apples are usually harvested in October, and peaches in August.

Apple Lane Orchard, 2641 Apple Lane, Julian. (760) 765–2645. Watch cider pressing on Thursday mornings, and apple slicing during "Apple Days." Open daily September through December.

Orfila Art Center, 4470 Highway 78, Julian. (760) 765–0102. Wine tasting and art gallery.

Wineries. Menghini Winery, 1150 Julian Orchards Drive, Julian. (760) 765–2072. Enjoy tasting locally produced wine and a guided tour of this family-run winery with picnic area, vineyard, and apple orchards. Open Monday through Friday from 10:00 A.M. to 4:00 P.M., Saturday and Sunday until 5:00 P.M.

Witch Creek Winery, on B Street in the KO Corral, Julian. (760) 765–2023. Drop by for wine tasting. Open daily 11:00 A.M. to 5:00 P.M.

Special Events

NOTE: All Julian events take place in Julian Town Hall unless otherwise noted.

January through mid-December. Art shows and crafts shows. Contact chamber of commerce for schedule.

February, March, and end of April. Spring wildflowers, Borrego Springs.

March. Daffodils bloom, Julian.

First week in March. R&B Bicycle Club Tour of Borrego, Palm Canyon Resort, Borrego Springs.

Mid-March. Historic Days Outfit Contest.

Late March to early April. Arts and Crafts Show.

April. Lilacs and wildflowers in bloom, Julian.

Early to mid-May. Annual Julian Women's Club Wildflower Show.

May. Julian Arts Guild Spring Fine Arts Show.

Last weekend in May. May Fest Celebration, Valley Independent Bank, Julian.

Late June to early July. Annual Julian Women's Club Heritage Quilt Show.

Fourth of July. Community Fourth of July Parade, Main Street.

July 17. Julian Blues Bash, Menghini Winery.

Late August to early September. Annual Weed and Craft Show, Julian Arts Guild Fall Fine Arts Show.

Mid-September. Julian Lions Club Bluegrass Jamboree and Banjo Fiddle Contest. Annual Grape Stomp, fiesta.

Mid-September through November. Julian Apple Harvest time.

Every weekend in October. Triangle Club Old Time Melodrama.

Second week in October. Oktoberfest, Valley Independent Bank, Julian.

Last weekend in October to early November. Borrego Days, Desert Festival, street parade. Borrego Springs.

End of November. Julian Annual Country Christmas, Victorian caroling, tree lighting.

December. Community Christmas with Santa, Victorian caroling.

Other Recommended Restaurants and Lodgings

Julian

Rongbranch Restaurant and Boar's Head Saloon, 2722 Washington Street. (760) 765–2265. This perennial family favorite is well known for steaks, BBQ, charbroiled burgers—also buffalo burgers made of lean ground buffalo meat. Variety of pies, convivial saloon, and attractive gift shop.

Julian Pie Company, 1921 Main Street. (760) 765–2449. Dine in the front yard on sandwiches and freshly baked pie. Open daily from 9:00 A.M. to 5:00 P.M.

Buffalo Bill's, 3rd and B Street. (760) 765–1560. Claims to serve the best buffalo burgers on the mountain. Other menu selections are great, too. Patio dining. Open Monday through Friday from 7:30 A.M. to 1:30 P.M. and Saturday and Sunday from 7:00 A.M. to 4:00 P.M.

Butterfield Bed and Breakfast, 2284 Sunset Drive. (800) 379-4262; (760) 765-2179. Snuggle up in this cozy five-bedroom bed-and-breakfast. Each guestroom has private bathroom, cable TV, VCR, DVD/CD players, Victorian charm, freshly baked cookies, and all of the amenities of home. Wood-burning fireplaces available in some rooms and in the parlor. Delicious gourmet breakfast served in the gazebo with abundant country charm.

Julian Lodge Bed and Breakfast, 4th and C Street. (800) 542–1420; (760) 765–1420. Two-story, modern, with warmth of antique furnishings and decor; twenty-three rooms with bath, cable TV, air-conditioning. Continental breakfast served in homey lobby.

Borrego Springs

NOTE: Summer hours and days are subject to change.

Kendall's Cafe, The Mall (in the center on the south side). (760) 767–3491. Opens at 6:00 A.M. to start your day with an excellent breakfast. The lunch menu continues through dinner. Varied menu features Mexican and American dishes, chef's salad. Open daily until 8:00 P.M.

Bernard's, Suite 503, The Mall (on the south side). (760) 767–5666. A favorite for savory continental and American Alsatian regional cuisine. Chicken specialties, fresh soup daily. Full bar. Open Monday through Saturday from 11:00 A.M. to 9:00 P.M.

Palm Canyon Resort, 221 Palm Canyon Drive. (800) 242–0044; (760) 767–5341. Western flair in sixty-one spacious rooms with king or two queen beds, in-room coffee, hair dryer, cable TV, refrigerator, private balconies and patios. Pool and spa, fitness center. Minimarket, laundry, gift shop; restaurant and saloon with live entertainment. Adjoining RV park. Sunday champagne buffet brunch.

Villas Borrego, P.O. Box 185, Villas Borrego, CA 92004. (760) 767–5371. One- and two-bedroom villas with patios, swimming pool. Daily, weekly, and monthly rates. Adjacent to The Mall.

Stanlands Resort Inn & Suites, 2771 Borrego Springs Road. (760) 767–5501. Near the village center. Twenty-one units with private patios, kitchens; pool; golf and tennis nearby. Complimentary breakfast December through April.

RoadRunner Golf & Country Club, 1010 Palm Canyon Drive, P.O. Box 3081, Borrego Springs, CA 92004. (760) 767–5374; www.roadrunnerclub.com. Family-owned, luxury, gated mobile-home retirement community, with eighteen-hole executive golf course, clubhouse, tennis courts, and large therapeutic swimming pool.

For More Information

Julian Chamber of Commerce, Town Hall, Washington and Main Streets, P.O. Box 1866, Julian, CA 92036. (760) 765–1857. Open daily from 10:00 A.M. to 4:00 P.M.

Julian Bed and Breakfast Guild guide to lodging. Information and reservations: (760) 765–1555. Open daily 9:00 A.M. to 9:00 P.M.

Julian Historical Society, P.O. Box 513, Julian, CA 92036. (760) 765–0436.

Julian Approved AAA Accommodations. (888) 765–0373.

Borrego Springs Chamber of Commerce, 622 Palm Canyon Drive, P.O. Box 420, Borrego Springs, CA 92004. (800) 559–5524; (760) 767–5555; www.borrego springs.com.

Wildflower Information, Borrego Springs. (760) 767–4684.

Anza Borrego Desert State Park, 200 Palm Canyon Drive, P.O. Box 299, Borrego Springs, CA 92004. (760) 767–5311. Visitor Center Program information, (760) 767–4205.

Island Getaway

Santa Catalina Island / 1 Night

- ☐ Ocean cruise to island
- ☐ Beach
- ☐ Pier
- ☐ Scuba/snorkel diving
- ☐ Boating and fishing
- ☐ Hiking
- ☐ Island and harbor tours
- ☐ Glass-bottom boat
- ☐ Wilderness
- ☐ Dance casino
- ☐ Horseback riding

On your two-day Santa Catalina Island escape, which begins with a brisk ocean voyage, you'll soon be seduced by an entirely different environment.

The island air, surrounded by the sea, is clearer; the sun is brighter; and there are no automobiles. Sunbathe and swim in a small protected beach area; scuba and snorkel in translucent waters; go sailing, fishing, or biking; and join a variety of scenic tours around the island, from the peaceful sparkling harbor to the undeveloped wilderness interior where buffalo and deer roam freely. Enjoy a glass-bottom boat trip; visit the world-famous Casino Building, which hosted many of the Big Bands of the 1930s and 1940s (Harry James, Woody Herman, and Jimmy Dorsey were just a few); and dine in fine style at water's edge.

Day 1 / Morning

From Los Angeles the fastest way to get to Catalina by boat (about one hour) is from Long Beach via the Catalina Express boats, which make frequent daily departures year-round from the *Queen Mary* port alongside the legendary ocean liner whose celebrity passengers included royalty, Hollywood stars, and millionaires.

Head south on Santa Ana Freeway I–5 to Long Beach Freeway 710 south to Long Beach. Follow signs to the *Queen Mary,* which lead you to the Catalina Express Port and *Queen Mary* parking lot: It's advisable to arrive twenty minutes or more before departure time. Lock up your car (daily rates for the lot) and board the *Catalina Express,* a double-deck, one-hundred-passenger cruiser. It's best to keep your luggage light or in small bags that you can stow in the ship's hold as you board or can carry on with you to place under your airline-style seat. This saves waiting for your luggage when you arrive in Catalina.

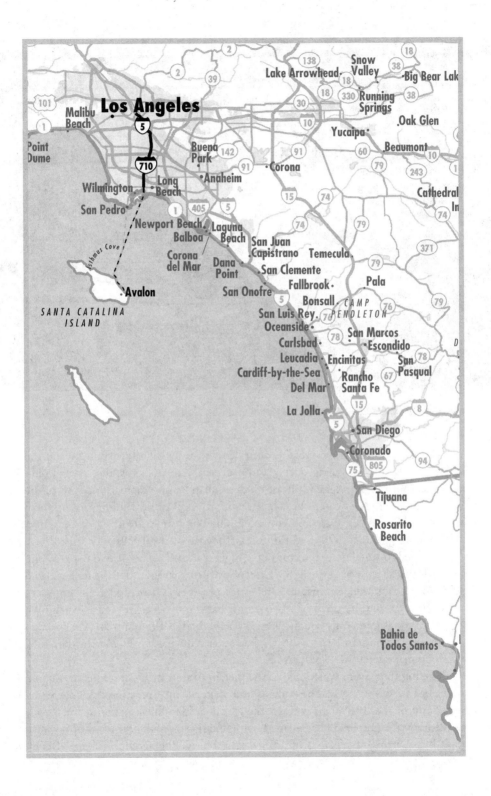

Beautiful Santa Catalina Island's Avalon Bay.

The 21.8-mile channel crossing may be a bit rough in a few spots but on the whole is fairly smooth sailing, as the fast boat seems to skim across the waves. Pretty soon you spot the tall, jagged hills of Catalina Island rising dramatically out of the limitless ocean; then you see the tall, graceful, round Casino Building in the blue bay encircled by small boats, and you're disembarking in **Avalon.**

Beginning in the 1920s and through its heyday of the 1930s and early 1940s, visitors sailed to Catalina Island from Los Angeles aboard either of two Great White steamers, the SS *Avalon* and the SS *Catalina,* which carried 2,000 passengers on a never-to-be-forgotten adventure. Orchestras played for dancing, and there were food, romance, and the thrill of a two-and-a-half-hour ocean voyage, even though the crossing was frequently rough. (The *Avalon* retired in 1956, and the *Catalina* discontinued its sailings in 1976. Both stopped service during World War II, when they were commandeered by U.S. forces.)

The big ships were welcomed at the pier in Avalon by entertaining, costumed mariachis, as well as by island residents and visitors, since meeting the boat was a high point of the day. When you left the island on the Great White steamer, your departure was sentimentally serenaded by the mariachis, and folks lined up to wave good-bye. During the glamorous Big Band era, all the famous names—Benny

Goodman, Count Basie, Harry James, Freddy Martin, Ray Noble, Tommy Dorsey, Jan Garber, Jimmy Dorsey, and others—played nightly for thousands of enthusiastic dancers at the elegant Casino Building overlooking Catalina Bay. The Casino made history in May 1940, when 6,200 people came to swing and sway to the lilting music of Kay Kyser and his orchestra.

Nowadays high-speed cruisers make multiple sailings to and from Catalina Island daily. Three boat companies service the island, with departures from Long Beach and San Pedro harbors, and the Balboa Pavilion at Newport Beach. You can also reach Catalina by helicopter service, from both San Pedro and Long Beach.

Most hotels arrange to meet their guests at the pier and transport them to the hotel via golf cart or taxi as a courtesy service. Upon arrival you may as well check in if your room is ready. You should inquire about check-out time, which is usually quite early, around 10:30 or 11:00 A.M.

Investigate **Crescent Avenue,** Avalon's main street, with its shops and cafes, palm trees, and postage-stamp-size beach that could probably fit in your backyard. The population in Avalon—the only city on the 21-mile-long, 8-mile-wide island—is about 3,200. Summer and weekend visitors increase this figure to more than 10,000 visitors who crowd the tiny, 1-square-mile city, feeling lucky to find a place to stand on its famed beach, let alone sprawl on the warm sand.

You'll soon be aware of the pleasant absence of cars, as automobile use is limited. There are no rental cars on Catalina Island. Vehicle permits are tightly restricted by the city, and the waiting list is said to be about eight years long. In Avalon you mostly walk, ride a bike, use a golf cart, or board a tram.

There are no traffic, no noise or congestion, no smog, and no freeways here— truly an island paradise. You'll really feel on vacation in this happy-go-lucky little seaside resort. There's a vague European Riviera feeling in its compactness, tall palm trees, and jumble of cottages covered with flaming bougainvillea climbing up the steep hillsides. Bells chime from a hilltop tower; small boats rock in the sunny bay. The air is soft, and the fragrant, caressing breeze is balmy. It's a bit funky, a bit scruffy—and relaxed, friendly, romantic, carefree, and disarming.

LUNCH: New Antonio's Pizzeria and Cabaret, 230 Crescent Avenue, Avalon. (310) 510–0008. Select a window table overlooking the blue postcard bay or sit out on the deck in this large, casual local hangout with 1950s decor and sawdust and peanut shells on the floor. Made-to-order thick-crust pizza with four cheeses is served hot and tasty. There are also pasta, steaks, and chicken. Individual jukeboxes at each table are where all the good 1950s music is coming from. Daily breakfast, lunch, and dinner; full bar.

Afternoon

Crescent Avenue, sometimes called Front Street, is made for leisurely window shopping or relaxing on a bench watching the action in the yacht-filled harbor. As the only offshore rendezvous for Southern California yachtsmen, Catalina originally gained popularity as a yacht haven and sportfishing mecca and is still a prestigious yachting anchorage. John Wayne and other celebrity outdoorsmen used to sail their yachts over to fish for swordfish and marlin. Author Zane Grey, who lived up in the hills for many years, was an ardent fisherman as well.

The tall, stately Casino Building dominates the far side of the bay. Shops and restaurants line both sides of the busy, broad, redbrick street. Stores feature beachwear, casual attire, souvenirs, T-shirts, and kitsch you never dreamed of. Avalon Bay Company has the largest selection of women's clothing, shoes, and accessories; good-looking Sugarloaf Books has magazines, gifts, and postcards. The staff at Visitors Discovery Tours, across from the green Pleasure Pier on Crescent Avenue, will be happy to help you line up sightseeing tours convenient to your busy schedule.

A leading island attraction and world-famous landmark is the twelve-story, art deco **Casino Building,** perched at the edge of Avalon Bay, which opened in 1929. Here's where all the Big Bands played during the swinging years. Throughout the 1930s the famous Casino Ballroom, on the twelfth floor, vibrated with 3,000 to 5,000 dancers on an average night. In a forty-minute guided tour of the historic Casino Building, you're waltzed out on the circular dance floor beneath its revolving mirrored chandelier for a nostalgic twirl, then onto the broad terrace for photogenic views of the harbor, city, and mountains. This tour also includes the **Avalon Theatre** and the **Catalina Art Association Gallery** in the building (fee for tour). There's another tour, of the **Catalina Island Museum,** also in the building (fee).

DINNER: Cafe Prego, 403 Crescent Avenue, Avalon. (310) 510–1218. Considered Avalon's finest Italian cuisine. Try to snag a streetside window table or one facing the water so you can watch the lights twinkling in the harbor. You could be in a small, romantic seaside cafe in Portofino, Italy. Dinners include soup, crisp salad, and a basket of fragrant, warm bread. Try the richly flavored pasta combo: manicotti and cannelloni with *aglio e olio* linguine. Dinner only; casual dress; best to reserve on weekends.

LODGING: Pavilion Lodge on Crescent Avenue, Avalon. (800) 428–2566 (from California, 8:00 A.M. to 5:00 P.M.); (310) 510–2500 (twenty-four-hour service). AAA three-diamond rated. Opposite the beachfront, seventy-three rooms cluster around a sunny, grassy courtyard. The lodge is sparkling clean, with cable TV, minirefrigerator, in-room coffeemaker, complimentary continental breakfast and coffee in the lobby, and courtesy baggage service to and from the boat terminal (no in-room telephone). Two-person, two-night packages from Sunday through Thursday include round-trip boat transportation and choice of two island tours. Reservations: (800) 626–5400.

Day 2 / Morning

BREAKFAST: The Busy Bee, 306 Crescent Avenue, Avalon. (310) 510–1983. If the sun's shining, you'll want breakfast outdoors at one of Catalina's oldest restaurants. At a deckside table over the shining water, you can savor pancakes and eggs, New Orleans Scramble with Cajun sausage, and other specialties on the one-hundred-item menu.

In summer Avalon is a splendid place to lounge on the beach or go for a swim. But after breakfast you'll probably have to check out of your room. The Pavilion Lodge will store your luggage and transport it to the boat in time for your departure. (Not all hotels include this courtesy service.)

To see more of Santa Catalina Island than just the downtown area, opt for the **Avalon Scenic Tour,** which takes you on a 9-mile, fifty-minute narrated tour from the waterfront up into the hills high above the harbor. Your driver tells the history of Catalina Island, which was discovered in 1542 by Juan Cabrillo, a Portuguese explorer, who named it San Salvador. It was rediscovered sixty years later by Spanish explorer Sebastian Viscaino, who renamed it Santa Catalina in honor of St. Catherine's Feast Day. Both explorers claimed the island for Spain, which did not attempt to colonize it.

The island has had many owners. At the end of the Mexican War in 1848, Pio Pico, California's last Mexican governor, allegedly deeded the island to an American, Thomas Robbins, in exchange for a horse and silver-trimmed saddle. Following a succession of private American owners, the island was finally sold to the Banning brothers, who formed Santa Catalina Island Company to develop the island as a pleasure and fishing resort.

Outside of Avalon, the rest of the island is largely uninhabitable and pretty much the same as it was when the island was discovered more than 450 years ago, thanks to the foresight of William Wrigley Jr., the chewing-gum magnate who purchased Catalina Island in 1919 and began improvements and conservation programs to preserve its natural beauty. In 1972 the Wrigley family established the Santa Catalina Island Conservancy to protect and preserve Catalina for future generations. The conservancy now owns about 86 percent of the island's 76 square miles.

Among other high points brought to passengers' attention is Zane Grey's "Pueblo Hotel." Built in 1926, it is the former hillside home of the prolific author of eighty-nine books, including *Riders of the Purple Sage, Call of the Canyon,* and other western novels. Also pointed out is the former Wrigley estate, now a popular four-star country inn. The bus winds up around the hills, and you have passed absolutely no other car on the road, which overlooks Catalina's 9-hole golf course, tennis courts, stables, and the baseball field where, from 1921, Wrigley's Chicago Cubs held their annual spring baseball training for about twenty-six years. View stops and photo opportunities are plentiful on this tour (tour fee).

LUNCH: **Armstrong's Fish Market and Seafood Restaurant,** 306 Crescent Avenue, Avalon. (310) 510–0113. Sit inside the small, cheery dining room with blue-and-white-checkered tablecloths or out on the broad deck over Avalon Bay. Lunch favorites are mesquite-charbroiled fresh seafood, steaks, and chicken specialties that come with rice pilaf, cole slaw, or steamed vegetable.

Afternoon

Stroll the green **Pleasure Pier,** where the visitors bureau can answer any questions and make suggestions. Along the pier you'll find boat rentals and Catalina Diver's Supply Shop. Eric's is known for burgers, sandwiches, and ice cream. At the end of the pier where the seagulls convene, Earl & Rosie's Seafood snack bar has, since 1967, been dispensing burgers and fries.

About midway along this broad, wood-planked pier, board the **Glass Bottom Boat,** where you can see through Catalina's crystalline waters below the surface of the sea to a marine preserve of brightly hued fish and giant beds of kelp. This cruise is best on a sunny day when visibility is generally 70 to 80 percent. The iridescent orange Garibaldi, California's state marine fish, is easy to spot. Sleek baby California sea lions do somersaults beneath the glass floor, so close you can count their whiskers. Occasionally you might see a cormorant, a large feathered bird that swims underwater, greedily feasting on fish as fast as it can catch them in its long beak. Night trips are also available (trip fee).

If there's time before you leave the island, browse Avalon's fascinating side streets. **The Steamer Trunk,** 125 Sumner Avenue, is a stunning shop, with contemporary handmade jewelry, mobiles, art objects, and T-shirts. On Metropole Street are Von's grocery and the multilevel **Metropole Market Place and Hotel,** a rambling complex of restaurants and specialty shops around a pretty courtyard.

Head for the boat pier about fifteen to twenty minutes before departing the storybook island to claim your luggage, if it's been forwarded by your hotel. The cruise back to the mainland is frequently smoother sailing than coming over. Disembarking in Long Beach, pick up your car and head for the 710 freeway north to Los Angeles.

There's More

Santa Catalina Island Company Discovery Tours, P.O. Box 737, Avalon, 90704. (310) 510–2500. This company offers a variety of island tours. The extremely popular Inland Motor Tour is a three-and-three-quarter-hour scenic adventure that includes an Arabian horse performance and visits the rugged and unspoiled wilderness interior, where you can see rare native plants and free-roaming buffalo herds, descendants of the fourteen brought over in 1924 for the filming of Zane Grey's book *The Vanishing American.* Today, about 300 buffalo roam freely here. Inquire about other exciting island tours.

The Wrigley Memorial and Botanical Garden/Catalina Island Conservancy, P.O. Box 2739, Avalon, 90704. (310) 510–2595. This honors William Wrigley Jr.'s life work in preservation of the island. The huge memorial is an almost forty-acre showcase of Catalina native plants. Open daily from 8:00 A.M. to 5:00 P.M. Tram service from Island Plaza.

Two Harbors at the Isthmus is a casual, secluded small village for camping and hiking; it has swimming beaches, a dive center, and a B&B as well. Among many movies filmed in this scenic area are *Hurricane, Mutiny on the Bounty,* and *MacArthur.* For information call (310) 510–0303.

Catalina Safari Bus, located in the Plaza, along Crescent Avenue. (310) 510–2800. Provides daily scheduled transportation between Avalon and Two Harbors, with stops throughout the island.

Catalina West End Dive Center in Two Harbors offers scuba and snorkeling trips, beach dives, equipment rental; group rates. (310) 510–0303, ext. 272.

Brown's Bike Rentals and Sales, 107 Pebbly Beach Road, Avalon. (310) 510–0986. Across from the basketball court. Open 9:00 A.M. to 5:00 P.M. Permit required outside of Avalon or Two Harbors.

Catalina Scuba LUV. 126 Catalina Avenue, Avalon. (310) 510–2350. Scuba diving with open-water instruction, kayaking lessons, and more.

Golf cart rentals. Island Rentals, (310) 510–1456.

Boats to Catalina from different ports:
  Catalina Express, from Long Beach, San Pedro, and Dana Point harbors. (800) 995–4386; (310) 519–1212.
  Catalina Flyer, from Newport Beach's historic Balboa Pavilion. (949) 673–5245.
  Catalina Explorer, from Long Beach. (877) 432–6276.

Island Express Helicopter Service. Daily flights from both Long Beach and San Pedro. (310) 510–2525.

Special Events

Early January. Benefit 50-mile Run, Avalon to Two Harbors. (909) 399–3553.

February. New Balance Buffalo Run. (714) 978–1528. Annual Avalon Harbor Underwater Clean-Up. (310) 510–2595.

March. Catalina Marathon. (714) 978–1528.

End of March. Annual Catalina Conservancy Ball, Casino Ballroom.

First week in April. Catalina Island Conservancy Ball. (866) 743–2761.

Beginning of April. Annual Rubber Ducky Derby. (310) 510–1987.

Mid-April. Earth Day Celebration. (310) 510–0954.

First week in May. Annual Catalina Island Rugby Festival. (800) 448–4050.

Mid-May. Catalina Island Hoe-Down. Live entertainment, games, and food. (310) 510–2595, ext. 0.

Mid-June. Swing Camp Catalina. Classes and performances by leading swing dancers from around the world, with 1940s-style Big Band Dance at Casino Ballroom. (626) 799–5689.

Mid-June to end of August. Kid's Fishing Derby. (310) 510–1987.

Last week in June. Classic Silent Film Benefit in historic Avalon Theater in the Casino Building. (310) 510–2414.

July 4. Parade and fireworks display over Avalon Bay, dinner dancing in the Casino Ballroom, golf cart parade, fireworks show, Two Harbors.

Mid-August. Catalina Tiki Fest. Hawaiian luau features music, food, and cultural workshops.

Mid-September. Annual Catalina Festival of Art, outdoors on Crescent Avenue. (310) 510–0808. Annual Catalina Wine Festival. (310) 510–1520.

Annual Pottery and Tile Expo. (310) 510–2414.

Early and mid-October. Annual three-day, three-weekend Catalina Jazz Trax Festival, in the legendary Casino Ballroom. Ticket information and dates, (866) TRAXTIX. Halloween Swing Fling and Costume Ball, Casino Ballroom. (800) 626–4804.

Late October. Annual Avalon Ball. Features music of the 1920s and 1930s.

Early November. Catalina Island Triathlon, premier end-of-season event. All participants must be a Tri-Fed member. Information: Pacific Sports, (714) 978–1528.

End of November. Thanksgiving Feast at Harbor Reef, a tradition at Two Harbors.

December. Annual "Shop in Avalon" night. Christmas carolers, holiday discounts, and tree lighting. (310) 510–1520.

December 31. Annual New Year's Eve Celebration, Casino Ballroom. (310) 510–1520. New Year's Eve Celebration with dinner, dancing, and gala party at Two Harbors. (310) 510–2800.

Other Recommended Restaurants and Lodgings

Avalon

NOTE: Catalina Island hotels offer various mid-week and seasonal rates and packages. The high-rate summer season is mid-June to mid-September. Some packages include round-trip boat passage, island tours, a courtesy taxi to and from the boat dock, and continental breakfast. It's best to inquire when making reservations.

Channel House, 205 Crescent Avenue. (310) 510–1617. Noted for savory European cuisine. Lunch and dinner specialties feature sandwiches, seafood, and steak.

Ristorante Villa Portofino, 111 Crescent Avenue. (310) 510–2009. This classy dining room with candlelight and white tablecloths opens to the beachfront street. A dinner favorite for northern Italian dishes of homemade pastas, lasagna, ravioli, and veal. Fine wine. Closed Wednesday.

Sally's Waffle Shop, on the beachfront opposite the green Pleasure Pier. (310) 510–0355. Breakfast headquarters for islanders and visitors who fancy its variety of omelettes and waffles.

Casa Mariquita Hotel, 229 Metropole Avenue. (800) 545–1192; (310) 510–1192. Spanish-style hotel, ¾ block from the beach, with twenty-two rooms, cable TV, minifridge, and complimentary coffee and tea. Two-night, midweek packages include boat trip and tours.

Hotel Metropole, 123 Crescent Avenue. (800) 300–8528 (California); (800) 541–8528 (United States); (310) 510–1884. In attractive Metropole Market Place; entrance is on Whitley Avenue. Forty-eight custom rooms plus two-bedroom beach house, cable TV, minibar, complimentary continental breakfast in the lobby. Various two-night, midweek seasonal rates and packages include round-trip boat passage.

Seacrest Inn, 201 Clarissa (P.O. Box 128), Avalon, 90704. (310) 510–0800. An eight-room, romantic retreat with Victorian decor themed for honeymoons, weddings, and anniversaries. All fresh, nonsmoking rooms; in-room whirlpool for two in most rooms and suites; refrigerator; air-conditioning; remote-control TV, HBO, VCR; complimentary continental in-room breakfast basket. Sundeck with view; 1 block to beach. Special romance and wedding packages. AAA rated.

For More Information

Catalina Island Visitors Bureau & Chamber of Commerce, P.O. Box 217, Avalon, CA 90704. (310) 510–1520; www.catalina.com.

NORTHERN
ESCAPES

NORTHERN ESCAPE ONE

Harbor Hopping

Ventura, Oxnard / 1 Night

- ☐ Historic sites
- ☐ Beaches
- ☐ Waterfront dining
- ☐ Shopping
- ☐ Farmers' markets
- ☐ Harbor and island cruises
- ☐ Whale-watching
- ☐ Marinas
- ☐ Antiques
- ☐ Water sports
- ☐ Mission

This two-day, one-night escape to a nearby pair of small, friendly coastal cities offers refreshing harbor and marina activities and lifestyles, a famous mission, historical sites, museums, and adventure cruises to scenic offshore islands. You'll shop, dine, and snack at the bubbling waterfronts; purchase fresh local produce at its source; and stretch out on splendid, sunny, uncrowded beaches.

Day 1 / Morning

Drive north on Ventura Freeway 101 through the San Fernando Valley. Along the Conejo Grade you can see the flat valley spread out to the foothills. Though much of the time the air is misty, you can still see across acres of citrus groves and farms and frequently spot workers in the fields picking the strawberries for which the area is famous—like a painting by Millet. Ventura County is a leading producer of lemons and strawberries and has a great deal of open space. In Oxnard, from the freeway and along roads leading to the ocean and beaches, are miles of lemon groves and fields of strawberries and celery, which flourish in the rich soil of the Oxnard Plain. After passing Oxnard, continue a short distance north to Ventura, alongside richly cultivated farms. Ancient, leafy eucalyptus trees with trunks as thick as a barn door stand tall astride the freeway.

In **Ventura** exit the freeway at California Street, turning right on California Street and then left on Main Street. Ventura's ongoing upscale downtown revitalization, with fine new restaurants, trendy boutiques, a live theater, palm trees, decorated sidewalks, and a movie complex, offers new interest to visitors. The city's noted **San Buenaventura Mission,** 211 East Main Street (805–643–4318), where the city of Ventura began, is a few blocks farther along Main, between Junipero and Palm.

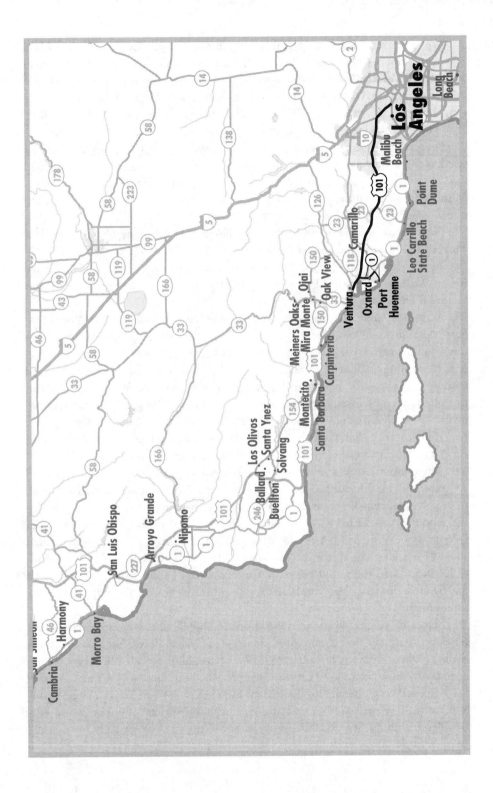

You enter the mission a few doors away, through its gift shop, at 225 East Main Street, which sells religious artifacts and cards. The gift shop leads to the small Museum of Vestments, which displays clothing worn by the missionary fathers over a 200-year period. Walk through the pleasant mission garden, with its Spanish-style fountain and tall shady trees. The small church, graced by a tall beamed ceiling, wrought-iron chandeliers, wall paintings, and lighted candles at the altar, holds services every Sunday. San Buenaventura Mission, founded in 1782, was the ninth of twenty-one California missions built during Spain's occupation of California, and it was the last mission founded by Father Junípero Serra. The mission, open Monday through Saturday from 10:00 A.M. to 5:00 P.M. and Sunday to 4:00 P.M., offers self-guided tours (donation $1.00).

Next door to the church, the red-tile-roofed **Albinger Archaeological Museum,** 113 East Main Street (805–648–5823), exhibits some of the 30,000 artifacts discovered in a 1974–75 dig. The oldest treasure is a bowl dating back 2,500 years. (Open Wednesday through Friday from 10:00 A.M. to 2:00 P.M. and Saturday and Sunday from 10:00 A.M. to 4:00 P.M.)

Across the street, the **Ventura County Museum of History and Art,** 100 East Main Street (805–653–0323), houses three galleries. The Smith Gallery features the George Stuart Historical Figures Collection of some 197 miniature figures in rotating exhibits. Authentically detailed and dressed in elaborate period costumes, the figures represent leading historical persons, including Abraham Lincoln, Queen Victoria, Marie Antoinette, and Louis XIV. The "Ventura County in the New West" exhibit explores Ventura from the Chumash era through the twentieth century, and there is a small, glass-enclosed statue of Father Junípero Serra. The Hoffman Gallery's changing exhibitions range from fine arts to local history. The museum store is nicely stocked with ethnic jewelry as well as a variety of art, travel, and local history books. (Open Tuesday through Sunday from 10:00 A.M. to 5:00 P.M.; docent-led tours by appointment; admission.)

About 5 blocks from the mission, **Ortega Adobe,** 215 West Main Street (805–658–4726), is the last of the downtown area's small, rustic, red-tile-roofed adobes. Built in 1857, this is the site where Emilio Ortega began fire-roasting his chiles and started the popular Ortega Famous Green Chiles Company, said to be the first commercial food manufacturing venture in California. (Open daily by appointment.)

Before driving down to the waterfront for lunch and sightseeing, check out some of Ventura's noted **antiques dealers** on Main Street. Nicholby Antique Mall, 404 East Main Street (805–653–1195) offers antiques and collectibles. (Open Monday through Saturday 10:30 A.M. to 5:30 P.M. and Sunday 11:00 A.M. to 5:00 P.M.) Times Remembered, 467 East Main Street (805–643–3137), is a large, good-looking mall of small dealers offering an intriguing variety of antiques and collectibles, including *Star Wars* memorabilia and old signs. (Open daily from 10:30

A.M. to 5:30 P.M., Friday and Saturday until 9:00 P.M.) *NOTE:* There is free parking all day at the city parking structure, at Santa Clara and California Streets.

To get to the waterfront and Ventura Harbor Village and Marina, 5 miles from downtown, turn right on California Street and continue to Harbor Boulevard; turn left and drive approximately 2 miles to the harbor entrance.

LUNCH: Milano's Italian Restaurant, in Ventura Harbor Village, 1559 Spinnaker Drive, Ventura. (805) 658–0388. Practically an institution for home-style family cooking and dining at waterside or indoors, with cozy red-and-white-checked tablecloths and friendly service. Favorite luncheon specialties, served with hot garlic bread and your choice of soup or salad, include baked lasagna layered with rich meat sauce and ricotta, Parmesan, and mozzarella cheeses; flavorful eggplant Parmesan is served with pasta.

Afternoon

Ventura Harbor Village, spread along thirty-three waterfront acres, is the area's largest harborside dining-shopping-entertainment showcase. Tall, red-roofed spires and arches envelop more than thirty-five shops, galleries, waterfront restaurants, and a carousel, amid bright flowers, colorful sailboats, and yachts swaying in the sparkling marina. For a spin across the water, board the *Dreamer* for forty-minute **cruises,** which leave hourly Saturday and Sunday between noon and 5:00 P.M., from 1575 Spinnaker Drive, Slip 14 (805–642–7753).

Drop by the gray, weathered, three-story **Channel Islands National Park Visitors Center,** 1901 Spinnaker Drive (805–658–5730). Park rangers offer information on what you'll see on trips to the five rugged, primeval Channel Islands, lying just 14 miles off Ventura's coast. Tidepool displays and topographic island exhibits point out the characteristics of each island. The elevator whisks you to the top-floor deck tower for a tremendous panoramic view of the harbor, the mountains, and the Channel Islands out in the Pacific. (Open daily from 8:30 A.M. to 5:00 P.M.; free.) For firsthand information on year-round excursions to the islands, visit adjacent **Island Packers Cruises,** the official commercial charter to the islands (information: 805–642–1393). There are also half-day whale cruises.

If you want to get out on the sand and in the water, practically next door to the Channel Island National Park Visitors Center is **Harbor Cove Beach,** the city's safest swimming beach, protected by a breakwater, with a children's play area and convenient restrooms. **Surfer's Point,** at Seaside Park, is one of the most popular surfing and sailboarding beaches. Closer by, the 1,500-foot-long **San Buenaventura City Pier,** completed in 1872, had its heyday when the harbor was filled with steamships whose passengers and cargoes waited to be loaded and unloaded. Nowadays visitors strolling, shopping, or dining on the extensively renovated, long, peaceful pier can watch anglers casting their lines for bass and bonita and enjoy spectacular coastline and mountain views.

DINNER: Alexander's Restaurant, adjacent to Four Points Sheraton Hotel, 1050 Schooner Drive, Ventura. (805) 658–2000. Alongside the boat-filled marina, it's a sleek lunch and dinner scene for such specialties as grilled rack of lamb and prime rib served with choice of soup or salad, baked potato or rice. Sunday champagne brunch extravaganza. Genial happy hour in the lobby bar; weekend entertainment.

LODGING: Four Points Sheraton Hotel in Ventura, 1050 Schooner Drive, Ventura. Reservations, (800) 229–5732 (in California); (805) 658–1212. A AAA three-diamond resort 1 block from the beach and edging the marina. The dynamic, rambling architecture was designed by the Frank Lloyd Wright Foundation. Harbor views from each of its 175 luxury guest rooms and suites with private balconies, hot tubs, kitchens, coffeemakers, room service, cable TV, iron and ironing board; restaurant, lounge; heated swimming pool, one lighted tennis court, a basketball court, Jacuzzi, fitness room, and nearby golf.

Day 2 / Morning

BREAKFAST: At the hotel. Alexander's Restaurant, overlooking the marina, offers tempting selections, from fresh fruit, scrambled eggs, and bacon to eggs Benedict and *huevos rancheros*.

Oxnard, 60 miles from Los Angeles and the "Strawberry Capital of the United States," is just minutes away along the scenic Gold Coast. Follow Harbor Boulevard south along the beautiful stretches of pale, near-deserted beaches from San Buenaventura State Beach, which begins at San Buenaventura City Pier, passing McGrath State Beach, with its sand dunes and lagoons, and Mandalay Beach to Channel Islands Boulevard and Channel Islands Harbor, a lively waterfront resort, recreation, and dining marketplace. Chumash Indians fished and hunted here in the dramatic, lonely marshes you can see from the highway.

The horseshoe-shaped **Channel Islands Harbor** complex comprises **Harbor Landing,** the **Marine Emporium Landing,** and **Fisherman's Wharf,** flagged by its white lighthouse and home to the Ventura County Maritime Museum. In this bustling area a variety of specialty shops, restaurants, and sidewalk cafes add to the appeal of the special and sunny seaside setting.

Channel Islands Harbor, considered one of the state's finest full-service facilities, has 2,600 boat slips, four yacht clubs, and nine full-service marinas. It also offers beautifully landscaped parks with attractive picnic areas and barbecues.

Stroll around the terra-cotta–colored buildings of **Harbor Landing Promenade** (2800 South Harbor Boulevard), with its cheery waterfront restaurants and chic shops, and watch the masts of boats and small craft bobbing in the pristine harbor. Along here you can buy a yacht, charter a sportfishing or cruise boat, take sailing lessons, rent a bike or a boat, and go whale-watching from December through March, when the Pacific gray whales pass through the channel

The lighthouse at Oxnard's Channel Islands Harbor.

on their annual migration from Alaska to Baja. For a change of scene, board the **Harbor Hopper Ferry** for a tour of the harbor. Hours are seasonal; call for a schedule (805–985–5828).

From Harbor Landing drive or walk alongside the water a few blocks to the Marine Emporium Landing, 3600 South Harbor Boulevard (805–985–5828), a gray-and-white-trimmed waterfront shopping-dining complex of New England–style clapboard architecture. Among the numerous shops, **Coast Chandlery** features traditional nautical items and supplies that are in sharp contrast to the unique clothing and gift boutique in **The Loft** upstairs.

The sprawling Casa Sirena Hotel and Marina complex is your next destination. To get there, turn right on Channel Islands Boulevard, turn right on Peninsula Road, and park.

LUNCH: The Lobster Trap Restaurant, 3605 Peninsula Road, Channel Islands Harbor. (805) 985–6361. Along with terrific panoramic views of the harbor, it's a trendy and popular spot, noted for fresh local seafood entrees, salads, crab cakes, steak, and prime rib. Sunday champagne buffet brunch. Best to make reservations.

Afternoon

On Fisherman's Wharf, the striking white lighthouse stores icing equipment for the commercial fishing boats that unload their catch at the dock. Pleasure boats also tie up here for provisioning.

Walk along the boardwalk to the **Ventura County Maritime Museum** (Fisherman's Wharf), 2731 South Victoria Avenue (805–984–6260), located in a large brick courtyard behind the small waterfront buildings. This museum is a seafarer's Valhalla. On display are twenty-four models of historic ships, including the *Golden Hinde, Old Ironsides,* the *Mayflower,* and the *Bounty,* as well as antique ship models and many other sailing exhibits and artifacts. Gift shop; self-guided or docent-led tours. (Open Monday and Thursday through Sunday from 11:00 A.M. to 5:00 P.M.; donation.)

En route back to Los Angeles, visit the **Seabee Museum,** Ventura Road at Sunkist (805–982–5163), in the Naval Construction Battalion Center, Building 99, in Port Hueneme, a commercial and military port. (Drive east on Channel Islands Boulevard to Ventura Road, turning right on Sunkist, to reach the museum.) The Seabees is the branch of the U.S. Navy that goes overseas and builds bridges, runways, and other immediate needs for the armed forces. The museum was established in 1947 to preserve its history and achievements.

Among the museum's exhibits of U.S. and foreign military memorabilia—from World War II and the Korean and Vietnam Wars—collected by the Seabees on foreign shores and donated to the museum are unusual musical instruments, coins, weapons, uniforms, and posters. Dioramas feature Seabee major construction jobs throughout the world; a gift shop sells Seabee T-shirts, caps, and souvenirs.

When you leave the museum, follow Ventura Road to Surfside Drive and **Port Hueneme Beach Park,** a beautiful, quiet beach ideal for swimming and surfing, with palm trees, a playground, a fishing pier, barbecue pits, picnic areas, and restrooms. **Port Hueneme Museum,** nearby at 220 Market and Hueneme Road (805–488–2023), displays the early days of the historic port. (Open Monday through Friday from 10:00 A.M. to 3:00 P.M.) Port Hueneme is the only deep-water facility between Los Angeles and San Francisco, a thriving international port where, among other goods, imported automobiles are unloaded for U.S. distribution.

To return to Los Angeles, take 4th Street to Pleasant Valley Road, turn right, and follow Pleasant Valley Road as it angles up toward Highway 34; turn right (south) on 34 until it intersects Freeway 101 south to Los Angeles.

There's More

Olivas Adobe, 4200 Olivas Park Drive, Ventura. (805) 644–4346. Built in 1847 by wealthy Don Raimundo Olivas for his family on his 4,700-acre rancho, when early California life revolved around working farms and ranches. Listed on the National

Register of Historic Places, the spacious, two-story, Monterey-style home, with its own chapel, is furnished with antiques of the period. Grounds open daily, with docent-guided tours on Saturday and Sunday, 10:00 A.M. to 4:00 P.M. A major portion of adjacent land is now Olivas Park Golf Course.

Ventura County Certified Farmers' Markets. (805) 529–6266. Held twice weekly, rain or shine, on Wednesday and Saturday, these fairly small markets offer good prices on fresh fruits and vegetables, eggs, seafood, plants, and cut flowers. Two outdoor locations: Pacific View Mall Lot, Mills Road and Main Street, Wednesday from 9:00 A.M. to 1:00 P.M., and the city parking lot on the corner of Santa Clara and Palm Streets, Saturday from 8:30 A.M. to noon.

Progressive Dining, Channel Island Harbor. (805) 985–4852. Enjoy a memorable evening on the water as you're whisked away to one restaurant for appetizers, another for the main entree, and a third for dessert. Cruise the harbor in between courses, and bring your friends, as the boat holds up to twenty-two people. Call for days and hours.

Jim Hall Kart Racing Schools, 1555G Morse Avenue, Ventura. (805) 642–1329. Everything for the novice or experienced racer.

Carnegie Art Museum, 424 South C Street, Oxnard, downtown next to Plaza Park. (805) 385–8157. On the National Register of Historic Places, built in 1906 as a Carnegie Library, this neoclassical-style museum, with stately pillars, houses a permanent collection of more than 200 paintings and sculptures focusing on California painters from the 1920s to the present; important changing exhibits. Open Thursday and Saturday from 10:00 A.M. to 5:00 P.M., Friday from 11:00 A.M. to 6:00 P.M., and Sunday from 1:00 to 5:00 P.M. Admission.

Gull Wings Children's Museum, 418 West 4th Street, Oxnard. (805) 483–3005. Alongside the art museum. Children love the hands-on, touchable exhibits, puppet theater, and stimulating activities. Gift shop. Open Tuesday through Sunday from 10:00 A.M. to 5:00 P.M. Admission.

Murphy Auto Museum, 2230 Statham Boulevard, Oxnard. (805) 487–4333. One of the oldest collections of Packards—dating from 1927 to 1958—and many others on display. Car buffs will love these classics; a 1903 Packard is the oldest car here. Buicks, street rods, and others, including a Ferrari. Saturday and Sunday 10:00 A.M. to 4:00 P.M.

Farmers' markets and produce stands. Experience Oxnard's wonderful agricultural bounties with visits to its weekly farmers' markets and the many fresh produce stands in the area. Sample seasonal fresh produce, especially strawberries, citrus, artichokes, and celery; seafood; gorgeous cut flowers; bakery goods; and gourmet items to take home. Farmers' Market Downtown, at Plaza Park, 300 West 5th Street. (805)

483–7960. Every Thursday rain or shine from 9:00 A.M. to 1:00 P.M., you'll find more than a hundred items on sale fresh from the farm.

Farmers' Market at Channel Islands Harbor at Marine Emporium Landing, 2810 South Harbor Boulevard, Oxnard. (805) 985–4853. Every Sunday, 10:00 A.M. to 2:00 P.M. rain or shine. Farmers' market, arts and crafts, BBQ, and entertainment.

Independently owned produce and flower stands are located throughout Oxnard. Here are three areas: Olivas Park Drive and Telephone Road, along Victoria south of Gonzales, and south of Olivas Park Drive.

Special Events

Beginning of February to end of March. Celebration of the Whales Week, Channel Islands; daily whale-watching trips from Channel Islands Harbor, Oxnard.

Arrival of Tall Ships, Ventura Harbor Village.

Mid–February. Rail to Romance Valentine dinner train, Fillmore. (800) 773–TRAIN.

March. St. Patrick's Day Parade & Festival, downtown Ventura.

Mid–April. Point Mugu Air Show. Point Mugu Naval Air Test Center. (805) 989–8548.

Early May. Ten-day Chamber Music Festival, downtown Ventura. (805) 667–2900.

Third weekend in May (Saturday and Sunday). Annual California Strawberry Festival, a statewide food event. Gourmet strawberry foods, contests, live entertainment. At Strawberry Meadows, Oxnard College Park. Minimal admission.

First weekend in June. "Annual Sidewalk Chalk One Up For Kids" Street Painting Festival. Plaza Park, Oxnard.

July 4. Street Fair, Main Street, downtown Ventura. Fireworks Show and Celebration, Ventura. Fireworks by the Sea and Farmers' Market, Channel Islands Harbor, Oxnard.

End of August. Annual Ventura County Fair, Ventura County Fairgrounds.

September. Channel Islands Film Festival, Ventura.

End of September. Annual California Beach Festival. Food, entertainment, sports, beer garden, crafts. California Street Promenade. Autumn Historic Home Tours. Visit lovely old Victorian and Craftsmen private homes. Oxnard.

October. Annual Taste of Ventura County Food and Wine Festival. Channel Islands Harbor, Oxnard.

Harvest Arts & Crafts Festival, Ventura. (805) 648–3376.

Kids Ocean Fest, Ventura Harbor Village. (877) 89–HARBOR.

Ventura's "California Cruisin'" Classic Car Show. (805) 766–0898

First week in November. Flea Market & Swap Meet, Ventura. (805) 648–3376.

Mid-November. Holiday Open House Wine Tasting, Ventura. (805) 656–5054.

First Sunday in December. Holiday Street Fair, downtown Ventura. Food, entertainment, really big arts and crafts show. Boat Parade of Lights, Ventura Harbor Village.

First weekend in December. Hometown Holiday Christmas Parade, downtown Oxnard.

First and second weekends in December. Annual Parade of Lights and Harborfest, Channel Islands Harbor, Oxnard. Victorian Christmas House Tours, six decorated beautiful Victorian-style houses, Heritage Square, Oxnard. Annual Parade of Lights, Ventura Harbor Village.

Mid-December to March. Whale-watching, Ventura.

Other Recommended Restaurants and Lodgings

Ventura

Joannafina's Mexican Cafe, 1127 South Seaward Avenue. (805) 652–0360. In a small cottage converted to a funky cafe with garden patios, Joannafina's has been said to have the best tamales in the county. But you should try the burritos and other delicious, authentic Mexican specialties made from family recipes. Sunday champagne brunch and roving Mexican trio.

Jonathan's, 204 East Main Street. (805) 648–4853. In the historic downtown district across from the mission. Owner-chef Jonathan's Mediterranean-style specialties favor lobster ravioli, spicy crab bisque; grilled chicken breast basted with Moroccan flavors is served atop savory vegetable risotto and accompanied by a red *coulis* sauce.

Holiday Inn Ventura Beach Resort, 450 East Harbor Boulevard. (800) 842–0800; (805) 648–7731. At the beach; 260 coastline-view guest rooms with balconies, satellite TV, coffeemaker, iron/ironing board, hair dryer; one restaurant, kids-eat-free program, cocktail lounge; oceanfront swimming pool, exercise room. Adjacent to the San Buenaventura City Pier. Special and seasonal rates; AAA rate discount.

Ventura Beach Marriott, 2055 Harbor Boulevard. (805) 643–6000; (800) 228–9290. Offers 283 luxurious guest rooms, including fourteen suites. Adjacent to

San Buenaventura State Beach. Heated swimming pool, whirlpool, fully equipped health club with saunas. Restaurant and lobby bar. Special rates available.

Oxnard

Casa Sirena Hotel and Marina, 3605 Peninsula Road, Channel Islands Harbor. (800) 447–3529; (805) 985–6311. Premier waterside hotel, offers 272 beautifully appointed rooms, including thirty suites, with coffeemaker, refrigerator, microwave oven (in the suites), cable TV, and hair dryer, among other amenities. Besides sailboats drifting past your window, facilities feature heated swimming pool and spa, tennis, putting green, and bicycles. Dine at adjacent popular Lobster Trap Restaurant (see listing on page 125). Romance and other getaway packages, meeting facilities.

Embassy Suites Mandalay Beach Resort, 2101 Mandalay Beach Road. (800) 362–2779 (nationwide); (805) 984–2500. Tropical lush gardens on the beachfront; 248 suites, wet bar, refrigerator, coffeemaker and coffee, microwave ovens, two TVs. Large heated pool, two spas, two lighted tennis courts, exercise facility. Restaurant, lounge; complimentary cooked-to-order breakfast and evening receptions. Special packages. Parking fee.

For More Information

Ventura Visitors and Convention Bureau, 89 South California Street, Suite C, Ventura, CA 93001. (800) 333–2989 (United States); (805) 648–2075; www.ventura-usa.com. Open Monday through Saturday from 9:00 A.M. to 4:00 P.M. and Sunday from 10:00 A.M. to 4:00 P.M.

Ventura Parks and Recreation. (805) 658–4726.

Oxnard Convention & Visitors Bureau, Connelly House at Heritage Square, 200 West 7th Street, Oxnard, CA 93030. (800) 269–6273 (visitor information); (805) 385–7545; www.oxnardtourism.com.

Channel Islands Harbor Visitor Center, 3810 West Channel Islands Boulevard, Suite G, Oxnard, CA 93035. (800) 994–4852.

Port Hueneme Chamber of Commerce, 220 North Market Street, Port Hueneme, CA 93401. (805) 488–2023.

NORTHERN ESCAPE TWO

Country Getaway

Ojai / 2 Nights

This sleepy little country village has a special tranquillity perfect for unwinding in a three-day outing. Creative people as well as fugitives of Los Angeles's fast lanes have long been drawn to Ojai (pronounced "O-hi") for its quiet, unhurried pace. Tucked in a deep coastal valley, extending from the 6,000-foot Topa Topa Mountains at the edge of Los Padres National Forest to the ocean, Ojai's miles of orange groves brim with golden fruit. Avocado trees drape the rolling foothills, and the hectic world seems far away. Small wonder that Ojai was the setting for the mystical, beautiful valley of Shangri-La in the movie *Lost Horizon,* starring Ronald Colman.

In this cozy town you can tee off at two championship golf courses, play tennis, browse and shop at fine galleries and boutiques, tour artist studios, and pedal a bike along a meandering creek down country lanes where horses graze in sunny pastures. You can visit a museum, "take it off" in style at a chic health spa resort, picnic in uncrowded parks, purchase just-picked oranges and avocados to tote home, and stay in a legendary world-class inn. Camping, fishing, and boating are available in nearby Lake Casitas, site of the 1984 Olympic rowing and canoeing events.

- ☐ Resort
- ☐ Golf
- ☐ Tennis
- ☐ Spa
- ☐ Parks
- ☐ Orange and avocado groves
- ☐ Museum
- ☐ Hiking and biking
- ☐ Antiques
- ☐ Galleries
- ☐ Fishing and boating

Day 1 / Morning

Drive north on Ventura Freeway 101 to Ojai, 76 miles through the rural San Fernando Valley. Traveling over the Conejo Grade, you see the vast fertile plain spread out below. Both sides of the highway are checkerboarded with farms, row crops, and citrus groves.

Immediately after seeing the signs for Ventura, exit to the right on Highway 33 north to reach Ojai, 14 miles inland along a divided country road framed by voluptuous hills that turn chartreuse in spring and are sere in winter.

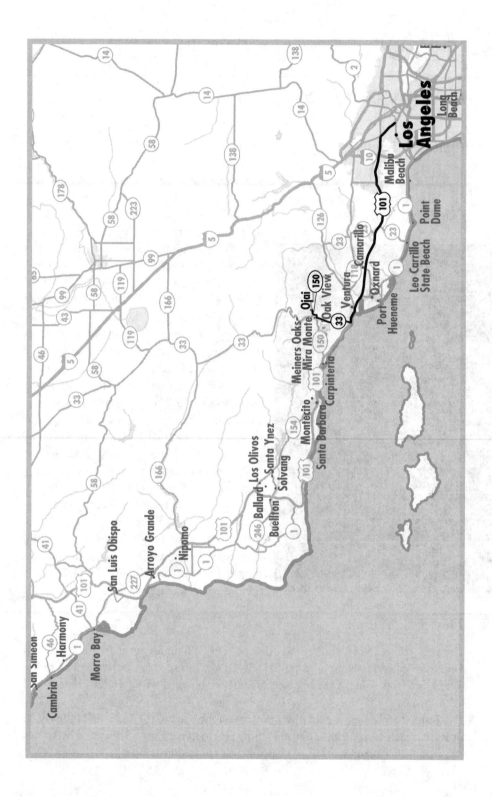

After Foster Park follow the one-lane rural road past Casitas Springs and small houses; you'll see bikers and horseback riders on the bike and equestrian paths that follow the road.

As you drive through Oak View, make note of **Oak Pit Barbeque,** on the right side of the road, to return to for sandwiches to eat there or take out on your way home (see "Other Recommended Restaurants and Lodgings").

Continue through the small village of Mira Monte, along Ojai Avenue, to the Ojai Valley Inn & Spa, on the right, and turn onto the private road to the inn.

LUNCH: Oak Grill, Ojai Valley Inn & Spa, 905 Country Club Road, Ojai. (800) 422–6524; (805) 646–5511; www.ojairesort.com. Dining on the broad terrace beneath a vine-covered pagoda surrounded by the giant oak trees and lush golf course marks a carefree beginning to your holiday. Relax in the beautiful surroundings over creative sandwiches, salads, tortilla soup, and other specialties.

Afternoon

Golfers won't waste any time teeing off on Ojai Valley Inn & Spa's renowned, challenging course. Nongolfers, with permission, enjoy tooling around this scenic, impeccably maintained course in a golf cart, rattling over rustic wooden bridges spanning picturesque creeks, and cruising fairways lined with giant sycamores and oaks. Tennis enthusiasts will soon be racing across the courts, and swimmers are equally at home in the sunny, uncrowded pools.

Others can drive, take the trolley, or borrow a bike from the inn and pedal about 1 mile into downtown Ojai. **Libbey Park,** with its splashing fountain smack in the center of town across from the Arcade, is the showcase for most local events and activities. In the charming, oak-studded small park, the secluded bowl beneath an ancient sycamore is the delightful setting for the city's prestigious annual Ojai Music Festival in June, year-round concerts, and theater. Libbey Park is also the site of the Ojai Tennis Tournament, held in April, and public courts.

Alongside, the post office, with its landmark 65-foot bell tower, was built in 1917, at the same time as the shaded, Spanish-style shopping arcade across the street. There are no parking meters, and you'll find plenty of parking places.

The best way to see Ojai is to stroll the small downtown area. The **Arcade,** between Signal and Montgomery Streets, is the city's main shopping stretch of stores, galleries, and some restaurants. You'll find more of everything on the small side streets, across from the arcade and behind it.

Rains, 218 East Ojai Avenue (805–646–1441), Ojai's largest store and family owned since 1917, is an attractive, well-stocked, upscale emporium featuring men's and women's apparel, giftware, kitchenware, pottery, and hardware. A few doors away, **Tottingham Court, Ltd.,** 242 East Ojai Avenue (805–646–2339), is a unique place to shop, have brunch, or both. Its small tearoom with dining patio offers quiche, sandwiches, salads, pastries, and true English scones with Devonshire cream from England. Among its multitude of import gift items are china, crystal, silver, baby wear, and tiny collectibles.

Across from the Arcade, **Barbara Bowman stores,** at 125 and 139 East Ojai Avenue, make their own exclusive and handsome clothing and accessories. **The Ojai Valley Museum,** 130 West Ojai Avenue (805–640–1390), is in the Old Catholic Church, built in 1919 and on the National Register of Historic Places. You get a delightful mixture of old and new from works of local artists displayed in a changing gallery to a glimpse of the city's past with the Native American artifacts discovered in nearby excavations of the Oak Grove and Chumash tribes, who settled here thousands of years ago. View the lifelike birds and animals, together with memorabilia depicting Ojai's early pioneer life. The museum's gift shop offers T-shirts, postcards, and great children's books. (Open Thursday and Friday from 1:00 to 4:00 P.M., Saturday 10:00 A.M. to 4:00 P.M. and Sunday noon to 4:00 P.M.) The **Ojai Valley Chamber of Commerce & Visitors Bureau** is just next door, where you can pick up maps, brochures, and other visitor information (see "For More Information").

Stop by the **Massarella Pottery & Gallery,** 105 South Montgomery Street (805–646–9453), a good-looking showroom and factory displaying the owners' classic stoneware and porcelain, glass, jewelry, and sculpture made on the premises. If you're lucky, you can watch the potters throwing the clay and firing it. (Closed Monday and Tuesday.)

DINNER: The Ranch House, South Lomita and Besant, Ojai. (805) 646–2360. This charming flower-and-plant-filled gourmet garden restaurant with meandering streams is a longtime special favorite for Ojai residents and visitors. Breads are baked daily, desserts come right from the kitchen, the wine list is notable, and herbs are from the garden. Dinner served Tuesday through Saturday; Sunday champagne brunch. (Pricey.)

LODGING: Ojai Valley Inn & Spa, 905 Country Club Road, Ojai. (800) 422–6524; (805) 646–1111; www.ojairesort.com. In 2004 a major $65-million renovation and expansion of this landmark resort was completed. You'll find four new restaurants and lounges, a new pub with wood-burning pizza ovens, new golf clubhouse, new pools, new conference center and ballroom, and other improvements. Atop 220 rolling acres, 308 guest rooms and suites, each with private balcony or terrace overlooking the fairways; hair dryer, coffeemaker, iron and ironing board; room service, television, minibar, turndown service. **Spa Ojai** has a luxurious experience, twenty-eight treatment areas, private guest quarters, a restaurant, hair salon, and retail shop. The Inn's Ranch & Stables offers guided horseback trail rides, guided hikes, and mountain-bike rides into the Los Padres National Forest, and a charming children's petting farm. Eighteen-hole championship golf course, driving range, putting green, golf shop; four tennis courts; tennis center; two heated swimming pools, whirlpool, exercise facility; concierge service; children's playground; basketball court; complimentary bikes and Ojai trolley shuttle to town. Sunday buffet brunch. Member of Historic Hotels of America. Golf, spa, and B&B packages available. Children's programs.

Day 2 / Morning

BREAKFAST: Ojai Valley Inn & Spa. Breakfast in the glass-walled dining room overlooking the sunlit golf course and the mountains begins your day with beauty and beautifully prepared specialties.

After breakfast golfers will soon be breaking par on the front nine. Or you can drive into and through the village for about another 2 miles east, to see the beautiful acres of orange groves and avocado groves, and then drive up into the foothills for spectacular vistas across the rich valley.

This most easterly end of town is where you can see the famous Shangri-La view as seen in the movie *Lost Horizon*. At Boccali's Pizza & Pasta, 3277 Ojai Avenue, turn right and drive partway up the hill to Dennison Grade. Stop at the stone bench on the right side of the road. The panoramic view down into the valley on a clear, bright day, as well as when the mountain ranges seem to be floating in clouds and mist, is gorgeous.

Return to Ojai Avenue and turn left to **Soule Park,** off Highway 150 on Boardman, adjacent to Soule Golf Course (pronounced "sole").

The spacious park, edging squiggly San Antonio Creek, provides shady picnic tables, barbecue pits, a playground, tennis courts, and serene expanses of lawn and trees. Local equestrian groups hold weekend shows in Soule's horse arena, considered one of the country's finest.

LUNCH: The Garden Terrace Restaurant, 1002 East Ojai Avenue. (805) 646–1133. This cheery place with tablecloths and fireplace is directly across from Soule Golf Course, with a view of the golfers on the emerald fairways. Its California cuisine menu features such delightful specialties as potato-crusted salmon, curried chicken crepes with pineapple chutney and baby green salad, daily specials, and sandwiches. Scrumptious homemade gourmet desserts lead off with chocolate hazelnut flourless cake served with raspberry sauce on the bottom and crème Anglais. Open daily. Reservations recommended.

Afternoon

Return to the Ojai Valley Inn & Spa for golf, tennis, or swimming and sunning. Later you might want to drive back into the village or pedal in for shopping or further sightseeing. **Bart's Books,** 302 West Matilija Street at the corner of Cañada (805–646–3755), has been a collector's delight and a town pride since 1964. Go inside to browse this unusual open-air bookmart, built around a huge oak tree and offering some 100,000 new and used books, magazines, and sheet music. Shelves of bargain-priced used books line the exterior walls to accommodate after-hours book lovers, who can buy them by tossing the marked price over the wall onto the patio. Open daily 9:30 A.M. to sunset.

A few blocks away are the **Biblical Gardens,** on the grounds of the graceful old Presbyterian Church, 304 North Foothill Road at the corner of Aliso (805–646–1437). The ecumenical garden features fifty varieties of plants mentioned in the Bible; all have been authenticated, and you're in for a few surprises. Join a guided tour, or pick up a map and wander about on your own. All plants are labeled, making them easy to identify.

If antiques hunting is part of your fun in visiting small villages, check out the **Treasures of Ojai Antiques,** 110 North Signal Street, at the corner of Matilija (805–646–2852). Here's where some twenty-five to thirty or more antiques dealers display treasures from estate jewelry, California pottery, and collectibles to Native American rugs, home accessories, and art nouveau pieces. Open daily from 10:00 A.M. to 5:00 P.M.

DINNER: Suzanne's Cuisine, 502 West Ojai Avenue, Ojai. (805) 640–1961. Join the locals who know the winners. Lunch and dinner selections favor Southwest salad with chili and feta cheese and rosemary-roasted rack of lamb. Bar, garden, and indoor dining. Closed Tuesday. Reservations suggested.

LODGING: At the Ojai Valley Inn & Spa.

Day 3 / Morning

BREAKFAST: Another splendid breakfast at Ojai Valley Inn & Spa.

Golfers will want to play another round on the well-manicured course, hit some balls on the driving range, or sharpen up their game on the putting greens near the dining terrace, with Ojai's warm sun on their backs.

Afternoon

If you'd like to tote home some of the luscious oranges, avocados, or any of the local seasonal fruits you see in the rich groves throughout the rural area, they're for sale at Ojai Certified Farmer's Market (see "There's More") and also in the small, attractive Starr Market downtown.

On your way home, try to allow time to stop at scenic **Lake Casitas.** Follow Highway 33 west to its junction with Highway 150; west from Mira Monte turn right (north) and drive about 3 miles to the park's entrance. The gleaming man-made reservoir, with 60 miles of shoreline, is surrounded by lush avocado groves.

Recreation is unlimited at Lake Casitas. Here, at one of the area's largest campgrounds, visitors can rent a boat; ride a bike; fish for trout, bass, or catfish; picnic and barbecue—but no swimming. A snack bar serves breakfast and lunch.

Admission. (805) 649–2233. At the lake, **Blue Heron Water Amusement Park** is for kids younger than twelve. Open from May through September from 10:00 A.M. to 5:00 P.M. Admission and parking fee. (805) 649–2233.

After your visit to Lake Casitas, take Highway 33 back to 101 and follow it south to Los Angeles.

There's More

Golf. Soule Park Golf Course, 1033 East Ojai Avenue. (805) 646–5633. An 18-hole public course threaded with old oaks and pine trees. Golf shop, driving range, carts; Clubhouse Restaurant; seniors' weekday rates.

Tennis. Tennis is a large part of Ojai's lifestyle. Besides courts at Libbey and Soule Parks, you can play at Nordhoff High School, 0.5 mile north of the Y intersection on Highways 150 and 113, or at Matilija Junior High, just off El Paseo Road.

The Oaks at Ojai, 122 East Ojai Avenue. (800) 753–6257; (805) 646–5573. Resident health and fitness spa retreat run by noted fitness expert Sheila Cluff, who can help you take it off and stay that way. Various programs and packages; spa cuisine.

Bike riding is one of the most pleasant ways to see the Ojai Valley, riding either through the downtown area or along the 10-foot-wide, paved bike path separated by a fence from the road and equestrian path. A 16.5-mile trail begins at Fox Street downtown and leads through scenic back roads, ending in Ventura. Pick up trail maps at the Ojai Valley Chamber of Commerce & Visitors Bureau or at Bicycles of Ojai, 108 Cañada Street (805–646–7736), which rents and sells bikes for adults. Hop on your bike and follow the trail.

Ojai's "Pink Moment." At day's end, look toward the soaring Topa Topa Mountains to watch the pink-orange sunset radiate over the peaks. It bathes the sky and mountains in a luminous, blushing glow that gradually diffuses and fades. Strictly an Ojai phenomenon.

The Pottery, studio gallery of Otto Heino, 971 McAndrews Road. (805) 646–3393. This internationally acclaimed potter welcomes visitors Tuesday through Sunday from 1:00 to 5:00 P.M. Go east on Ojai Avenue, past Soule Park; turn left on Reeves Road to McAndrew Road.

Ojai Certified Farmer's Market, downtown in the parking lot at 300 East Matilija, behind the Arcade Plaza. (805) 698–5555. Fresh vegetables and fruits, delicious breads, arts and crafts, and more. Every Sunday from 9:00 A.M. to 1:00 P.M.

Special Events

NOTE: Call for admission fees.

Early April. Renaissance Faire & Shakespeare, at Lake Casitas. (805) 496–6036.

Last weekend in April. The Ojai Tennis Tournament, Libbey Park. (805) 646–7421. The oldest amateur tennis tour, since 1895.

First Saturday in May. Self-guided Annual Ojai Garden Tour of private gardens. (805) 646–8126.

June. Annual five-day Ojai Music Festival, Libbey Park. (805) 646–2094. Day and evening concerts.

Mid-June. Annual Ojai Wine Festival, Lake Casitas. (800) 648–4881. Crafts and arts plus a supervised children's play area.

Mid-September. Ojai Valley Mexican Fiesta. Mariachis, folkloric dances, crafts, and food. Libbey Bowl. (805) 640–1692.

Annual Bowlful of Blues Festival, on the shores of Lake Casitas; regional blues styles. (805) 646–7230.

Mid-October. Annual Ojai Studio Artists Tour. (805) 646–8126. Popular two-day tours of private studios of Ojai's finest painters, sculptors, potters, printmakers.

Other Recommended Restaurants and Lodgings

Ojai

L'Auberge Restaurant, 314 El Paseo. (805) 646–2288. Between Cañada and Rincon; entrance on Rincon. This vintage 1910 white mansion, half hidden by oak trees, is home to L'Auberge, which enjoys an excellent reputation for noteworthy French Belgian cuisine. Specialties include New York pepper steak flambé, *poulet cordon bleu,* and desserts of raspberry ice cream dipped in chocolate. Luncheon Saturday and Sunday; dinner nightly. Reservations suggested. Terrace dining offers stunning view of the rugged Topa Topa Mountains. Open Wednesday through Sunday starting at 5:30 P.M.

The Clubhouse Restaurant at Soule Park Golf Course, 1033 East Ojai Avenue. (805) 646–5685. Wrapped around a dramatic fireplace in a dining room overlooking sunny fairways. Medium-priced continental menu includes sandwiches, pasta, seafood, salads, fresh pastries. It's quite busy weekends; best to reserve. Lunch weekdays only. Dinner Saturday and Sunday. Closed Monday.

Best Western Casa Ojai Inn, 1302 East Ojai Avenue. (800) 255–8175; (805) 646–8175. Across from Soule Park Golf Course. Forty-five guest rooms, in-room coffeemakers, cable TV, nonsmoking rooms available; heated pool and spa; complimentary continental breakfast of muffins, pastry, orange juice, and coffee in lobby hospitality suite. Freshly baked cookies served each afternoon.

Hummingbird Inn, 1208 East Ojai Avenue. (800) 228–3744; (805) 646–4365. Thirty-one nonsmoking guest rooms in attractive, Spanish-style architectural and garden setting; kitchen units available. Cable TV; swimming pool and spa; complimentary bakery breakfast, fresh baked cookies served every afternoon; senior citizen rates. AAA approved. One block from Soule Park Golf Course.

The Lavender Inn, 210 East Matilija Street. (805) 646–6635. Historic inn overlooking gardens has eight rooms, five with private bath. Complimentary wine and cheese between 5:00 and 6:00 P.M.; complimentary continental breakfast served overlooking landscaped grounds.

Blue Iguana Inn. Highway 33, 117947 Ventura Avenue. (805) 646–5277. Southwestern-style villa inn has twelve rooms, including one- and two-bedroom suites with fully equipped kitchens, perfect for an extended getaway. Courtyard swimming pool and Jacuzzi. Complimentary continental breakfast served Saturday and Sunday. Pets on approval.

Oak View

The Oak Pit, 820 North Ventura Avenue, Highway 33. (805) 649–9903. This is your best pit stop on your way to or from Ojai for Texas barbecued pork ribs and hefty hand-carved beef and ham sandwiches, barbecued beans, and chili, to eat there or take out. Help yourself to the array of fiery sauces, including "Smokey" and "Killer." Open daily.

For More Information

Ojai Valley Chamber of Commerce & Visitors Bureau, 150 West Ojai Avenue (in the old church chapel), P.O. Box 1134, Ojai, CA 93023. (805) 646–8126 9:00 A.M. to 4:00 P.M.; www.the-ojai.org.

For further information about parks and camping, call the City of Ojai Recreation Department (805–646–1872) or the Ojai Ranger Station, 1190 East Ojai Avenue, Los Padres National Forest (805–646–4348).

American Riviera

Santa Barbara / 2 Nights

- ☐ Beaches
- ☐ Fine dining
- ☐ Mission
- ☐ Museums
- ☐ Wharf
- ☐ Children's zoo
- ☐ Botanical garden
- ☐ Sailing
- ☐ Biking
- ☐ Whale-watching
- ☐ Antiques shopping

Here's a three-day getaway to Santa Barbara, Southern California's own Riviera, a small, prosperous seaside resort community with a special panache, tucked between the Pacific Ocean and the rugged Santa Ynez Mountains. Sleek yachts dance in its snug, flag-festooned harbor, and tall, skinny palm trees frame miles of white-sand beaches dotted with picnic tables and barbecue pits.

With its festive air, profusion of flowers, slower pace, and old-world flavor, Santa Barbara is a cultural community of style, old money, and gracious living blended with the romance and tradition of its ancient Spanish heritage.

Santa Barbara's temperate weather began luring wintering Eastern socialites back in the late 1880s. Moreover, the city has always been a retreat for celebrities (the late Julia Child, Michael Douglas, Jonathan Winters, Jeff Bridges, Rob Lowe, and Oprah Winfrey among them), who unwind in the casual lifestyle and anonymity of a small town. And when the Reagan administration's hilltop Rancho del Cielo was nicknamed the "Western White House," Santa Barbara became a world-renowned, glamorous Southern California destination.

Few cities can boast such a robust, historic past and different cultures, dating from 1782, when Spanish soldiers accompanied by Franciscan Father Junípero Serra founded Santa Barbara, establishing a military presidio and a mission. Remnants of the ancient fort still remain, and Mission Santa Barbara is the city's greatest treasure and most famous landmark.

The city was an important Spanish stronghold in the New World for forty years, until California became a Mexican territory. During the Mexican-American War, Santa Barbara became part of the United States, in 1845, and the sleepy pueblo began to stir and grow.

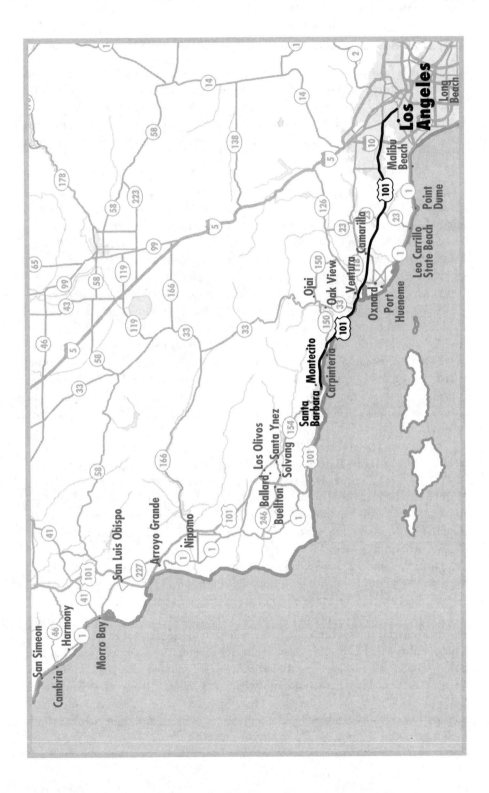

Day 1 / Morning

Drive north from Los Angeles 90 miles to Santa Barbara on Freeway 101, also known as Ventura Freeway 101. As the road traverses the rural San Fernando Valley, through fringes of small towns like Calabasas, the low, rolling hillsides are studded with clusters of large oak trees, native to the area. Approaching Camarillo, the dramatic downswing of Conejo Grade presents a panoramic sweep of the misty green valley spread out below.

After Ventura the freeway, enlivened with a flowered divider strip of colorful oleanders, borders the glistening ocean, and there is the graceful curve of white beaches and small coves. Oil tankers far out on the horizon are camouflaged to resemble small tropical islands, even with tall palm trees waving in the distance.

The blue ocean fades in and out of sight as you note the cutoff to Lake Casitas. Passing Carpinteria, you'll no longer see the 20-foot-high figure of Santa Claus saluting passing drivers, which had been a landmark figure in the town since 1950. It was removed. However, the charming enclave of gift and toy stores, bakery, the Candy Kitchen, and Beau Rivage Antiques remains; as does the Garden, a lovely outdoor luncheon spot for sandwiches, quiche, salads, and wines.

Arriving in Santa Barbara, note **Stearns Wharf,** at the foot of State Street, the town's main thoroughfare. Built in 1872, it is the West Coast's oldest operating wharf, really a 3-block-long extension of State Street over the Pacific Ocean. The engaging dolphin fountain marks the beginning of State Street, as well as the entrance to the busy pier, where one can fish, shop, dine or snack, browse, and drive or stroll.

Along the pier, **Stearns Wharf Vintner's** is fun for wine tasting on its sunny terrace, and **Madame Rosinka** can read your palm with true gypsy finesse.

In the **Sea Center** (805–682–4711), operated by the Museum of Natural History, exhibits feature live marine animals in saltwater tanks and awesome, life-size models of whales and dolphins. Regular children's activities and special events. (Open daily 10:00 A.M. to 5:00 P.M. Closed major holidays; admission. Public parking available on the wharf.)

From the pier the scene inland is an enchanting Dufy painting—cushy yachts preen in the sunlit harbor along the curved waterfront, and the little city spreads up into the mauve foothills and the protective embrace of the mountains.

The lively area around the wharf is a fine starting point to explore Santa Barbara's charming beachfront, where cycling and jogging paths weave through **Chase Palm Park** beneath soaring palm trees, where the antique carousel is ever popular. Bikes, roller skates, and **Pedalinas** (jaunty four-wheel cycles with surrey on top) are rentable across from the wharf at Cycles 4 Rent, 101 State Street (888–405–BIKE). In this same area, every Sunday from 10:00 A.M. until sunset hundreds of regional artists sell and exhibit their work in a bustling arts and crafts show held along a sunny, 1-mile oceanfront stretch.

Santa Barbara is noted for its beaches, and each has its own attractions: **East Beach/Cabrillo Pavilion** is the most popular, with bike paths, volleyball courts, and picnic areas, plus a great cafe. **West Beach,** on the other side of the wharf, offers the best sailboarding, swimming, and sunbathing as well as beginning sailboarding lessons and rental equipment. **Leadbetter Beach,** at the breakwater with a landscaped picnic area and the Sea Cove cafe right on the sand, is well known for some of the best surfing and sailboarding.

L U N C H : **East Beach Grill,** 1118 East Cabrillo Boulevard, Santa Barbara. (805) 965–8805. An upbeat spot right on the sand, with good sandwiches and grilled food, where you can watch the action on the bike paths and in the ocean.

Afternoon

The **Andree Clark Bird Refuge,** at 1400 East Cabrillo Boulevard (805–564–5433), is near the intersection of Cabrillo Boulevard and Highway 101. At this charming lagoon and gardens adjoining the Child's Estate Zoo, you can feed and watch the many varieties of freshwater fowl. A bikeway and footpath fringe the lagoon. Park on the north side of the lagoon. (Free.)

The adjacent **Santa Barbara Zoological Gardens,** 500 Niños Drive (805–962–6310), on a clifftop in a delightful garden setting off Cabrillo Boulevard at East Beach, was designed primarily for children. The zoo features more than 700 animals from around the world, including baby elephants, big cats, giraffes, monkeys, and sea lions as well as exotic birds. A restaurant, playground, and picnic area are here, too. Kids particularly love the petting park and the miniature train ride. (Open daily from 10:00 A.M. to 5:00 P.M. Closed Thanksgiving and Christmas Day. Admission fees, parking fee.)

Before leaving the beach area, pick up a handy destination guide at Santa Barbara Visitors Information Center, 1 Santa Barbara Street (805–965–3021), at the corner of Cabrillo Boulevard. These guides are also available at the courthouse, most restaurants, and shops.

Incidentally, from the beach at Stearns Wharf you can ride the electric Downtown Waterfront Shuttle bus east and west on Cabrillo Boulevard to Coast Village Road and back as well as up State Street to Sola Street, just past the Museum of Art. It runs round-trip every fifteen minutes from 10:00 A.M. to 5:00 P.M. and until 8:00 P.M. on Friday and Saturday (fare). Or you can hop on the open Santa Barbara Trolley at the wharf for a ninety-minute narrated sightseeing tour of the city (fare). City lots in the downtown area provide free parking for the first seventy-five minutes.

State Street, Santa Barbara's foremost promenade, is truly one of the most attractive main streets anywhere and a favorite shopping and browsing stroll for visitors and residents alike. State begins at the ocean and leads you through the Old Town historic section and the city's important dining and shopping hub of specialty shops, galleries, and upscale department stores. You'll soon notice that traffic moves at a slower pace in sedate Santa Barbara. Along this appealing boulevard, large trees in huge planters share sidewalk space with tall eucalyptus and palm trees, decorative iron grillwork, arched passageways, and lots of flowers.

It is a planned harmony and beauty. The people of Santa Barbara are determined to preserve their city's Spanish inheritance in timeless, graceful architecture of red-tiled roofs, arched facades, benches, and courtyards. The city acquired this distinctive look following a severe earthquake in 1925 that destroyed much of the downtown section. Everything was rebuilt in a unified motif still adhered to. Even sidewalk telephone booths must conform to the red-tiled-roof theme. There is a noticeable absence of glitz. No high-rise buildings intrude into Santa Barbara's clear blue skies, and billboards have long been banned.

Along State Street you'll want to browse the charming **Paseo Nuevo,** bordered by Chapala Street, an engaging, two-level, Spanish-style mall of restaurants, upscale department stores, cafes, fountains, courtyards, galleries, and numerous boutiques. Farther along in the 1100 block, the 16-foot-tall sidewalk clock, with Westminster chimes, and inviting shade trees enhance the entrance to **La Arcada Court,** with its specialty shops, cafes, galleries, fountains, plants, and Acapulco Mexican Restaurant, a convenient upbeat place to snack and people-watch at the outdoor tables.

Continuing up State Street, you'll arrive at the **Santa Barbara Museum of Art,** 1130 State Street (805–963–4364), whose colorful banners welcome you to one of America's foremost small museums, boasting a prestigious permanent collection of art and ancient sculpture, plus important changing exhibitions. The Museum Bookstore is a good bet for art books and distinctive jewelry made by local artisans. The new **Peck Wing,** showcasing nineteenth- and twentieth-century European art, features a gift shop, cafe, and children's gallery. (Open Tuesday through Sunday from 11:00 A.M. to 5:00 P.M. Docent gallery tours Tuesday through Sunday at 1:00 P.M. Admission. Free admission Thursday and the first Sunday of the month.)

DINNER: **Wine Cask Restaurant,** 813 Anacapa Street, Santa Barbara. (805) 966–9463. Tucked in downtown's charming and historic El Paseo in a majestic dining room with a hand-painted beamed ceiling and a baronial fireplace. Imaginative bistro-style cuisine offers delightful appetizers, such as grilled fresh Hudson Valley *foie gras* with apple risotto. Dinner entrees include pan-seared Alaskan halibut and grilled filet mignon. Extensive wine list features selections from the restaurant's adjacent wine store. Sunday brunch.

LODGING: **Four Seasons Resort Santa Barbara,** 1260 Channel Drive, Santa Barbara. (800) 332–3442; (805) 969–2261. The city's most luxurious hotel, with 210 rooms, suites, and cottages, on twenty-one rambling garden acres. Three lighted tennis courts, swimming pool and Jacuzzi. Guest-room amenities include TV, refrigerated minibar, clock radio, terry robes, and hair dryer. Complimentary putting green, bikes, croquet, and shuffleboard. Twenty-four-hour room and concierge service, two restaurants, elegant Sunday champagne buffet brunch. Golf arrangements with local courses. Complimentary overnight shoeshine.

Day 2 / Morning

BREAKFAST: Esau's, 403 State Street, Santa Barbara. (805) 965–4416. Hungry patrons line up out the door of this small, genial cafe for great hotcakes, omelettes, and hash browns made with *real* potatoes. Fine service, too.

All visitors want to see the city's most famous landmark, **Mission Santa Barbara,** Laguna and Los Olivos Streets (805–682–4713). Take State Street to Mission Street or to Los Olivos Street. Turn right toward the mountains and continue to the mission, situated in the scenic rural foothills overlooking the city; both streets run into it. Known as the "Queen of the Missions" for its graceful symmetry and tall twin bell towers, it is the tenth of twenty-one California missions, founded in 1786 by the Spanish Franciscan Fathers and still a Catholic parish church. The annual Italian Street Festival is held on its broad terrace. A self-guided tour encompasses the gardens, museum, courtyards, chapel, and cemetery. The small gift shop features pretty fans, books, T-shirts, souvenirs, and religious objects. (Open daily from 9:00 A.M. to 5:00 P.M. Closed holidays. Admission; children younger than twelve get in free.)

Since it's just 2 blocks north of the mission, you're within walking distance of the **Museum of Natural History, Planetarium, and Observatory,** 2559 Puesta del Sol Road (take Mission Canyon Road and follow the signs; 805–682–4711). The museum is housed in a rambling ranch-style building around a courtyard. The highlight is the knockout 72-foot skeleton of a giant blue whale, outside to the right of the entrance. Exhibit halls include the West's largest collection of Chumash Indian artifacts. Check out the full-scale model of a 33-foot giant squid, suspended from the ceiling in the Marine Hall. The Museum Store offers pottery, T-shirts, Native American and Southwest jewelry, and souvenir items. (Open daily from 10:00 A.M. to 5:00 P.M. Closed holidays. Admission; free admission the last Sunday of each month.)

In the same quiet area, about 1.5 miles north of the mission, is the spectacular **Botanic Garden,** 1212 Mission Canyon Road (805–682–4726). Take Mission Canyon Road to Foothill Road, go right 1 block, then left on Mission Canyon Road to the garden. You'll find some sixty-five acres of beautiful California wildflowers and native flora, a redwood forest, and miles of nature trails. The gift shop features books, souvenirs, and native plants. Docent-guided tours are offered daily. (Open daily 9:00 A.M. to 5:00 P.M. Fee; children younger than five get in free.) Closed some holidays.

Drive back to the city center for lunch.

LUNCH: Chase Grill Downtown, 1012 State Street, Santa Barbara. (805) 965–4351. Here for more than twenty years, Chase's is continually voted as having the best Caesar salad in town and keeps customers happy with good pasta and other Italian specialties.

Afternoon

While you're downtown, head over to another famous landmark, the **Santa Barbara County Courthouse,** in the 1100 block of Anacapa Street (805–962–6464). Considered one of the most striking public buildings in the United States, the handsome, impressive Spanish-Moorish building, completed in 1929, boasts an 80-foot clock tower and grand-scale archways and turrets, all surrounded by spacious lawns, palm trees, and lush tropical plants. The attractive interior is rich in its hand-painted ceilings, wrought-iron chandeliers, murals, and historical exhibits. From the observation deck the panoramic city view sweeps from the lavender Santa Ynez Mountains over the carpet of red-tiled roofs to the sparkling Pacific Ocean and occasionally to the Channel Islands floating in the mist 20 miles offshore. Free guided tours daily at 2:00 P.M., except Sunday. (Open Monday through Friday from 8:00 A.M. to 4:45 P.M., weekends and holidays from 10:00 A.M. to 4:45 P.M. Free. Tour information: 805–962–6464.)

El Paseo, "The Street" in Spanish, in the 800 block of State Street between State and Anacapa, remains one of the city's loveliest and oldest Spanish-style shopping and dining complexes. Built in the 1920s around the 1827 adobe home of the historic De la Guerra family, it houses art galleries, specialty shops, fine restaurants, and an outdoor cafe in the colorful central courtyard.

For those interested in history, the compact downtown area is rich in landmarks of Santa Barbara's colorful past. Among historical highlights is **El Presidio de Santa Barbara State Historical Park,** 122 East Cañon Perdido Street (805–965–0093). This is where the city began in 1782 and includes buildings that were part of the Presidio Real, the original fortress. In addition to a slide show, there are a scale model of the old fort and a gift shop. (Open daily 10:30 A.M. to 4:30 P.M. Free.)

Just south of the Presidio, the **Santa Barbara Historical Society Museum,** 136 East De La Guerra Street and East Cañon Perdido (805–966–1601), is a complex of colonial Spanish houses built in the 1800s. The museum features many exhibits, as well as memorabilia of the city's four cultural eras: Native American, Spanish, Mexican, and American. (Open Tuesday through Saturday from 10:00 A.M. to 5:00 P.M. and Sunday from noon to 5:00 P.M. Guided tours. Free.)

Antiques buffs will admire the string of little shops on **Brinkerhoff Avenue** at Cota, between Chapala and De La Vina. This nostalgic, charming, tree-shaded, 1-block-long street, named after Santa Barbara's first physician, Samuel Brinkerhoff, is a designated Special Historic District. The original Victorian-style clapboard houses line the street in an array of bright sherbet colors, and white picket fences border old-fashioned gardens. The homes are now antiques and specialty shops, plus some galleries, to browse for memorabilia, old treasures, and gifts. Most are open Tuesday through Sunday from 11:00 A.M. to 5:00 P.M.

DINNER: The Palace Grill, 8 East Cota Street. Santa Barbara. (805) 963–5000. A lively longtime local favorite for hot, Louisiana-style Cajun, Creole, and Caribbean cuisine. Look for jambalaya, fresh fish, *andouille* sausage, and Key lime pie for dessert. Closed Monday.

LODGING: Four Seasons Resort Santa Barbara.

Day 3 / Morning

BREAKFAST: In your hotel or at **Tutti's,** 1209 Coast Village Road, Montecito. (805) 969–5809. This Italian deli-restaurant is a bright, airy local breakfast hangout, great for huge fresh muffins, pancakes, waffles, and such. Quite busy.

You're in the heart of lively **Coast Village Road,** an intimate, tree-shaded strip of posh cafes, galleries, wine shops, designer boutiques, and long-legged blonds driving gleaming Jaguars and Ferraris. After browsing the shops, take the time to drive around the residential section of affluent **Montecito,** where the wealthy Easterners and Midwesterners drawn to Santa Barbara during the 1890s established their luxurious estates. The millionaire migration included Rockefeller, Carnegie, Du Pont, McCormick, Cudahy, and other barons of industry, who built palatial vacation mansions in Montecito's rolling woodlands. For the scenic hillside drive, take Olive Mill Road at the end of Coast Village Road to Alameda Padre Serra. Along "APS" the famed Riviera view is a photogenic panorama over the city that reaches to the palm trees along the beachfront. Then drive back to the ocean for lunch.

LUNCH: Pascuccis. 729 State Street, Santa Barbara. (805) 963–8123. For that mouthwatering Tuscany flavor, try any variety of pizza, pasta, salads, antipasti, and sandwiches. Casual dining at its finest.

Afternoon

At oceanside on West Cabrillo Boulevard, the **yacht harbor and breakwater,** home to around 1,200 pleasure and working craft, grab your attention with strikingly colored flags flapping high overhead. The broad, paved walkway atop the breakwater offers a scenic 0.5-mile walking tour around the harbor, the Yacht Club, marine stores, and restaurants, along with fine views of surfers and boats. This is the departure point for shoreline tour boats and sportfishing excursions, as well as a source of boats for rent and charter.

Retrace your way south to Los Angeles.

There's More

Farmers' market, each Tuesday and Saturday, is a fun place to shop. Local growers sell fresh fruits, vegetables, nuts, eggs, flowers, and plants at reasonable prices, with puppet shows and other entertainment enlivening the scene. The Tuesday market takes place in Santa Barbara's Old Town in the 500 and 600 blocks of State Street from 4:00 to 7:30 P.M., later in summer. The Saturday market—larger and more crowded—is held downtown at the corner of Santa Barbara and Cota Streets from 8:30 A.M. to 12:30 P.M. In Montecito it's at the 1100 and 1200 blocks of Coast Village Road on Friday from 8:00 A.M. to noon. For information call (805) 962–5354.

Boating, sailing, and fishing opportunities are at the breakwater. The Santa Barbara Sailing Center (800–350–9090) offers sailing classes, boat rentals, coastal sunset dinner cruises, whale-watching parties, and more.

Golf. You can hit the sticks at two 18-hole municipal courses open for daily play (reserve in advance):

Santa Barbara Golf Club, 3500 McCaw Avenue at Las Positas Road. (805) 687–7087. Bordering the Earl Warren Showgrounds.

Sandpiper Golf Course, 7925 Hollister Avenue, Goleta. (805) 968–1541.

Hang gliding and paragliding. Keep a lookout for the daring hang gliders near the bluffs at Arroyo Burro Beach. Fly Above All, 1221 State Street (805–965–3733), gives lessons.

Whale-watching. Track the big grays off the coast during their southward migration to Baja, mid-November through March, and again when they head back north, during February, March, and April. Best viewing spots are along the bluffs at Shoreline Park. Several commercial charters offer cruises, among them Sea Landing Aquatic Center, Santa Barbara (888–77–WHALE; 805–963–3564).

Polo. Santa Barbara Polo & Racquet Club, 3375 Foothill Road, Carpinteria. (805) 684–8668. Polo games/matches every Sunday, April through October, at 1:00 P.M. and 3:00 P.M. Admission. Phone for information and schedule. Open to the public.

Lotusland, 695 Ashley Road, Santa Barbara. Reservations (taken between 9:00 A.M. and noon): (805) 969–9990. Tucked in the rolling hills of Montecito, the legendary thirty-seven-acre garden estate of opera singer Ganna Waleska features thirteen distinct gardens, which display botanical environments from all parts of the world, including dramatic and exotic trees and the famed lotus-and-water-lilies pool. Docent-led tours from mid-February to mid-November are by advance reservation only. Admission.

Special Events

First week in January. Hang Gliding and Para Gliding Festival. Daring local pilots fly in precision contests and demonstrations off the ocean bluffs.

Late January to early February. Santa Barbara International Film Festival. Premieres and screenings of international and U.S. films; citywide festivities. (805) 963–0032.

February. Santa Barbara Opera, 123 West Padre Street. (805) 898–3890.

March. Whale Festival. (805) 897–3187. From the bluffs along Shoreline Park, you can watch the big gray whales on their northern migration.

End of March, early April. Annual Santa Barbara International Orchid Show, at Earl Warren Showgrounds. One of the world's most prestigious horticultural events.

Mid-April. South Coast Earth Day Festival. (805) 963–0583.

Sea Festival and Tall Ships Visit, Maritime Museum. (805) 962–8404.

Late April. Presidio Days. Three-day celebration of Santa Barbara's birthday and multiethnic heritage, held at the historic Presidio. (805) 965–0093.

May. Santa Barbara Renaissance Faire. (805) 962–6222.

End of May. I. Madonnari, three-day Italian street painting festival, attracts thousands of visitors and some 400 local artists, who get on their knees to create vibrant chalk paintings on the pavement of the Old Mission courtyard terrace. Entertainment; Italian marketplace; Italian cuisine. (805) 964–4711.

June. Santa Barbara Antiques and Fine Arts Show, Santa Barbara County College. (805) 730–4401.

End of June. Santa Barbara Writer's Conference, Westport campus. Weeklong creative-writing workshop; lectures by best-selling authors. Summer Solstice Celebration Parade on State Street with costumes, dancers, and music. (805) 684–2250.

July 4. Independence Day Celebration. Parade and Classic Car Show, on State Street, celebration throughout the city. Outstanding fireworks at the harbor.

July. Santa Barbara National Horse Show, Earl Warrens Fairgrounds. (805) 687–8711.

California Wine Festival, Chase Palm Park. (800) 850–4370.

Mid-July. Santa Barbara County Fair, Santa Maria Park. Carnival, food, crafts, music.

Early August. Old Spanish Days (Fiesta). Santa Barbara's biggest event, begun in 1926. A five-day celebration of Santa Barbara's Spanish heritage, featuring a grand parade with gaily decorated horse-drawn carriages; children's parade; Spanish marketplaces; and carnival, rodeo, and Spanish dancers. (805) 962–8101.

August. Santa Barbara City Triathalon, Oak Park. (805) 966–6950.

September. Santa Barbara Book and Author Festival. (805) 962–9500.

Zoo-B-Que Festivities at Santa Barbara Zoo. (805) 962–6310.

October. Santa Barbara Festival of Art and Jazz, Santa Barbara Courthouse. (805) 695–8686.

October 31. Halloween Festival, De La Guerra Plaza. (805) 962–2098.

November. Inspired by Nature Holiday Marketplace, The Botanic Garden. (805) 682–4726.

Santa Barbara Native Arts Festival. (805) 403–0744.

Early December. Downtown Holiday Parade and Parade of Lights. Extravagantly decorated boats and fireworks near Stearns Wharf.

Other Recommended Restaurants and Lodgings

Santa Barbara

Brophy's, 119 Harbor Avenue. (805) 966–4418. Near the water, this place bustles with friendly locals and other happy diners. The menu of fresh seafood selections changes daily. Popular grilled halibut is served with roasted garlic, basil, and tomato vinaigrette. Other favorites include scampi, sea bass, ahi, and salmon. Good-looking salads are prepared with or without seafood.

Café Buenos Aires, 1316 State Street. (805) 963–0242. Conveniently located in the heart of downtown, with romantic decor. Treat yourself to exciting South American food with fine Argentinian specialties. Dine indoors or in the lovely courtyard.

The Harbor Restaurant, 210 Stearns Wharf. (805) 963–3311. At the end of the wharf, it's just right for grilled fish, salads, steaks, and cocktails while you enjoy some of the best views of Santa Barbara. Lunch and dinner daily; Sunday champagne brunch.

Bacara Resort & Spa, 8301 Hollister Avenue. (877) 422–4245; (805) 968–0100; www.bacararesort.com. About a twenty-minute drive north of the city, this posh hacienda with luxe spa spread across seventy-eight acres caters to guests. Three hundred sixty luxurious guest rooms and suites feature fireplace, balcony or patio, minibar, personal safe, robes and slippers; three restaurants; four tennis courts, three swimming pools, plus adjacent golf course; boutique shops; concierge service. Spa packages. Sunday buffet brunch.

Fess Parker's Doubletree Resort, 633 East Cabrillo Boulevard. (800) 879–2929. On the boulevard across from the beach, newly remodeled in 2006, and sprawled over twenty-four acres, this resort has 360 rooms and suites with private patio and mini-bar, clock radio, hair dryer, iron/ironing board, robes upon request, TV, and VCR. Concierge service, swimming pool, spa, Jacuzzi, gym, three lighted tennis courts, putting green, two restaurants, and lounge.

Montecito Inn, 1295 Coast Village Road. (800) 843–2017. Charming small hotel with European ambience; built by Charlie Chaplin and friends in the 1920s. Located 2 blocks from the beach; sixty-one well-furnished guest rooms and suites with refrigerator, VCR, and nice bathrooms; swimming pool, Jacuzzi, sauna, exercise room; lounge, complimentary bikes, and trolley passes. Additionally available are seven one-bedroom luxury suites (four with fireplaces) and Italian marble bathrooms that feature Jacuzzi tubs.

For More Information

Santa Barbara Conference and Visitors Bureau, 12 East Carrillo Street, Santa Barbara, CA 93101. (800) 927–4688; www.santabarbara.com. Ask for destination guide.

Hot Spot, 36 State Street, in the visitor bureau. (800) 793–7666; (805) 564–1637. For free reservations and information about lodgings, attractions, and events.

Windmills and Wineries

Solvang and the Santa Ynez Valley Wine Country / 1 Night

This two-day itinerary takes you north to "Little Denmark," where windmills spin lazily in blue skies in a fairy-tale village of curving streets lined with shops and cafes. You'll visit and tour wineries in acres of vineyards flourishing in rural Santa Ynez Valley, which has become one of California's richest grape-growing and wine-making regions, and you'll visit small, quiet pioneer villages that haven't quite marked the turn of the nineteenth century.

- ☐ Historic villages
- ☐ Shopping
- ☐ Mission
- ☐ Wineries
- ☐ Lake boating and fishing
- ☐ Resort
- ☐ Golf
- ☐ Horseback riding
- ☐ Ethnic dining
- ☐ Open-air theater

Day 1 / Morning

Drive north from Los Angeles on Ventura Freeway 101 about 132 miles to **Solvang,** the delectable smorgasbord of Denmark tucked in the peaceful Santa Ynez Valley of rich farmlands and vineyards, located less than an hour past Santa Barbara.

Follow 101 through dramatic Gaviota Pass, with its soaring cliffs; go through the tunnel; and continue past the turnoff for splendid Nojoqui Falls Park, named for the 164-foot waterfall and including a playground and picnic area. Take the Buellton/Solvang exit, turn right onto Highway 246, and continue for about 5 miles to Solvang.

LUNCH: Greenhouse Cafe at Petersen Village, 457 Atterdag Road, Solvang. (805) 688–8408. In Petersen Village Square, the heart of the village, with delightful garden patio. Select from the varied menu of Danish and American dishes, or savor the house specialties: *aebleskiver*—a ball-shaped pancake—hefty sandwiches, and those thin Danish pancakes. Open daily; hours vary. Dinner Saturday only. Delightful dining patio.

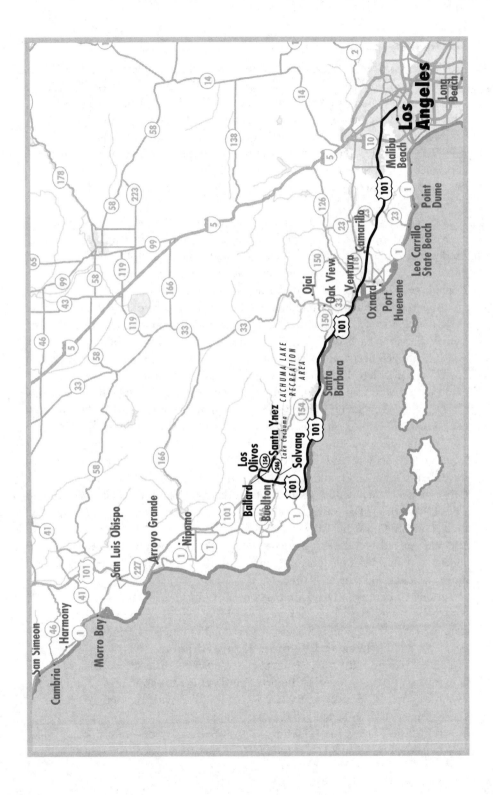

Afternoon

After lunch explore Solvang's sunny streets with their brightly colored buildings and brick and cobblestone sidewalks. Danish half-timbered farm-style buildings have tall, steeply pitched roofs of simulated thatch or heavy shake shingles adorned with weather vanes, dormer windows, steeples, and hand-carved storks. Gas street-lamps glow in the evening, and buildings are outlined with tiny lights.

"The Danish Capital of America" has a storybook quality, as you stroll past fairy-tale murals on building facades and tall, country-style windmills that creak in the soft breezes. Some windmills house gift shops or restaurants, and all provide ideal photo opportunities.

Solvang's inviting streets are lined with more than 200 tempting shops, whose open Dutch doors reveal arrays of fine imports, including crystal, pewter, porcelain, handcrafted candles, antiques, and clocks. You'll find dolls, trolls, leather fashions, music boxes, old-world bakeries, and famous designer names such as Royal Copenhagen, Georg Jensen, Hummel, and Rosenthal.

Appealing restaurants and bubbling sidewalk cafes with colorful umbrellas offer great dining variety. You'll never have a better opportunity to enjoy authentic Danish specialties such as *gravlax,* smorgasbord, *frikadiller* (Danish meatballs), and *bof med log* (chopped beef with onions), and don't overlook *smorrebrod,* the hefty Danish open-face sandwich that can feed a small battalion. Additionally, change-of-pace menus offer American, Italian, Mexican, continental, and even Chinese cuisine. Many Solvang restaurants close between lunch and dinner (usually 3:00 to 5:00 P.M.), European fashion; most have menus posted outside.

Solvang, meaning "Sunny Field," was founded in 1911 by a group of Midwest Danish educators who wanted to establish a Danish colony and folk school to preserve their culture and traditions in an area where settlers could farm the rich soil. Other pioneers included carpenters and workers who built the first buildings and school. The strong Danish heritage is evident in local customs and holidays. The lively **Danish Days,** held the third full weekend in September, is when the city celebrates its old-world ties. Residents dress in Danish costume and prepare, cook, and serve traditional *aebleskiver* and sausage on the streets. There is entertainment, music, dancing, and parades.

Along Copenhagen Drive, on the corner of Alisal Road, **Rasmussen's** (1697), with wide arches and a tall roof steeple—the oldest, most complete department store in town—is known for Swedish crystal, Danish porcelain, handmade sweaters, gift items, and kitchenware. **Frogmore House Antiques** (1683) features antiques and collectibles from the sublime to the ridiculous. The **Blue Windmill,** at Hamlet Square, has a fine assortment of T-shirts. You don't get to shop in a windmill every day, so explore the large one on Alisal Road; it's filled with a variety of gift items, many suspended from its tall ceiling.

On Mission Drive, the **Jul Hus** (1580) is Solvang's most unusual store, selling only Christmas merchandise year-round. This festive store where you hear Christmas music is filled with a large assortment of Christmas ornaments and decorations, toys, nutcrackers, music boxes, and the Dickens Ceramic Houses surrounding a fully trimmed Christmas tree with twinkling lights.

Stop by any of the city's four **bakeries,** where they use old-country, centuries-old recipes for favorite pastries. Don't overlook the popular, large, pretzel-shaped *Kringler,* as big as a suitcase, filled with almond paste and raisins, topped with sliced almonds and drifts of sugar. Small, friendly **Solvang Park,** at the corner of Mission Drive and 1st Street, is where Solvangers picnic and relax on the grass alongside the bust of Hans Christian Andersen, Denmark's prince of fairy tales, in his famous top hat. You'll also find a small replica of the *Little Mermaid,* the famous bronze sculpture in Copenhagen's harbor, perched atop a rock and fountain at the corner of Mission Drive and Alisal Road.

Cross the street to visit the **Hans Christian Andersen Museum,** upstairs in the Book Loft building, 1680 Mission Drive (805–688–2052), which honors the noted Danish fairy tale writer, Denmark's favorite son and most famous figure. The small museum upstairs in the bookstore's loft is filled with copies of Andersen's beautifully illustrated books, and many photos, letters, and memorabilia, including photographs of the beautiful singer Jenny Lind, the "Swedish Nightingale" with whom Andersen was said to have been hopelessly in love. This tall, stringy, long-nosed man wrote 156 fairy tales and was greatly honored during his lifetime. The museum is open from 9:00 A.M. to 5:00 P.M. and is always accessible through the **Book Loft/Kaffe Hus.** Browse the bookstore's wide selection of current, used, and collector's classics while you sip a cup of gourmet coffee at the Kaffe Hus.

Drive or walk to the **Old Mission Santa Inés,** 1760 Mission Drive (805–688–4815), established in 1804, the nineteenth of the twenty-one California missions and one of the best preserved and restored—it still celebrates daily Mass. The graceful old parish church, with its beautiful gardens around a large fountain, evokes the valley's Spanish missionary beginnings. Explore on your own through the Chapel of the Madonnas, which has the original worn tile floors, a 29-foot-high beamed ceiling, and hand-painted wall murals. The museum displays extensive artifacts of the Chumash Indian mission era; the gift shop shows religious artifacts and pottery. Frequently called the "Mission of the Passes," Santa Inés is the focus of many yearly events in the Santa Ynez Valley. (Open in the summer daily from 9:00 A.M. to 5:00 P.M. and in the winter Monday through Friday from 9:00 A.M. to 5:00 P.M. and Saturday and Sunday from 9:00 A.M. to 5:00 P.M.; admission.) Gift store.

An easy, fun way to get around town is to ride the popular **Surrey Bike**—a four-wheel cycle with a red surrey on top, and all passengers pedaling together like the Radio City Rockettes down the curving streets. Other offbeat sightseeing includes a twenty-minute narrated tour around town aboard Solvang's *Honen,* replica of an authentic Danish streetcar of the 1900s that is pulled by two massive, blond Belgian draft horses. Board at the visitor center on Copenhagen Drive and

Solvang's windmills are delightful old-world sights.

2nd Street, every half hour daily during the summer season and weekends during the winter (fee). Romantics can see the city in an open, horse-drawn white carriage on weekends and holidays; board it off Copenhagen and 1st Street.

DINNER: Bit O' Denmark, 473 Alisal Road, Solvang. (805) 688–5426. Start your own tradition at the oldest restaurant in town. This lovely, warm, and pleasant place, offering fine food and service, features a gourmet Danish smorgasbord feast with an extensive variety of hot and cold delectables, plus American entrees. Full bar, wine and espresso bar.

LODGING: Petersen Village Inn, 1576 Mission Drive, Solvang. (800) 321–8985; (805) 688–3121. AAA four-diamond rating. Discover old–world flavor in each of the thirty-nine spacious, individually decorated rooms (and one tower suite with Jacuzzi and fireplace), featuring canopied beds, antique and period furniture, TV, and turndown service. One restaurant. Complimentary European buffet breakfast and dinner for two served in dining room. Midweek packages, corporate and group rates. Complimentary wine-tasting or theater tickets.

Day 2 / Morning

BREAKFAST: At the inn. Beautifully presented, generous complimentary buffet in the dining room includes juice, coffee, Danish pastry, rolls, ham, and cheese.

After breakfast select foods for a picnic lunch at the wineries by stopping at the **El Rancho Market,** 2886 Mission Drive at Refugio Road (805–688–4300). It's just out of the village, but it's on your way to Santa Ynez and the wineries. There's a fine selection of hot and cold deli items, sandwiches, and picnic baskets. Open daily.

There's a mystique and romance about wine, often associated with the pleasurable and better things in life. The experience is enriched by driving along the peaceful backcountry roads of **Santa Ynez Valley,** with its natural beauty of pastures, orchards, and acres of lush vineyards. As you visit the unpretentious wineries and unchanged, hundred-year-old villages, you are far removed from the daily bustle.

Pick up a "Santa Barbara County Wineries" map from your hotel or the Solvang Visitors Bureau (1511 Mission Drive) and follow the wine route. This one-night itinerary doesn't visit all the wineries, as you won't have sufficient time unless you plan to stay over another night, but you might mark the rest for a return visit to Solvang.

From Solvang take Highway 246 to the sleepy little town of **Santa Ynez,** off Highway 246, founded in 1882. There's not much traffic in its 2-block-long business center. Drop by the **Santa Ynez Valley Historical Society Museum,** on Sagunto Street and Farady (805–688–7889), where eight rooms ramble around a shady courtyard and fountain. Immerse yourself in early California history and memorabilia. The Indian Room exhibits a diorama of Chumash Indian life; the Pioneer Room displays century-old furnishings; and the West Room shows saddles, guns, and other items. (Open Wednesday through Sunday from noon to 4:00 P.M.)

Parks-Janeway Carriage House, part of the museum, displays an outstanding collection of more than thirty-five gleaming carriages and buggies that seem right out of western movies, including the "Wells Fargo" and the "United States Mail"; silver-mounted saddles and equestrian gear are here, too, as is a gift shop. (Open Wednesday through Sunday from noon to 4:00 P.M.)

From Santa Ynez take Edison Road north, turning left at Baseline Avenue to **Ballard,** the valley's oldest and first town, founded in 1880. Turn right on Cottonwood Street to see its landmark, two-room little red schoolhouse, set back on a broad lawn shaded by two ancient trees. The school has been in continuous use since its dedication in 1883.

From Ballard continue a few miles on 154 through a soft countryside of apple orchards, farmhouses, and ranches to **Los Olivos,** which has a flagpole in the center of the main street, inviting cafes, and wine shops. Once a major Butterfield stagecoach stop, the town, with its many resident artists, has evolved into a lively fine-arts center for the Santa Ynez Valley. Visit historic **Mattie's Tavern** on Highway 154, built in 1896 as an overnight inn and still a warm, intimate restaurant for fine dining.

After driving around Los Olivos, go back through Ballard, turning right on Edison Road to Highway 246 to the **Gainey Vineyard**, 3950 East Highway 246 (3 miles east of Solvang), Santa Ynez (805–688–0558). The family-owned winery, begun in 1984, sits atop the family's 1,800-acre ranch. Gainey is one of the most visitor-oriented and popular facilities and features the largest tasting room in the area and good-size picnic gardens. The beautiful 12,000-square-foot winery and visitor center are surrounded by sixty-five acres of premium varietal grapes, producing Chardonnay, Sauvignon Blanc, Pinot Noir, Merlot, Johannisberg, and Cabernet Franc. Daily tours. Tastings all day. Open daily from 10:00 A.M. to 5:00 P.M. A logo glass is your souvenir. The gift shop sells T-shirts and gift packs.

Afternoon

LUNCH: Picnic at the Gainey Vineyard.

To visit more wineries, go east on Highway 246 to 154; turn left, staying on Highway 154 to 101; then turn right on Zaca Station Road and left up the hill to **Firestone Vineyard**, 5080 Zaca Station Road, Los Olivos (805–688–3940), the largest winery in the valley. The impressive building sits atop 260 acres of estate vineyards, enhanced by an attractive garden patio, a fountain, and picnic tables. The daily twenty-minute guided tours from 11:15 A.M. to 1:15 P.M. begin in the vineyard, go to the fermentation room, and then end in the large tasting room. Sampling of Firestone's most popular varietals: handcrafted Chardonnay, Merlot, and other premium varietals available only at the winery. The gift shop features logo T-shirts, tote bags, and wine accessories.

After sampling the wines, turn left on Zaca Station Road; continue on it until the name changes to Foxen Canyon, about 3 miles, to **Fess Parker Winery & Vineyard**, 6200 Foxen Canyon Road, Los Olivos (800–841–1104; 805–688–1545). The family-owned and -operated winery's award-winning wines include Chardonnay, white Riesling, Syrah, Pinot Noir, and Viognier. Tours are from 11:00 A.M. to 5:00 P.M. daily, in the barrel room, with a fee and tours for tasting three or four wines; you keep the logo glass. If celebrity owner Fess Parker ("Davy Crockett" of TV fame) is around, he'll autograph a bottle of wine for you. Gift shop; picnic area.

Foley Estates and LinCourt Vineyard, 2.5 miles north of Highway 246, at 1711 Alamo Pintado Road, Solvang (805–688–8554), is framed by mountains and beautiful old trees and surrounded by twenty-three acres of estate vineyards. The boutique winery was established by a family of doctors who refurbished an old dairy barn into a winery and had their first harvest in 1978. Foley's tasting room is in a small, rustic farmhouse with a homey front porch and a picnic area. Open daily from 10:00 A.M. to 5:00 P.M. for visitors to sample its award-winning Chardonnay, Sauvignon Blanc, Cabernet Sauvignon, Pinot Noir, and Merlot.

To return to Los Angeles, get back on Highway 246 through Buellton/Solvang and pick up Highway 101 south.

There's More

Bethania Lutheran Church, 603 Atterdag Road, Solvang. Built in 1928, the Danish-style, rural church reflects tradition with its handcrafted oak pulpit and altar and replica of a fully rigged Danish sailing ship suspended symbolically from the ceiling. Regular Sunday worship; Danish services once a month.

Elverhoj Museum of History and Art, 1624 Elverhoy Way, Solvang. (805) 686–1211. On a quiet residential street 2 blocks from the shops, this Danish-style farmhouse cultural museum is very browsable. Gallery and period rooms depict Solvang's pioneer past and how the city evolved, with early photos, antique furnishings, and artifacts. Open Wednesday through Sunday from 1:00 to 4:00 P.M.

Hans Christian Andersen Park, on Atterdag Road, 3 blocks north of Mission Drive, Solvang. (805) 688–PLAY. The rustic creekside setting is relaxing for fun, picnics, and barbecues. Children's playground and tennis courts are here, too.

Festival Theatre, 2nd and Oak Streets, Solvang. (800) 727–2123; (805) 922–8313. The Pacific Conservatory of the Performing Arts (PCPA) Theaterfest presents five productions in repertory under the stars, June through mid-October, in a 780-seat, open-air theater-in-the-round. Inquire about hotel-theater-dinner packages (800–468–6765).

Solvang Motorcycle Museum. (805) 686–9522. Features classic European motorcycles, displaying about twenty-five bikes at a time in a changing monthly display. Open Saturday and Sunday from 11:00 A.M. to 5:00 P.M. or by appointment. Admission.

Ostrich Land, 610 East Highway 246, Buellton. (805) 686–9696. Meet some of the largest birds in the world—8 to 9 feet tall—and learn about some of their characteristics. Open daily from 10:00 A.M. to 5:00 P.M.

Glider rides. Windhaven Glider Rides, Santa Ynez Airport. (805) 688–2517. Soar over the valley and above the scenic Santa Ynez mountains with FAA-certified pilots. Open Wednesday through Sunday.

Miniature horse ranches. Quicksilver Miniature Horse Farm, 1589 Alamo Pintado Road, Solvang, welcomes visitors daily from 10:00 A.M. to 3:00 P.M. (805) 686–4992.

Chumash Casino Resort. Three miles east of Solvang on Highway 246 in Santa

Ynez. (800) 728–9997; (805) 686–0855. Las Vegas–style video gaming, high-stakes bingo, smoke-free card room; restaurant; valet parking. Open twenty-four hours daily.

Cachuma Lake Recreation Area, 12 miles east of Solvang, off scenic Highway 154. If you're an angler, like to camp or go boating and hiking, and enjoy other year-round outdoor recreation, this 8-mile-long lake and environs are for you. Snack bar, general store, picnic areas. Admission per car. Two-hour "Eagle Cruises" from November through February; "Wildlife Cruises" conducted from March through October. Reservations: (805) 686–5050. General information: (805) 686–5054.

Golf. River Course at the Alisal, 150 Alisal Road, Solvang. (805) 688–6042. On the banks of the Santa Ynez River; open to the public as well as guests of the Alisal Guest Ranch and Resort next door. Four lakes enhance the naturally scenic, 18-hole championship course, which also features driving range, practice greens, and well-stocked pro shop. The River Grill Restaurant, in the rugged clubhouse setting, with expansive patio overlooking the rolling greens, is the perfect spot for relaxing after a round of golf or for breakfast, lunch, dinner, and Sunday brunch. Not all meals are served daily; call for details.

Special Events

January. Blues Festival, Solvang, Royal Scandinavian Inn. (805) 688–8000.

February. Solvang Custom Knife Show, Solvang Royal Scandinavian Inn. (805) 688–3612. Annual Easter Egg Hunt, Hans Christian Andersen Park.

End of February. Annual two-day Flying Leap Storytelling Festival, Solvang Park. (805) 688–9533. International storytellers spin delightful tales in selected venues throughout the city.

Early March. Solvang/SCOR. Century Bike Ride. (562) 690–9693. One-hundred-mile bike ride with thousands of cyclists begins and ends in Solvang.

Mid-March. Annual Taste of Solvang. Food festival weekend, "Dessert Reception," walking smorgasbord, wine and cheese tasting, and more. Live entertainment throughout the village. Limited tickets; call (800) 468–6765.

Mid-April. Santa Barbara County Vintner's Festival. (800) 218–0881; (805) 688–0881. Wine, food, and entertainment. Advance tickets only.

Early May. Los Rancheros Visitadores Annual Santa Ynez Valley Trek. Hundreds of riders parade through Solvang. Art Under the Arches at Old Mission Santa Inés. Arts and crafts, food, entertainment.

June–October. Solvang Theater Fest, 420 Second Street. This outdoor summer theater festival includes live dramatic shows and musicals. (805) 922–8313.

June. Old Santa Ynez Day. (805) 688–4878. Celebrate the town's birthday in Old West style; cowboy shoot-outs, food, entertainment, parade.

July 4. Independence Day Parade. Fireworks show and activities at Santa Ynez High School.

Mid-August. Old Mission Santa Inés Fiesta. (805) 688–4815. Festive weekend of food and fun, mariachi *folklorico* dancing, and entertainment.

Third weekend in September. Annual Danish Days Festival. (805) 686–6144. Velkommen! Celebrate Solvang's Danish heritage; folk dancing, music, food, fun, parades, entertainment. All weekend.

Mid-October. Day in the Country, Los Olivos. (805) 688–1222. Old-fashioned fun, games, entertainment, food and crafts.

Early November. Solvang Prelude. Twenty-five-mile, 50-mile, or 100K bike ride SCOR event, through beautiful Santa Ynez Valley. Two-Day Peppertree Ranch Art Show, entertainment.

Mid-November through Christmas. Winterfest celebration events in Solvang. For a schedule call (800) 486–6705 or (805) 688–6144.

Early December. Christmas Tree Lighting and Ceremony, Solvang Christmas Parade, traditional Danish Christmas celebration at Elverhoj Museum. "Olde"-fashioned Christmas in Los Olivos, open house hosted by art galleries and merchants, with hundreds of glowing luminarias.

Second week in December. Nativity Pageant, hosted by Efrem Zimabalist Jr., Solvang Theatre Fest. (805) 688–6144.

Other Recommended Restaurants and Lodgings

Solvang

Mustard Seed, 1655 Mission Drive. (805) 688–1318. Home-style American cooking, featuring sandwiches, salads, soups, and daily specials. Patio dining. Breakfast and lunch.

New Danish Inn & Lounge, 1847 Mission Drive. (805) 688–4311. The distinctive windmill at the door signifies what's to come: a delectable Danish smorgasbord. You'll also find favorite American dishes as well: steak, fish 'n' chips and other seafood, veal, and lamb.

Paula's Pancake House, 1531 Mission Drive. (805) 688–2867. Popular for good food. Extensive breakfast and lunch menu features thin Danish pancakes, waffles, omelettes, homemade soups, salads, burgers, and daily specials. Patio dining.

The Alisal Guest Ranch and Resort, 1054 Alisal Road. (800) 425–4725; (805) 688–6411; www.alisal.com. Three miles down the road from city center. There's a genuine western flavor to this 10,000-acre, upscale resort. Seventy-three well-furnished cottages with studio rooms or two-bedroom suites feature wood-burning fireplace, coffeemaker, wet bar, refrigerator with icemaker, clock radio, hair dryer, turndown service. There is no in-room TV or telephone to mar your peaceful escape. Play golf on the renovated 18-hole championship course, where deer watch you tee off. Swimming pool, Jacuzzi, seven tennis courts with pro shop, riding stable for daily trail rides, hayrides, private lake for fishing and boating, children's petting zoo and activities, library, recreation/TV room, Oak Room lounge offers evening entertainment, conference center. Full breakfast or buffet breakfast and hearty dinner included in two-night-minimum stay. Seasonal packages.

Holiday Inn Express, 1455 Mission Drive. (800) 44–RELAX; (805) 688–2018. Warmly decorated; eighty-two rooms and suites with refrigerator, TV, and hair dryer (upon request); heated pool and spa. Full complimentary continental breakfast in the attractive dining room.

Wine Valley Inn, 1564 Copenhagen Drive. (800) 824–6444; (805) 688–0559. Look for the distinctive clock tower. Fifty-six AAA three-diamond rooms nicely furnished with antiques, TV, and refrigerator; six enchanted cottages, most with private spas, kitchens, and fireplaces. Complimentary continental breakfast, senior AAA discounts, golf packages.

For More Information

Solvang Conference and Visitors Bureau, 1511 Mission Drive, P.O. Box 70, Solvang, CA 93464. (800) 468–6765; (805) 688–6144; www.solvangusa.com. Pick up a handy walking map of the village.

Two handy visitor centers: 1639 Copenhagen Drive and 1511 Mission Drive.

Coastline and Hearst Castle

San Luis Obispo, San Simeon, Cambria, Morro Bay / 2 Nights

This packed, three-day excursion takes you about 200 miles north through California's richly scenic central coast of rolling hills and pastoral land to a lovely, small college town. You'll also stop at a noted winery for a taste of its premium wines or bubbly; visit a legendary, art-filled castle; have lunch in a seaside artists' colony in the pines; and see California's "Gibraltar of the Pacific."

NOTE: This itinerary visits Hearst Castle in San Simeon, where reservations are required. Tours (about two hours long) are always available and can be reserved anywhere from a few hours to weeks or months in advance. Call (800) 444–4445 for information.

☐ Mission

☐ Wineries

☐ Farmers' markets

☐ Artists' colony

☐ Museum

☐ State university

☐ Castle/gardens

☐ Galleries

Day 1 / Morning

Leave Los Angeles via Ventura Freeway 101 north, driving through rural San Fernando Valley. After the turnoff for Ojai, the freeway follows the unruffled, mist-covered ocean. You're soon past Santa Barbara with no congestion, thanks to the revamped freeway, which bypasses the city. Curving inland, you drive through dramatic Gaviota Pass, where the road is framed with tall, rugged mountains. Exit Highway 246/Buellton (on the outskirts of Solvang) on Avenue of the Flags, a landscaped parkway decorated with a tall row of American flags waving in the breeze.

LUNCH: Pea Soup Andersen's, 376 Avenue of the Flags, Buellton. (805) 688–5581. The original 1924 home of split-pea soup. This large, very busy restaurant includes pea soup or salad with all sandwiches and entrees. For those in a hurry, the coffee shop serves the same food but has faster service than the dining room. Open daily 7:00 A.M. to 10:00 P.M.

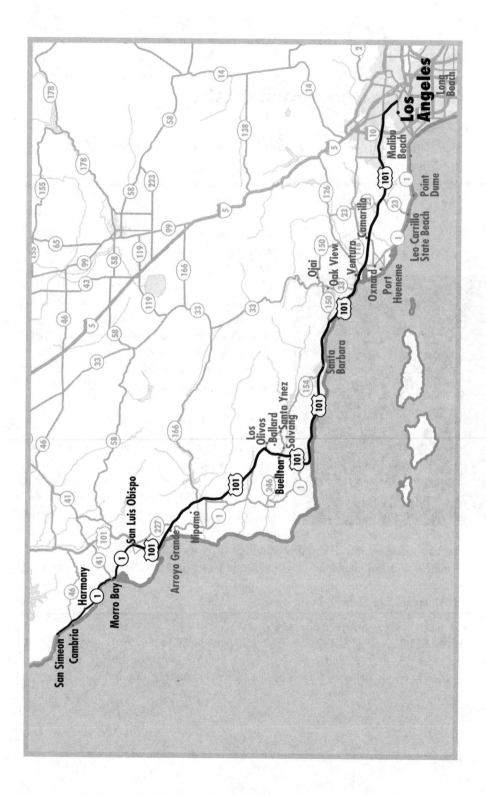

Afternoon

For the nearly 60 miles to San Luis Obispo, continue north on 101 in a tranquil, pastoral countryside where stately old oak trees dance gracefully over the hillsides. Just past Nipomo and about 3 miles south of Arroyo Grande, look for the winery on the right.

Beautiful **Laetitia Vineyard & Winery,** 453 Tower Grove Drive, Arroyo Grande (888–809–8463), welcomes you with complimentary daily tastings (from 11:00 A.M. to 5:00 P.M., until 6:00 P.M. in summer) of its estate-grown Pinot Noir, Chardonnay, and other premium wines as well as sparkling wine produced a la *methode champenoise,* accompanied by crackers and appetizers. Guided tours are by appointment only. Visit the gourmet gift shop and picnic grounds.

After your visit to the winery, return to Highway 101 north to San Luis Obispo.

Friendly and hospitable **San Luis Obispo** (say "Lewis," not "Looey") may well be one of the most likable small towns you've visited. Its rather old-fashioned, prosperous downtown area, distinguished by tree-shaded streets, offers a large, pleasant variety of shopping and dining, with good food served in generous amounts. Fortunately, local restaurants tend to bypass expensive nouvelle cuisine entrees of small portions and barely cooked cauliflower, favoring moderately priced, robust American-style fare instead. The city glows during its annual summer Mozart Festival; the weekly farmers' market is the hottest ticket on a Thursday night; and a rural creek meanders through the city.

Along Higuera Street, the main thoroughfare, stately, well-preserved old buildings add stability and harmony. Many buildings have been attractively recycled to trendy new lives.

Home to California Polytechnic State University, or Cal Poly, this is a walking town. Stroll through the **Network**'s skylit arcade, which has ceiling banners, bright shops, and a sandwich bar at the rear, where you tote your order out to the dining patio overlooking San Luis Obispo's picturesque creek. You'll have to go a long way to find a prettier, more natural setting.

To see where the city was founded in 1772, when Father Junípero Serra established **Mission San Luis Obispo de Tolosa** (782 Monterey Street), drive around the corner or walk across the footbridge over the creek. The mission was the fifth in the chain of twenty-one California missions and is still the focal point of the city. In the chapel the statues and Stations of the Cross along the walls are all original. The first California olive trees still grow in the pleasant mission garden. (Open daily from 9:00 A.M. to 4:00 P.M. in winter and to 5:00 P.M. in summer; bookstore, gift shop, and museum.)

Mission Plaza, the grassy landscaped area between the mission and San Luis Creek, is the focus of community events and a quiet creekside park of benches and shade trees. Visit the adjacent Community Art Center (open Tuesday through Sunday from 11:00 A.M. to 5:00 P.M.) and Children's Museum.

DINNER: F. McLintocks Saloon and Dining House, 686 Higuera Street, San Luis Obispo. (805) 541–0686. This western-style saloon, with long bar and moose-head decor, is where locals meet to eat and schmooze. Hearty, delicious nightly specials include beef ribs and BBQ chicken as well as hamburgers and BBQ beef sandwiches—and the chili has plenty of authority. Large portions, excellent service.

LODGING: La Cuesta Inn, 2074 Monterey Street, San Luis Obispo. (800) 543–2777 (in California); (805) 543–2777. Conveniently located across from Apple Farm Restaurant (see "Other Recommended Restaurants and Lodgings"); features seventy-two good-size rooms, bathroom with extra mirrored makeup vanity table, ample storage, small balcony, clock radio, TV, dining table and chairs; heated swimming pool, spa. Complimentary continental breakfast and afternoon tea and cookies served in the lobby. Friendly, efficient staff.

Day 2 / Morning

BREAKFAST: At the inn. Continental breakfast served in the lobby is included in your room rate. Help yourself to orange juice, coffee, mini muffins, and sliced bagels and cream cheese. You can also tote a tray to your room.

Leave for Hearst Castle, about a 45-mile drive. Drive down Monterey Street to Santa Rosa; turn right to the freeway, taking Highway 1 to **San Simeon.** Alongside the rolling hills and farms in the peaceful, open country, you become aware of California's grandeur and size. You'll pass several towns to visit on your return to San Luis Obispo—Morro Bay, Harmony, and Cambria, where an array of tall pine trees are raggedy green giants marching in place on the slopes. After a WELCOME TO SAN SIMEON sign where the ocean is as blue as Paul Newman's eyes, Hearst Castle is the next right.

At the visitor center, board your tour bus for the fifteen-minute, 5-mile trip to the hilltop castle; the trip is accompanied by an audiotape program. (Tours begin at 8:00 A.M. and leave every ten minutes. The last tour starts at 3:00 P.M. in winter, later in summer.)

Legendary **Hearst Castle,** "La Cuesta Encantada—The Enchanted Hill," with its lofty twin towers atop the four-level Spanish-Moorish mansion, was designed by architect Julia Morgan. Built by newspaper publishing tycoon William Randolph Hearst as a summer home between 1919 and 1947, this magnificent, art-filled, 165-room estate has 127 acres of gardens, pools, and terraces.

It's certainly not your everyday owner-built home, with its thirty-eight bedrooms and thirty-one baths on a quiet hilltop with an ocean view. In a forty-year spending orgy of millions of dollars and repeated forays to Europe, Hearst gathered art objects, Renaissance tapestries, paintings, silver, and ancient carved ceilings from everywhere. Entire castles and monasteries were dismantled and shipped stone by stone to San Simeon.

Back in the 1930s Hollywood's star-studded guest list for lavish weekends at the castle included Clark Gable, Charlie Chaplin, John Barrymore, and Greta Garbo, plus Hearst's mistress, actress Marion Davies. There were fabulous costume balls, deluxe barbecues, picnics, and nightly banquets. Those were the golden days of Hollywood. Today's guests take guided tours for a glimpse of the lifestyle of the flamboyant millionaire who, for twenty years, lived in regal splendor atop his private mountain kingdom.

The place is so vast that there are five separate tours to see all of it. Each tour includes the two pools and takes about an hour and three-quarters. Tour 1, the Experience Tour, is suggested for first-time visitors for an overall look. You'll begin at the serene, 104-foot-long, exquisite marble-faced Neptune Pool, filled with pure spring water. Then you'll see the eighteen-room guest cottage where Hearst lived during construction of La Casa Grande (the castle), your next stop.

The baronial, 100-by-42-foot Assembly Hall, where guests gathered for evening cocktails, is the castle's largest room, with Renaissance furnishings and ancient choir stalls. In the 67-foot-long Refectory (dining room)—whose fireplace is large enough to roast a rhinoceros—silk Sienese banners flutter from the 27-foot-high wooden ceiling imported from a sixteenth-century monastery.

The indoor Roman Pool, big enough to float the *Queen Mary,* is made of tiny blue Venetian tiles sprinkled with twenty-two-karat gold leaf. And on and on you go, viewing a mind-boggling collection of priceless art and furnishings, Egyptian pottery, mirrors, statues, and bathrooms with real gold fixtures. At the one-hundred-seat movie theater, you finally get to sit down, to watch a short movie of the good life at the castle, featuring famous stars and celebrities. All in all, it's the kind of place that makes you want to go home and burn the furniture.

Tour 2, the Upper Floors of Casa Grande, covers La Casa Grande's upper floors, including the Library, the Gothic Suite and study, the Doge's Suite, Cloister Rooms, and the Pantry and Kitchen, where all the sumptuous meals were prepared.

Tour 3, the North Wings Tour of Casa Grande, guides visitors through the north wing of La Casa Grande, three floors of guest suites with marble bathrooms and gold fixtures, and La Casa del Monte, a ten-room guest cottage; a short video is included.

Tour 4, the Garden Tour (offered April through October), takes in the extensive gardens; walkways; the Wine Cellar; La Casa del Mar, the largest, most elaborate guest cottage; and the Neptune Pool dressing rooms.

Tour 5, the Evening Tour, a two-hour Friday- and Saturday-evening tour offered March through May and September through December, includes a living-history program, with docents in period dress who appear as guests and staff; illuminated pools and gardens; and highlights of La Casa Grande and La Casa del Mar.

All tours entail considerable walking and stair climbing; be sure to wear comfortable walking shoes. The castle is open daily, except Thanksgiving, Christmas, and New Year's Day; the busiest season is late spring and summer. Hearst Castle was given to the state of California in 1958 and is a State Historical Monument. Close to one million people tour the castle every year, making it one of California's most popular attractions. Free parking is provided. Reservations are necessary and can be charged to your credit card. Since the castle holds more treasures than King Tut's tomb, toting along a camcorder and tape recorder will help you bring it all back for future reminiscing. No photo flash or tripods are permitted, however.

To extend your Hearst Castle experience, the National Geographic Theater at the visitor center presents a forty-minute movie on a five-story-tall screen, shown every forty-five minutes. *Building the Dream* tells the story of the creation of Hearst Castle, from inspiration to creation. Admission. (805) 927–6811.

Leave Hearst Castle, drive across the highway, and turn right along a narrow road to **Sebastian's General Store** and small **Patio Cafe,** adjacent to the post office and a Union 76 gas station. Sebastian's, built in 1852, is a State Historical Landmark. In addition to stocking groceries and wines, the store has a small section filled with attractive souvenirs, toys, and postcards half the price of those in the Hearst Castle gift shop.

Return to the highway, turning right (south) on Highway 1, and continue to Cambria, 6 miles down the road. At the Burton Drive traffic signal, turn inland into this small, appealing artists' colony surrounded by pine trees.

Cambria (locals call it "Camm-bria") is frequently compared with Carmel-by-the-Sea but seems more natural, not as cutesy or as thronged with tourists. Be sure to explore both sections of Main Street–East Village, up the hill, and West Village, more in the center of town. For lunch drive up the hill on Main Street to East Village.

LUNCH: Linn's Main Bin Restaurant, Bakery, Gift Shop, 2277 Main Street, Cambria. (805) 927–0371. A big sunny room with a gourmet gift shop and a bakery producing luscious berry pies. Linn's is noted for homemade chicken and beef potpie served with fruit or green salad. Other tempters include quiche, sandwiches, and Oriental chicken salad. Sunday brunch.

Afternoon

Cambria's converted Victorian buildings of the 1870s house one-of-a-kind shops, cafes, galleries, and lodgings. Besides Main Street, the side streets are worth browsing as well. On Bridge Street, **Simple Pleasures** features gifts, ornaments, and folk art for year-round holiday celebrations. **Banbury Cross,** alongside, displays old English decorative items, china, crystal, and linen.

Drive back down Main Street to Cambria's **West Village,** which resembles a faded movie set, with its small stores tucked in pretty cottages of soft colors, towers, dormer windows, and Dutch doors. In this very browsable stretch, you'll find a variety of galleries; antiques, gift, flower, and basket shops; and jewelers and clothing stores.

The **Soldier Gallery,** 789 Main Street (805–927–3804), here since 1973, makes tiny toy soldiers (54 mm size). Hundreds of different tiny military figures, painstakingly modeled and costumed, represent various wars, regiments, and so on. The store is open daily from 10:00 A.M. to 5:00 P.M. You'll find the chamber of commerce a few doors away, should you need brochures or information (see "For More Information").

Return to Highway 1 south. In barely ten minutes, turn left at the little town of **Harmony,** population eighteen. The former century-old dairy community is now a one-street artists' colony, with artisans working in the old warehouses along Harmony Valley Road. Watch glassblowers at work in Phoenix Studio Art Glass. Next door, Harmony Cellars Wine and Tasting Room, a small family-owned boutique winery, features handcrafted wines made on the premises. Stop by for a taste—the fee is applied toward your purchase—and browse the gift shop inside the winery, open from 10:00 A.M. to 5:00 P.M. Be sure to stroll the old brick paths around to the Pottery Works large, airy showroom.

Continue south to **Morro Bay,** where the enormous, 576-foot-high **Morro Rock** (the "Gibraltar of the Pacific"), a State Historical Monument, juts out of the water. Take the Main Street exit to the fascinating waterfront of this small fishing village and meander along the Embarcadero, with its shops, art galleries, restaurants, boat activity, and brunch and dinner harbor cruises. Watch the players at the giant (16-foot-square) chessboard in **Centennial Park** on the Embarcadero, then take the youngsters to the **Tidelands Children's Park** to clamber on the big sculptures and the Pirate Ship, while you watch the boats in the marina. Afterward, drive back to San Luis Obispo to relax before dinner.

DINNER: **Cafe Roma,** 1020 Railroad Avenue, San Luis Obispo. (805) 541–6800. Located near the restored train depot, Roma is consistently praised for rustic Italian specialties and good service in its romantic, candlelit dining room. Daily homemade pastas and breads; excellent veal dishes; fine wine list. Lunch Monday through Friday; dinner nightly.

LODGING: La Cuesta Inn.

Day 3 / Morning

BREAKFAST: Have the complimentary continental breakfast served in your hotel, or try a town favorite: **Louisa's Place,** 964 Higuera Street (805–541–0227), where everything's made from scratch. The specialties are omelettes, the hotcakes are saucer size, and the grilled ham is as tender as a new mother's smile. (Open daily from 6:00 A.M. to 3:00 P.M.)

If there's time before leaving for Los Angeles, take a walking tour or two of San Luis Obispo's **Heritage Walks,** which begin in Mission Plaza and cover many historical buildings and areas. A brochure is available from the chamber of commerce, 1039 Chorro Street, or inquire at your hotel.

Morro Bay's 576-foot-tall "Gibraltar of the Pacific."

Afternoon

En route home on Highway 1 south, stop for a look at the **Madonna Inn** (800–543–9666), with its own freeway exit on Madonna Road, and perhaps mark it for future visits. Sprawled across 2,200 acres, each of its 109 rooms is completely different, romantically awash with cupids, hearts, stained glass, and bacchanalia bathrooms. In the lobby twinkling lights cascade over a pink marble balustrade, a rose flowered carpet, and artificial plants and trees. See the powder room, of course, but the pièce de résistance is the waterfall urinal in the men's room. Also on-site are a cafe, restaurant, and gift shop.

Retrace your way south to Los Angeles.

There's More

Farmers' market, San Luis Obispo. Festive, popular, open-air market is held every Thursday evening (except Thanksgiving Day or if it's raining) from 6:00 to 9:00 P.M. on Higuera Street, between Osos and Nipomo, with streets closed to traffic.

Also held on Saturday from 8:00 to 10:30 A.M. at the Promenade shopping center parking lot off Madonna Road. Local farmers bring just-picked fruits and vegetables as well as fresh cut flowers and pressed cider. Restaurateurs barbecue chicken, ribs, and hot dogs on massive outdoor curbside grills; food booths offer pizza, sandwiches, and desserts. There's entertainment, too: jugglers, street dancers, clowns, and musicians.

Farmers' market, Morro Bay. Every Thursday, 3:00 to 5:00 P.M., at Young's Giant Food, 2650 North Main Street. Also Fishermen & Farmers Market, 850 Main Street, Saturday 3:00 A.M. to 6:00 P.M.

Farmers' market, Cambria. Veteran's Memorial Building, parking lot on West Main Street. Held every Friday from 2:30 to 5:00 P.M., rain or shine. Fresh produce, nuts, flowers, and fun.

The San Luis Obispo Trolley offers rides (fee) from noon to 5:00 P.M. daily, as it loops through downtown from the Civic Center or Monterey Street. (805) 541–0286.

Morro Bay Aquarium and Marine Rehabilitation Center, 595 Embarcadero, Morro Bay. (805) 772–7647. Fourteen tanks are filled with all kinds of ocean life, and it's fun to feed the seals. Open daily.

Morro Bay State Park Museum of Natural History, Morro Bay State Park, Morro Bay. (805) 772–2694. Realistic mammals, other animals, and fish; plus nature video, art gallery, museum store. Open daily except Thanksgiving, Christmas, and New Year's Day. Admission.

Paddle wheeler bay cruise, Morro Bay. (805) 772–2257. Daily cruises aboard the *Tiger's Folly;* Sunday champagne brunch.

Special Events

January. Winter Bird Festival, celebrating the winter bird migration to Morro Bay's Estuary. (800) 231–0592.

Mid–February. Mardi Gras Festival, San Luis Obispo.

End of February. Tall Ships Visit, Morro Bay.

Mid–March. Chili Cook–Off & Car Show, Cambria.

Mid–April. Children's Day in the Plaza, San Luis Obispo. Easter Egg Hunt, Cambria. Easter Egg Hunt, Del Mar Park, Morro Bay.

Late April. Annual I Madonnari Italian Street Painting Festival, San Luis Obispo.

Mid–May. Cruisin' Car Show, Morro Bay.

July. Shakespeare Festival, Cambria. Renaissance Festival, San Luis Obispo.

July 4. Fourth of July in Mission Plaza, San Luis Obispo. Picnic and fireworks display, Cambria. Art in the Park Parade and fireworks, Morro Bay.

Mid-July. Annual Mozart Festival, San Luis Obispo.

August. Annual Pinedorado Parade and Festival, Cambria, since 1948.

September. Annual Central Coast Wine Festival, San Luis Obispo. Annual Woodcarvers Show, Cambria.

First weekend in October. Harbor Festival, with wine and seafood, Morro Bay.

November 4–7. Harvest Wine Festival, San Luis Obispo.

November–December. Art Center Craft Art Market, San Luis Obispo.

Late November. Merchants Christmas Street Faire, Morro Bay.

December. Christmas in the Plaza, San Luis Obispo. Lighted boat parade, Morro Bay.

Month of December. Hearst Castle Holiday Decorated Tours, San Simeon.

Other Recommended Restaurants and Lodgings

San Luis Obispo

Apple Farm Restaurant, 2015 Monterey Street. (800) 225–2040; (805) 544–6100. A breakfast winner for home-style buttermilk pancakes, Belgian waffles, fresh muffins. Lunch and dinner American-style entrees include sandwiches, chicken and dumplings, turkey, fresh seafood. Top it all off with hot apple dumplings and fruit cobbler. Early-bird dinners from 2:00 to 5:00 P.M. Monday through Friday. Best to reserve for all meals.

Linnaeas Cafe, 1110 Garden Street. (805) 541–5888. A young hangout, with garden dining, for offbeat salads, soups, and burritos. Open daily. Hours vary.

Buone Tavola, 1037 Monterey Street. (805) 545–8000. Next to the Fremont Theater downtown. A steady favorite for northern Italian cuisine, featuring homemade pastas and all your favorite dishes. Garden seating. Open daily for lunch and dinner.

Apple Farm Inn and Trellis Court, 2015 Monterey Street. (800) 374–3705; (805) 544–2040. Victorian-style, 104-room hotel, with fireplaces and romantic country decor. Complimentary coffee, TV, radio, terry robes, turndown service, and souvenir gift. Heated swimming pool, spa; charming country store, restaurant, gift shop, working Mill House. Seasonal and group rates.

Quality Suites, 1631 Monterey Street. (800) 228–5151; (805) 541–5001. Has 138 two-room suites, each with two TVs, VCR, microwave, stereo, honor bar, refrigerator; complimentary cooked-to-order breakfast; swimming pool, spa; cocktail lounge. Senior and group rates.

Cambria

The Brambles Dinner House, 4005 Burton Drive. (805) 927–4716. West Village. The small red cottage was built in 1874 as a family residence. Everything is home-made in this multi-award-winning restaurant. Medium-priced entrees feature prime rib, grilled steaks, smoked ribs, fresh seafood, English trifle. Open Sunday through Friday from 4:00 to 9:30 P.M. and Saturday from 4:00 to 10:00 P.M.; Sunday champagne brunch served from 9:30 A.M. to 2:00 P.M. Reservations suggested.

The J. Patrick House, 2990 Burton Drive. (800) 341–5258; (805) 927–3812; www.jpatrickhouse.com. Tucked in the woods above Cambria's East Village, this authentic log-cabin bed-and-breakfast with country garden and carriage house features eight appealing guest rooms, each with private bath, antique furniture, queen-size bed, and wood-burning fireplace. Complimentary breakfast in the airy, glass-enclosed garden room includes fresh orange juice and fruit, yogurt, Irish oat-meal, homemade muffins, and breads. Early-evening hospitality of wine and assorted homemade hors d'oeuvres is served fireside in the cozy living room, and at bedtime, "killer" homemade chocolate-chip cookies and milk are waiting in the lounge. Two-night minimum stay on weekends.

For More Information

San Luis Obispo Chamber of Commerce, 1039 Chorro Street, San Luis Obispo, CA 93401; (805) 781–2777.

San Luis Obispo County Visitors & Conference Bureau, 1037 Mill Street, San Luis Obispo, CA 93401. (800) 634–1414; www.sanluisobispocounty.com. Open 8:00 A.M. to 5:00 P.M., till 8:00 P.M. Thursday, Friday, and Saturday. Free brochure.

Cambria Chamber of Commerce, 767 Main Street, Cambria, CA 93428. (805) 927–3624.

Hearst Castle. (800) 444–PARK, www.hearstcastle.com.

San Simeon Chamber of Commerce, P.O. Box 1, San Simeon, CA 93452. (805) 927–3500.

Morro Bay Chamber of Commerce, 880 Main Street, Morro Bay, CA 93442. (800) 237–0592 (in California); (805) 772–4467.

Mozart Festival, San Luis Obispo. (805) 781–3008; www.mozartfestival.com.

EASTERN ESCAPES

EASTERN ESCAPE ONE

Sun and Snow at Mountain Lakes

Lake Arrowhead, Big Bear Lake / 2 Nights

This three-day outing in the rugged and scenic San Bernardino Mountains takes you from city noise and traffic to a pair of sparkling, mile-high resort communities. Amid clear, invigorating mountain air and quiet pine forests, you'll find year-round boating, swimming, hiking, fishing, and other outdoor recreations that make these communities so stimulating to visit. The area prides itself on distinctive shopping, hearty mountain dining, and hospitality.

- ☐ Lake cruises
- ☐ Zoo
- ☐ Mountain biking
- ☐ Alpine slide
- ☐ Pine forests
- ☐ Water sports
- ☐ Hearty dining
- ☐ Golf
- ☐ Skiing and snowboarding
- ☐ Antiques

Lake Arrowhead, a bustling summertime getaway, becomes a serene winter wonderland with nearby skiing and snow fun. While Big Bear Lake is Southern California's major ski and winter sports center, it is a popular, refreshing destination in all seasons. Both rural mountain cities are easily toured in this change-of-pace itinerary.

Day 1 / Morning

For the 90-mile drive up to **Lake Arrowhead,** your first destination, head east from Los Angeles on I–10 toward San Bernardino, a pleasing drive through rolling countryside toward the majestic mountains. You'll probably find gasoline prices at least 15 cents per gallon higher in the mountains than in Los Angeles, so it's wise to fill your gas tank before leaving the city. Exit at California 215 Junction North/San Bernardino/Barstow. Drive through San Bernardino city and take the Highland Mountain Resorts 30 exit. Follow California 30 east to the Waterman/18 exit. Turn left on California 18 to Lake Arrowhead and ascend toward the mountains as you drive through the San Bernardino National Forest.

The marvelously scenic **Rim of the World Highway** is aptly named, as it climbs and winds around the San Bernardino Mountains up to Lake Arrowhead, at 5,200 feet. The panoramic view over the city is unparalleled as the road climbs and

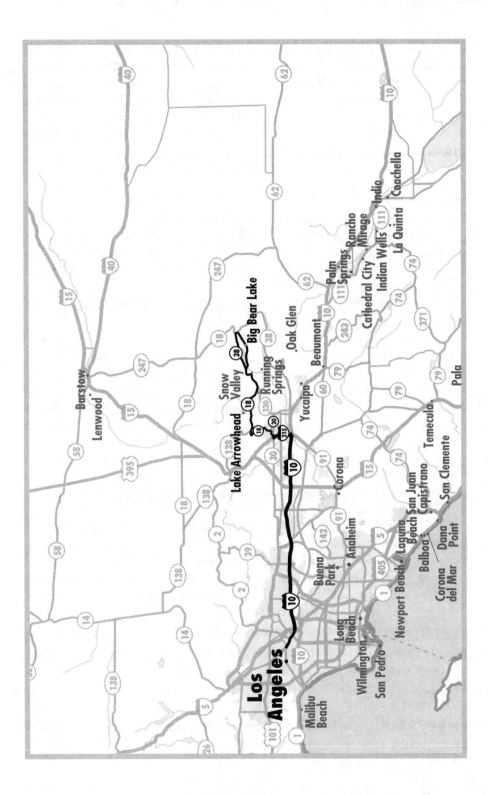

curves. The scenery is stark and indomitable, with tall pines covering the mountain-side. Massive sand-colored boulders tower alongside the road, and the mountain air is brilliantly clear and sparkling.

After you pass the turnoffs for the familiar small hamlets of Crestline, Lake Gregory, and Twin Peaks, framed by dense forests, the road narrows and makes a few downhill squiggles. Suddenly, there's the dramatic sight of the gleaming blue Lake Arrowhead, hidden in a dense forest of sky-touching pine trees.

Continue ahead to **Lake Arrowhead Village,** an attractive, bustling, multi-level complex of some eighty shops, galleries, and restaurants sprawling around the lakeshore.

Everything in this friendly, sunny mountain town focuses on the man-made, glittering blue lake. Lake Arrowhead, developed in the 1920s, became a glamorous, popular, year-round resort area for sailing and swimming in summer and for skiing in winter. The exclusive North Shore attracted wealthy vacationers and privacy-seeking celebrities. Almost everyone who was "somebody" had a second home in Arrowhead. Film studios used the area for frequent movie locations and found the perfect setting for *Heidi,* starring Shirley Temple.

The privately owned, thriving village you see today is, like a Hollywood movie, a remake of the original 1923 community. The village was completely rebuilt in 1979, except for the eye-catching, red-roofed, former 1920s dance pavil-ion, which was restored as the Theme Building and now houses upscale boutiques.

The lower lakeshore level is the busiest, with its cluster of shops and restaurants that snuggle close to the water's edge. **Just Browsing** is the big main store in the village, ideal for gifts, candles, mobiles, and postcards. Dreyers Grand Ice Cream, Harry and David, Pendleton, and the Rocky Mountain Chocolate Factory keep busy dispensing what you like best. Surrounding stores feature souvenirs, posters, clothing, T-shirts, and gifts; about a dozen factory-outlet stores offer discounts on national chain items.

Among the Pavilion boutiques, the Harvest offers country Americana furnish-ings of crystal, linens, and pretty afghans. Galleries, restaurants, and stores present still more variety on the traffic-free Peninsula level.

Lake Arrowhead Children's Museum (within the village Peninsula; 909–336–3093), alongside the lake, is for ages twelve and younger, who'll enjoy the hands-on exhibits, various activities, and puppet theater. (Open daily; admission.)

LUNCH: Papagayos, Lake Arrowhead. (909) 337–9529. Mexican food at its finest, with all items prepared daily. For those who love margaritas, they make their own from scratch. Open daily 11:00 A.M. to 9:00 P.M.

Afternoon

Cruising Lake Arrowhead is a memorable way to appreciate the beauty and seren-ity of the lake in its forest setting. During a one-hour narrated **cruise** aboard the

The Arrowhead Queen *paddle wheeler cruises the serene lake.*

sixty-passenger paddle wheeler *Arrowhead Queen,* your captain points out historical sites and landmarks. (Hourly departures from 10:00 A.M. to 6:00 P.M.; purchase tickets at Leroy's Sports Store.)

After your delightful cruise around the lake, take a short drive to **Blue Jay Village** to explore its many shops, restaurants, and its ice-skating rink. Drive uphill from Lake Arrowhead Village; turn right past the Lake Arrowhead Resort on Highway 189 for about 1.5 miles, along a quiet country road where chalet-style homes are sheltered among tall trees.

In Blue Jay Village, Front Street's row of stores includes Jensen's Finest Foods gourmet supermarket, Pat's General Store, antiques stores, a deli, and many other specialty shops and restaurants. Across the highway you'll find Rite-Aid drug store, Radio Shack, and a strip of choice dining places.

DINNER: Bin 189, in Lake Arrowhead Resort, 27984 Highway 189, Lake Arrowhead. (800) 800–6792; (909) 336–1511. A large, comfortable room with attractive decor. Choice dinner entrees besides New York steak and prime rib include broiled half chicken served with soup or salad, hot muffin, baked or fried potatoes; Southwestern Pasta Chicken and Rotelli is zesty with tomato, and tomatillo atop cilantro.

LODGING: Lake Arrowhead Resort, 27984 Highway 189, Lake Arrowhead. (800) 800–6792. Adjacent to the village, sprawled along the lakeshore, and featuring a private swimming beach and fishing dock, plus 177 luxurious rooms and suites. This is the largest hotel on the mountain. Heated swimming pool, health and fitness spa; restaurant; other recreational activities.

Day 2 / Morning

BREAKFAST: At your hotel. Or opt for **Belgian Waffle Works** (909–337–5222), in the village at the edge of the lake, for delectable waffles and croissant sandwiches. Try the fruit waffle with strawberries and sliced bananas topped with whipped cream with your cappuccino or espresso. Twice voted the number-one breakfast restaurant in the area.

Leave for Big Bear Lake by driving out of Lake Arrowhead Village; turn left to Rim of the World Highway 18 and continue for about 26 miles. The road zigzags to Big Bear Lake, curving down the heroic San Bernardino Mountains; past Running Springs, which has many roadside stores; and past forests and Green Valley Lake. Massive boulders loom on both sides of the highway. The road winds and curves, the air is very clear, and the forest trees march tall on buff-colored slopes. You'll spot the sign to Big Bear Lake to the right and then glimpse the placid blue lake in its travel-brochure setting beneath tall pine trees.

Big Bear Lake is considered a premier year-round recreation area because of its variety of activities for outdoor enthusiasts of all ages—sailing, fishing, hiking, lake tours, mountain biking, water sports, snow skiing, shopping, dining, and sightseeing. From mid-November through early April, its two skiing facilities, with miles of snowy slopes, have made it a major winter sports headquarters.

Friendly and unhurried, Big Bear Lake is the ultimate escape, a world removed from crowds and freeway traffic, secure in its beautiful mountain valley on the fringe of a fairy-tale forest. So far the small frontier town hasn't been prettified or boutiqued. It just meanders around the glittering, 7-mile-long man-made lake, with 27 miles of undulating shoreline.

There's a satisfying feeling of open space, similar to that of small towns in Alaska, throughout this sparsely built community, sheltered beneath the tall mountains that provide the long ski runs in winter. Flashes of the cobalt lake are visible through towering pines; the quiet, rural atmosphere is relaxing; the sun is richly warm, even in October; and the air is gorgeous and clear, at a nearly 7,000-foot altitude. Restaurants with sunny dining patios abound, featuring excellent food in generous portions, and there's a large choice in lodging accommodations of all types.

The focus of the city is the **Village,** a lively area along Pine Knot Avenue, which runs at right angles away from the lake toward the mountains and is the main drag, filled with shops, dining places, and people. The Village continues as Pine Knot ends up at another Big Bear Boulevard, this one having several busy blocks of more shops and restaurants. Then you're in wide-open space at the foot of the mountains and ski areas at the edge of the forest.

LUNCH: Old Country Inn Restaurant, 41126 Big Bear Boulevard, Big Bear Lake. (909) 866–5600. Dark walnut paneling, a peaked ceiling, and plants provide a just-right atmosphere for large-portioned specialties, such as Wiener schnitzel with potato pancakes, red cabbage, and sauerkraut; or go for the savory Italian entrees of veal, chicken, and pasta.

Afternoon

For shopping and browsing after lunch, drive back along Big Bear Boulevard to **Pine Knot Avenue** (the Village) and turn left toward the mountains. Among the many select shops along this vibrant stretch is **Der Weihnachts Markt** (The Christmas Mart), 652–654 Pine Knot Avenue (909–866–8468). Here for more than twenty years, the shop, with jolly Christmas music and a beautifully decorated Christmas tree, sells only imported Christmas merchandise year-round. Big sellers are the little village houses, beer steins, and colorful, fierce-looking nutcrackers.

A few doors away, the charming **Adora Bella,** 625 Pine Knot Avenue (909–866–3033), sells just about everything, from collectibles and clocks to stuffed animals, ceramics, picture frames, and a myriad of gift items. In **Mountain Country House,** 633 Pine Knot Avenue, you'll find a large selection of hand-crafted country-style items, from rag dolls, stationery, teddy bears, and birdhouses to afghans, pillows, and giftware. **North Pole Fudge and Ice Cream Co.,** in the heart of the village at 618 Pine Knot Avenue (909–866–7622), boasts fifteen different kinds of fudge and Dreyer's ice cream, and don't forget the yummy caramel apples. An excellent choice for anyone with a sweet tooth.

For a relaxing respite you can tour the calm blue lake in a one-hour narrated **cruise** on the ten-passenger *Serena,* which leaves from Pine Knot Landing at the foot of the village (909–866–6478), or on the sixty-passenger *Big Bear Queen* paddle wheeler, which leaves from Big Bear Marina, Paine Road at Lakeview (909–866–3218). Both charge the same rate.

DINNER: Evergreen Restaurant, 40771 Lakeview Drive, Big Bear Lake. (909) 878–5588. Dine with a view. This popular restaurant overlooks a lake and serves international cuisine, including steaks, seafood, beef Wellington, prime rib, shrimp tempura, rack of lamb, and a mouthwatering array of salads and burgers. Dinner Monday through Thursday, lunch and dinner Friday through Sunday.

LODGING: Northwoods Resort, 40650 Village Drive, Big Bear Lake. (909)

866–3121. Conveniently located in the heart of the Village, this resort has 148 guest rooms, including eight suites. The rustic wood decor reflects the natural beauty of Big Bear Mountain. Rooms are equipped with coffeemakers, hair dryers, clock radios, color television, with in-room movies and Nintendo games, fax, and computer access; some rooms have fireplaces. Restaurant and lounge, outdoor pool, spa, fitness facility, and huge conference center with extensive meeting and banquet facilities. Restaurant features Saturday buffet breakfast and Sunday champagne buffet brunch.

Day 3 / Morning

BREAKFAST: At the resort. Try the continental breakast.

Drive up Moonridge Road to the 9-hole **Bear Mountain Golf Course** (909–584–8082) and freshen up your game. Just beyond is **Moonridge Animal Park,** a small, charming zoo in a rustic, hilly clearing at the foot of Bear Mountain Ski. Look for silvery timber wolves; bobcats; huge, black-feathered golden eagles as big as turkeys; and, of course, the big, husky black grizzly bears that gave the region its name. (Open daily from mid-May through October; admission.)

In this same area shop at the **Bear Mountain Trading Co.,** 42646 Moonridge Road, a big log cabin treasure chest filled with old-fashioned gifts, turquoise jewelry, bears of all sizes, Navajo rugs, and other temptations.

LUNCH: Boo Bear's Den Restaurant, 572 Pine Knot Avenue, Big Bear Lake. (909) 866–2162. You can't resist the inviting, sunny parasoled patio, which lures lots of diners for daily seafood catches, sandwiches, ribs, steaks, and a great salad bar.

Retrace your way back to Los Angeles. Take Highway 18 south to California 30. Go west on 30 to I–215 and then south on I–215 to I–10 west. Follow I–10 west into Los Angeles.

There's More

Antiques shopping. Lake Arrowhead and its tiny neighboring hamlets are a hub of antiques stores. Among those nearby are Creekside Cottage, on Highway 189 out of Blue Jay in Agua Fria, featuring wonderful decorative gift items and fine glassware. Timberline in the Glen, in Cedar Glen, offers unique custom new and antique furniture items.

Skiing. Snow Valley Ski Resort (Lake Arrowhead), 14 miles east toward Big Bear Lake, from mid-November through March or April. Thirty-three runs, serviced by five double chairlifts, eight triples; longest run is 1.5 miles. Snowboarding with half-pipe available. Snow-making machine capability of more than 170 acres. Full facilities include cafeteria, bar, après-ski music, rentals. General information, (909) 867– 2751; recorded ski and snow report, (909) 867–5151.

Big Bear Lake's two full-service ski resorts are open throughout its long season, from mid-November through early April, whether or not there's snow. One ticket is good for both resorts. They each have high-tech snow-making systems for miles of snowy slopes:

Big Bear Mountain Ski Resort, P.O. Box 5812, Big Bear Lake, CA 92315. (909) 585–2519. In the Moonridge area, about 1 mile east of Snow Summit, is Southern California's highest major resort, with the biggest vertical rise. At an 8,805-foot elevation, Bear Peak, the highest and most challenging, has nearly 1,700 vertical feet of continuous skiing. Eleven chairlifts include one high-speed detachable quad, one quad chair, three triples, four double chairs, and two surface Pomas. Also snowmobiling, food, instruction, rentals. Ski hot line, (310) 289–0636.

Snow Summit Mountain Resort, P.O. Box 77, Big Bear Lake, CA 92315. (909) 866–5766. One mile east of the Village center. Well rated by *Ski* magazine, the resort is one of the most popular. Eleven chairlifts and more than 18 miles of ski runs—the most of any Southern California ski area. Night skiing and snowboarding. Food, rentals, ski school, licensed day-care center. Ski hot line, (310) 613–0602.

Mountain biking. In Lake Arrowhead at Snow Valley, from Memorial Day through Labor Day.

In Big Bear Lake, mountain-biking terrain covers miles of forest trails and roads. During the summer riders take their bikes on Snow Summit Mountain Resort's Sky Chair to the mountaintop, enjoy the valley views, have lunch, and hit the riding trails. Rentals and information: Team Big Bear, in Big Bear Lake, (909) 866–4565.

Boat rentals for sailing, waterskiing, fishing, and cruises. Big Bear Lake. Call Dock Club in Big Bear Lake, (909) 866–6463.

The MARTA Trolley in Big Bear Lake runs through the Village with three routes and convenient places to board (fee). Bus makes daily runs to Arrowhead and San Bernardino.

Horse-drawn carriage rides are a romantic, leisurely way to sightsee Big Bear Lake. Contact Victoria Park Carriages, Ltd., at the carriage stand location, corner of Lakeview and Bartlett. (909) 584–2277.

Hiking and gold-fever trails in Big Bear Lake offer historic insight into the 1864 gold rush in nearby Holcolmb Valley. Maps available at the Big Bear Ranger Station on the North Shore and at the chamber of commerce (see "For More Information").

Alpine Slide at Magic Mountain, on Big Bear Boulevard, 0.5 mile west of the Village in Big Bear Lake. (909) 866–4626. Hop on a scenic chairlift above the lake, then shoot down a thrilling toboggan-style slide with controlled speed. Also a water slide, miniature golf, and a snack bar. Open year-round, weather permitting.

Special Events

Early April. Easter in the Village, Lake Arrowhead. Easter-egg hunt, musical entertainment, candy. Spring Fest, Snow Summit, Big Bear Lake.

Mid-May. Trout Classic, Big Bear Lake Fishing Association. (909) 866–6260.

Wildflower Tours, Big Bear. (909) 866–3437.

End of June. Annual Premier Motorcycle Event, Big Bear Lake. (909) 878–4340.

Rotary Art and Wine Festival, Tavern Bay, Lake Arrowhead.

July 4. Festival of Lights Boat Parade, Fourth of July Gala and Celebration, Lake Arrowhead. Fourth of July Celebration, BBQ, and fireworks display over Big Bear Lake. (909) 585–3000.

Mid-August. Antique Car Club Fun Run, Big Bear Lake. (909) 866–1420.

Annual "National Marina Day," Big Bear Lake. (909) 866–1420.

Renaissance Faire, Big Bear Lake. (909) 585–7824.

A Tribute to the Legends of Rock and Roll, plus Oldies Classic Car Show, Big Bear Lake. (909) 866–4970.

Labor Day weekend to the last weekend in October. Annual Oktoberfest, Convention Center, Big Bear Lake. (909) 585–3000.

Early September. Fall Festival Crafts Faire, Convention Center, Big Bear. (909) 585–3000.

Mid-September. Big Bear International Film Festival.

September through October. Oktoberfest, in the Lake Arrowhead Village. Each weekend. (909) 585–3000.

October 31. Halloween in the Village, Big Bear Lake. (909) 866–4607.

Third Saturday in November. Tree Lighting Ceremony, Lake Arrowhead Village. (909) 337–2533.

End of November. Annual Holiday Jubilee, Big Bear Convention Center. (909) 585–3000.

Christmas Tree Lighting in the Village, Big Bear.

End of November through December. Annual Dickens Christmas Celebration, Lake Arrowhead Village. (909) 337–2533.

Mid-December. Festival of Lights, *Arrowhead Queen*. (909) 336–6992.

Tree Ornament Party and Lighting Ceremony, Big Bear Lake.

Other Recommended Restaurants and Lodgings

Lake Arrowhead

Woody's Boathouse Restaurant, P.O. Box 1845, Lake Arrowhead, 92352. (909) 337–BOAT. Dine lakeside with booths shaped like antique wooden boats. Scrumptious salad bar, seafood, prime rib, and steaks. Woody's Boathouse Breakfast Buffet, Sunday only.

Saddleback Inn–Arrowhead, 300 South State Highway 173; (800) 858–3334; (909) 336–3571; www.lakearrowhead.com/saddleback. Totally restored, 1917 historical landmark at the entrance to the village. Thirty-four guest rooms and cottages, with stone fireplaces, double whirlpool baths, minirefrigerator. The Nest Restaurant and bar. Several guest rooms are named after previous celebrity guests, including Howard Hughes and Mae West.

The Lakeview Romantique Lodge, 28051 Highway 189. (800) 358–5253; (909) 337–6633. A Victorian B&B that's a nine-room hideaway offering lake views, antique furnishings, and fireplaces. Continental breakfast features huge cinnamon rolls from local bakery. Ski and beach packages available.

Big Bear Lake

The Iron Squirrel, 646 Pine Knot Avenue. (909) 866–9121. Country French cuisine in this intimate dining room favors excellent salmon and other fresh fish entrees. For dessert there's puff pastry filled with ice cream and drenched in chocolate sauce. Dinner nightly.

Cowboy Express, 40433 Lakeview Drive. (909) 866–1486. Experience dining Western style at this family-friendly steak house. Enjoy steaks, burgers, sandwiches, ribs, chicken, salads, and the world's tiniest sundae. Scrumptious desserts and appetizers. Open for lunch and dinner.

Golden Bear Cottages, 39367 Big Bear Boulevard. (909) 866–2010. Twenty-five one- and two-bedroom cottages all with fireplace, color cable TV, VCR, and telephone. This all-season, AAA-approved resort specializes in family groups, with heated pool and spa, spacious children's playground, picnic areas, barbecues at each cottage, and large fire pit. Recreation activities include Ping-Pong, sand volleyball, and basketball. Midweek/off-season rates.

Best Western Big Bear Chateau, 42200 Moonridge Road, P.O. Box 1814, Big Bear Lake, 92315. (800) 232–7466. Between Bear Mountain and Snow Summit Ski Resorts, eighty-room European chateau with four-star amenities: fireplaces, antique furnishings, and heated towel racks in the bathrooms. Restaurant and lounge with dancing Friday and Saturday nights. Attractive ski package available.

For More Information

Lake Arrowhead Communities Chamber of Commerce, P.O. Box 219, Lake Arrowhead, CA 92352. (800) 337–3716; (909) 337–3715 (lodging information); www.lakearrowhead.net. In Lake Arrowhead Village, building F290.

Big Bear Lake Resort Association, P.O. Box 1936, 630 Bartlett Road, Big Bear Lake, CA 92315; (800) 424–4232; (909) 866–6190.

Big Bear Lake Chamber of Commerce & Visitors Center, 630 Bartlett Road, Big Bear Lake, CA 92315; (909) 866–4607.

Forest Ranger Station 76. (909) 866–3437 (for information on camping and hiking).

Apple Holiday Time

Oak Glen / 1 Night

If you think Southern California doesn't have a change of seasons, you'll discover otherwise in this one-night escape to rural Oak Glen. Located about 120 miles from Los Angeles (on the way to Palm Springs), the sequestered glen is tucked in the San Bernardino Mountains between Yucaipa and Beaumont, at an elevation of almost 5,000 feet.

Oak Glen is the Southland's largest mile-high apple-growing community. More than a million visitors come up year-round for its peace and beauty; to smell the lilacs and pink and white apple blossoms covering the slopes in springtime; to enjoy the cool summers in the mountains; to marvel at the brilliant fall foliage amid towering pines, cedars, and oaks; and to throw snowballs in winter. Above all, they come to enjoy the fall harvest of some forty million apples (40,000 bushels) of more than sixty-five varieties, all sold directly to the public in one of the largest operations of its kind in the country. The apple growers also press several hundred thousand gallons of fresh cider and sell their own blends. In all the friendly apple sheds, you can taste the different apples and ciders before you buy.

- ☐ Apple ranches and orchards
- ☐ Fresh-pressed cider
- ☐ Apple pie
- ☐ Mountain scenery
- ☐ Museums
- ☐ Animal petting farms
- ☐ Gift shops

In an 8-mile loop, you can visit twelve apple ranches and orchards. During apple harvest season, September to New Year's, you can buy fresh, crisp apples in the apple sheds by the bag, the box, or the bushel and buy fresh-pressed cider, apple butter, apple jelly, and other apple products; browse fifty specialty shops; enjoy hearty country food in five family restaurants, always highlighted by freshly baked, hot apple pie; have picnics; visit a candy factory and animal petting parks; and take part in seasonal festivities. On your return home you will visit an elegant and delightful decorative-arts museum.

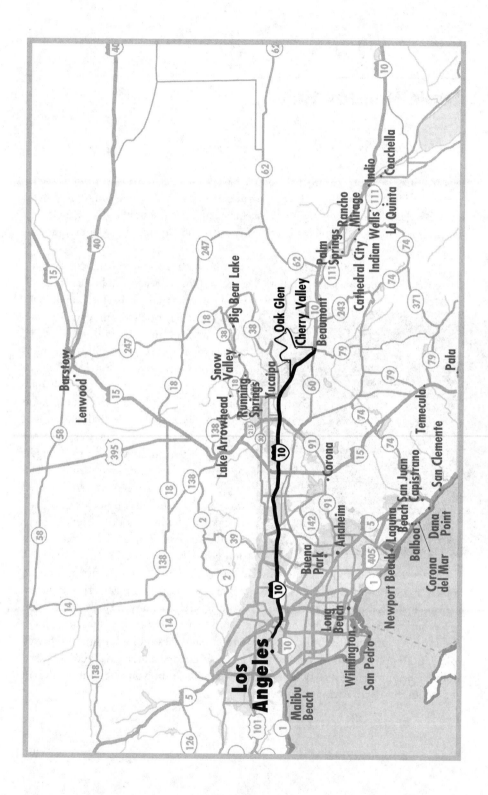

Day 1 / Morning

Drive east from Los Angeles on I–10 and exit Yucaipa Boulevard. Follow Yucaipa Boulevard east to Oak Glen Road, turn left, and continue on up to Oak Glen. The quiet rural road is nearly deserted during the week as it meanders past horses and cows grazing in sun-dappled fields and continues up the valley to an altitude of 5,000 feet to Oak Glen, then loops down the other side of the glen to Cherry Valley and Beaumont.

Oak Glen families have been growing apples in this beautiful sheltered canyon for more than a hundred years, on 450 rolling and fertile acres. The descendants of persevering mountain pioneers and their families run many of the original orchards and ranches in traditional, unsophisticated mom-and-pop operations that preserve the glen's authentic and unpretentious rustic character. They are reminders of the time when horse-drawn wagons filled with apples plodded down dusty dirt roads and a handful of homesteaders held out against fierce weather, Indian warfare, and marketing setbacks. Remnants of Oak Glen's spirited pioneer days linger everywhere.

Though the area is delightful to visit in any season for an old-fashioned holiday in the country, from September to October is when roadside sheds and ranchers' apple barns are crammed with fresh, just-picked apples (not waxed), plus tangy, fresh-pressed cider to tote home. This is delicious, unsweetened, and micro-flash pasteurized cider, far superior to that sold in your local supermarket. And everywhere there's the tantalizing, fruity aroma of apples and freshly baked apple pie. The glen's apple orchards are open daily during apple harvest season. Varieties of apples include MacIntosh, Jonathon, Gravenstein, Rome Beauties, Red and Gold Delicious, Fuji, Gala, Granny Smith, and other familiar names, as well as some new ones. Additionally, several ranches invite the public to join in the fun of seasonal U-pick crops on weekends for raspberries, pears, apples, and pumpkins. The ranch shops are treasures to browse for handmade and imported gifts, candles, American antiques, and much more.

NOTE: Days and hours are subject to change.

One of the first ranches you come to is **Parrish Pioneer Apple Ranch,** 38561 Oak Glen Road (909–797–1753), where in fall a tumble of fat golden and orange pumpkins brighten the entrance to the vintage red barn and salesroom of the oldest apple ranch in the canyon. It was founded in 1866 by Enoch Parrish, who traded his four-mule team and wagon for a homestead site of 160 acres, built a three-room log cabin, and planted the first apple trees in Oak Glen in the late 1860s. He later bought additional land and built a large house for his family of nine children; it is the oldest all-wood house in San Bernardino County.

Parrish Ranch Apple Shed is open daily year-round from 9:00 A.M. to 7:00 P.M.; seventeen varieties of apples are on sale from late autumn into the new year. The apple barn is stocked with apple cider, apple butter, dried fruits, jams and jellies, and Granlund's hand-dipped chocolates. There's a good restaurant and bakery, snack bar, and Granny's Attic.

The 1876 Parrish House, now an antiques and gift shop, displays American furniture, kitchen decor, glassware, old trunks, and collectibles from the Victorian era to the present.

Farther along, **Law's Cider Mill and Ranch,** 39392 Oak Glen Road (909–771–6903), is where the Law family opened Oak Glen's first apple shed, in 1938, and is still growing many varieties of apples. The small restaurant began in the apple packing shed when Teresa Law started baking apple pies to sell with coffee to customers in the early 1950s. The pies proved so popular that the family soon built a larger restaurant above the shed and added other buildings.

LUNCH: Law's Oak Glen Coffee Shop. (909) 797–1642. The chalet-style building's dining room offers views over the valley. Lunch favorites are homemade split-pea soup and meat loaf sandwiches. The menu also offers hamburgers, a variety of sandwiches, good chili, and chicken salad. Save room for Law's famous apple pie; about 200 are baked on weekends during harvest season. Before leaving the restaurant, take a peek at the fascinating apple-peeling-and-coring machinery in a small room adjacent to the kitchen, where apples are prepared for the pies. Enjoy breakfast buffet first Sunday of the month, and Saturday and Sunday during fall. Closed Monday and Tuesday. Call for hours.

Outdoors, the cider mill and apple shed are filled with bags and boxes of a variety of apples, gallons of apple cider, apple butter and preserves, gourds, Indian corn, and pumpkins. After September, open daily from 9:00 A.M. to 5:30 P.M.; closed most weekdays after December 1. The Apple Tree country gift shop, run by Teresa Law, features Beatrix Potter books and figurines, baskets, and pretty kitchen items.

Just up the road, **Oak Tree Village,** 38550 Oak Glen Road (909–797–4020), with fourteen acres of family fun, began in 1961 when a young couple were successful selling apples and apple pies from a shed on their orchard and built a small restaurant. They later added a delightful animal park—where children can still feed deer, sheep, goats, and pigs—then added Mountaintown, where lifelike wolves, Kodiak and polar bears, and rare birds are in a simulated natural habitat. The yellow clapboard complex features a sweet-scented Candy Kitchen where you can watch candymakers hand-dipping chocolates and making caramel apples and fudge, while you inhale the delectable scent of chocolates and other sweets simmering in the big copper kettles. Browse the eighteen specialty shops, two restaurants, and snack bars. There are also train and pony rides. During apple season live country music is presented weekends at the Peacock Pavilion. (Open daily year-round, 10:00 A.M. to 5:00 P.M.)

Afternoon

Around the curve of the road, **In-Line Orchard,** 39400 Oak Glen Road (909–797–3415), here since 1898, features thirty varieties of apples, chestnuts, and U-pick raspberries. Look for fresh cider, honey, apple butter, mini-doughnuts, syrups, and decorator baskets. (Open daily after September 1, through November from 9:30 A.M. to 5:00 P.M.; weekend barbecues.)

At the crest of the hill, an ancient wagon overflowing with big golden pumpkins highlights **Los Rios Rancho,** 39160 Oak Glen Road (909–797–1005), the largest apple ranch in Southern California and a family-operated spread since 1906, when Howard Rivers bought his 350-acre ranch. It offers twenty-six varieties of apples in the packing shed salesroom, a cider press, and fresh cider. Gourmet gift shop features apple blossom honey, apple butter, jams, even apple noodles; exotic baskets; and gourds, squash, and minipumpkins. The popular bakery is fragrant with its fresh, three-pound, hot apple pies; applesauce cake; and sandwiches. Country barbecues and special events on weekends feature arts and crafts festivals. Additionally, there are U-pick raspberries every weekend during August and early September and U-pick apples on weekends mid-September through October. Seasonal produce.

As you continue down the loop, you're soon at Oak Glen's greatest historical landmark, the old one-room, two-story **Oak Glen School House Museum,** 11911 South Oak Glen Road (909–797–1691), built of stone in 1928. Photos of Presidents Calvin Coolidge and Herbert Hoover hang on the walls above the still-in-use wood-burning stove. The schoolhouse has been restored as a museum and offers insight into the area's past. Weekend tours during apple season. There's a picnic area, tennis, and playground. Open Saturday noon to 4:00 P.M. and Sunday 1:00 to 5:00 P.M.

Below the crest of the hill, **Wilshire's Apple Shed,** 11925 Oak Glen Road (909–797–8731), has been growing apples since Joseph Wilshire bought his land in 1876 from a Native American for $50; the grant deed to his acreage was signed by President McKinley. The apple shed has been open since the early 1950s and is still run by the Wilshire family. Apples are still sold in pretty paper bags with handles. Additionally, you'll find fresh cider, gourmet food, coffee, gift items, antique apple labels, and cookbooks. (Open daily, 9:00 A.M. to 5:00 P.M., September through December.)

Another downward curve in the road leads to **Riley's Farm & Orchard,** 12253 South Oak Glen Road (909–797–7534). Here's where thousands of people show up yearly during different seasons to pick their own apples, pears, raspberries, corn, and pumpkins. Grab a U-pick bag at the store, hop into the wagon (or walk out to the orchard), and pick fresh produce right from the tree or the raspberry patch. You can press your own cider, pet the country animals, and browse the

General Mercantile store. Tours and theme dinners available by reservation. Monday to Saturday June to late September from 9:00 A.M. to 5:00 P.M. and late September to November from 10:00 A.M. to 5:00 P.M.

DINNER: The Cider Barrel Restaurant & Bakery, 38490 Oak Glen Road. (909) 797–7910; (871) 625–4536. Award-winning highlights from the expansive menu include Maine lobster, fresh halibut steak, pizzas, and other tasty Italian specialties in addition to steak, prime rib, and chicken. Lunch and dinner; weekend champagne brunch.

LODGING: Sage Herb Farm, 39796 Pine Bench Road, Oak Glen. (909) 797–7920. This New England–style inn has five guest rooms, each with private bathroom, balcony, and antique furniture. Beautiful scenic views. Reservations a must.

Day 2 / Morning

BREAKFAST: At the Inn. Join the others for delicious cottage fries and frittatas made with fragrant fresh herbs from the farm. Have your coffee or tea with mouth-watering cranberry muffins with cheesecake filling and orange sauce, or try the seasonal apple muffins with caramel sauce.

Later, go off to the village to browse the stores and visit other ranches and orchards. Be on the lookout for old farm implements, wagons, and numerous historic relics of the early days of apple farming. Then treat yourself to a hearty country-style brunch.

BRUNCH: Apple Dumplins Restaurant & Bakery, located in the old converted equipment barn built in 1867 at Parrish Pioneer Apple Ranch. (909) 797–0037. Stained-glass apples gleam in the windows, and the original ceiling beams are visible. Country-style breakfast buffet is served until 11:00 A.M. on Saturdays, Sundays, and holiday Mondays, year-round. Help yourself at the long buffet table to apple crisp, apple muffins, fresh melons, strawberries in season, pancakes, French toast, hot and spiced apple slices and cherries, scrambled eggs with cheese, seasoned potatoes, sausage, bacon, country gravy, biscuits . . . and more. The prized apple dumplings, served daily, are cored and peeled apples stuffed with sugar and spices, baked in a pie crust, and served hot in a bowl; topped with cider-cinnamon sauce and ice cream. Open daily 9:00 A.M. to 4:00 P.M. Seniors' 10 percent discount.

Afternoon

Departing Oak Glen to visit the **Edward–Dean Museum & Gardens** (9401 Oak Glen Road, Cherry Valley; 951–845–2626) en route home, continue down Oak Glen Road toward Beaumont. Driving through the piney San Bernardino National Forest, you'll find that the air is crisp and cold, the sycamore trees are a hundred shades of gold in the pale winter light, and the panoramas of the tall mountain ranges in the near distance are constantly changing.

As you drive down the rural valley following a woodsy stream, the museum is on the right, set well back from the road in the midst of sixteen beautifully land-scaped acres, including a sculpture garden and a picnic area. In the modern eight-room museum, the stunning permanent antique collection consists primarily of nineteenth-century European and Asian decorative arts—furniture, paintings, tapestries, porcelains, important Oriental pieces, and sculpture dating from the third century B.C. to the present.

The best part, however, is that you feel you've somehow stumbled into an eighteenth-century home and are a guest, not a museum visitor, where the charm of the period is evoked by the arrangement of furnishings and art objects. The museum was built in 1957 by Edward Eberle and Dean Stout, an interior decorat-ing team, to showcase their growing personal collection of antiques. When the partners retired, they gave the museum in its entirety to Riverside County, in 1964, for an art and cultural center.

Each room is named for a distinctive feature. In the spacious Pine Room, with its splendid seventeenth-century carved pine paneling, and an impressive eighteenth-century Waterford crystal chandelier, are cabinets displaying Chinese and Tibetan bronzes, Wedgwood, Meissen, and Spode porcelains. A rare 1804 pianoforte and an unusual paperweight collection are highlights in the Blue Room. The North Gallery's changing art exhibits combine works of current artists with those of artists of the past. (Open Friday, Saturday, and Sunday from 10:00 A.M. to 5:00 P.M.; closed legal holidays.) Group tours may be arranged. Admission.

From here follow Beaumont Avenue to I–10 west to Los Angeles.

There's More

Wood Acres, 38003 Potato Canyon Road. (909) 797–8500. A unique small family orchard specializing in gourmet dessert and antique apples. Visit Stone's Throw Gift Shop above the apple shed for antique furniture, pottery, and flower and garden accessories. Open Tuesday through Sunday after September 1 through apple season; open Friday through Sunday in the off-season.

Yucaipa Regional Park, 339 Oak Glen Road, Yucaipa. (909) 790–3127. At the gateway to Oak Glen, this lovely park offers a variety of recreational activities. In a scenic setting surrounded by the nearby San Bernardino and San Gorgonio moun-tain ranges, the park features a unique one-acre swim lagoon with two 350-foot water slides, white sandy beaches, two lakes stocked seasonally for year-round fish-ing, shady picnic grounds, snack bars, pedalboat rental, overnight campgrounds, equestrian trails, and summer concerts under the stars. Admission.

Special Events

NOTE: Call for admission fees and specific dates.

February. Valentine gifts and goodies.

Early March. Apple trees begin to bloom.

Last weekend in April. Annual Oak Glen Apple Blossom Festival throughout the glen. Activities at Law's Cider Mill and Ranch. Apple Blossom Festival arts and crafts at Los Rios Rancho. Annual Apple Pancake Breakfast, crowning of Apple Blossom Queen at Oak Tree Village. (951–845–9641).

End of May. Memorial Day Arts & Crafts Fairs.

Memorial Day to end of June. Cherry picking and buying. For information and orchard locations, call Cherry Grower's Association, (951) 845–3628.

Early June. Annual Gem and Mineral Show, Yucaipa Community Center, 1st Street and Avenue B. Two days.

Mid-June. Annual Corn Feed, Saturday and Sunday at Parrish Pioneer Apple Ranch. Annual Cherry Festival, since 1978, to celebrate cherry harvest: carnival rides, live music, parade, food and game booths. Admission. Call Beaumont Chamber of Commerce (951–845–9541) or Cherry Valley Chamber of Commerce (951–845–8466), or write to Beaumont–Cherry Valley Cherry Festival Association, P.O. Box 126, Beaumont, 92223.

Early August through September. Oak Glen Raspberry/Blackberry Festival. (909) 797–1005. Raspberry U-Pick on weekends begins at four ranches.

Mid-August. Oak Glen Annual Western Days. Country music, stunt shows, western-style BBQ at Apple Dumplins Restaurant, Parrish Pioneer Apple Ranch. (909) 797–1005.

Labor Day weekend (start of the apple season) through late December. Arts & Crafts Show, Los Rios Ranchos. Annual Arts & Crafts Fair—pony rides, clowns, and live entertainment at Oak Tree Village.

Beginning of September. Annual Oak Glen Fall Harvest Festival begins. (909) 797–6833. Hog Heaven Hoedown, Riley's Farm & Orchard.

Mid-September. U-pick apples at Los Rios.

End of September. Art in the Glen, Yucaipa Art Association, at Oak Tree Village.

Early October. Mountain Music Festival, Saturday and Sunday. Folk singers, children's concerts at Peacock Pavilion, Oak Tree Village. (909) 797–4020. Wagonloads of pumpkins at Los Rios.

Early November. Yucaipa Art Association Show, Oak Tree Village.

Mid-November. Blue-Gray (civil war) Cotillion, Riley's Farm & Orchard. Antebellum attire; reservations required.

End of November. Annual Lighting of the Glen Thanksgiving Weekend, Parrish Pioneer Apple Ranch. Carolers sing, Santa Claus visits; complimentary hot cider.

Early December. Breakfast with Santa, Puppet Show, Parrish Pioneer Apple Ranch. Two days, by reservation only. (909) 797–1753.

Mid-December. Old St. Nick Christmas caroling, Riley's Farm & Orchard. Cherry Valley/Beaumont. (909) 797–7534.

Other Recommended Restaurants and Lodgings

Apple Annie's Restaurant, in Oak Tree Village. (909) 797–7371. Known for their original five-pound "Mile-High Apple Pie," this restaurant serves it up home-style. Popular menu items include chicken-fried steak and meatloaf. Their helpings are huge and dinner is served family-style. Their motto is "If you're hungry, seconds are on us!" Full-service bakery on premises. Open daily 8:00 A.M. to 8:00 P.M.

Creekside Kitchen, 38493 Oak Glen Road. (909) 790–4559. Good soups, handsome sandwiches, and first-rate fresh-baked apple pie, pastries, and breads. Breakfast and lunch. Hours and days vary.

The Oak Glen Resort, 38955 Oak Glen Road. (909) 790–1801. Private membership campground and RV park; all recreational vehicles, including tents. Also, a general store. The Oak Tree Tavern/Restaurant (closed Wednesday and Thursday) serves breakfast, lunch, and dinner; open to the public. Reservations required. Free camping.

Best Western El Rancho Motel, 480 East 5th Street, Beaumont. (951) 845–2170. AAA and AARP; fifty-two units, with four two-bedroom units, shower or combination baths; air-conditioned; refrigerator, microwave, coffeemaker; heated swimming pool; large-screen TV; restaurant and bar; complimentary continental breakfast. Ask about bringing pets.

Best Value Inn, 625 East 5th Street, Beaumont. (951) 845–2185. Twenty-four guest rooms, including two-bedroom units; air-conditioned; HBO and ESPN. Small pool, whirlpool; pets. Seniors' discounts.

For More Information

Oak Glen Information. (909) 797–6833. Year-round events; www.oakglen.net.

Oak Glen Apple Growers Association. (909) 797–1005.

Yucaipa Valley Chamber of Commerce, 33733 Yucaipa Boulevard, P.O. Box 45, Yucaipa, CA 92399. (909) 790–1841.

Beaumont Chamber of Commerce, 450 East 4th Street, Beaumont, CA 92223. (951) 845–9541.

Cherry Valley Chamber of Commerce, 10700 Jonathan Avenue, Cherry Valley, CA 92223. (951) 845–8466.

Cherry Growers Association, 10700 Jonathan Avenue, Cherry Valley, CA 92223. (909) 845–3628.

Desert Retreat

Palm Springs, Coachella Valley / 2 Nights

- ☐ Golf, tennis, swimming, and sunbathing
- ☐ World-class resorts
- ☐ Fine dining
- ☐ Shopping
- ☐ Botanical garden
- ☐ Desert wildlife center
- ☐ Indian Canyons
- ☐ Aerial tramway
- ☐ Water park
- ☐ Horseback riding
- ☐ Casinos

Palm Springs's dry desert climate and radiant sunshine have lured sun-worshipers since the 1930s, when it was a small-town winter haven for movie stars. Its natural splendor, glamour, deluxe resorts, and lush golf courses enhance its reputation as a posh playground and home for presidents and celebrities, who frequent local shops and restaurants and have city streets named for them. But you don't have to be Elizabeth Taylor or a VIP to enjoy the seductive sunshine in this cactus paradise. There are accommodations and restaurants for all budgets.

The desert area is one of Southern California's most popular weekend getaways, boasting winters of more sunny days and less rainfall than other regions. Summer temperatures soar to one hundred degrees or higher, but the evenings are always cool. Drastically reduced hotel rates are irresistible, and the season is getting longer.

The Palm Springs season begins October 1 and runs through the end of May. The busy "high season" is from mid-January through mid-April.

Favorite good-life pursuits are swimming and lounging around the pool in the lazy sun, as well as swinging a golf club or tennis racquet. You'll also visit Indian Canyons, tour wildlife and garden centers, bike along sun-washed streets, shop in indoor air-conditioned malls, and enjoy people-watching from sidewalk cafes.

This three-day desert jaunt explores the mystique and romance of Palm Springs and the neighboring desert communities of the widespread Coachella Valley, where snowcapped lavender mountains frame groves of towering date palms and emerald golf fairways.

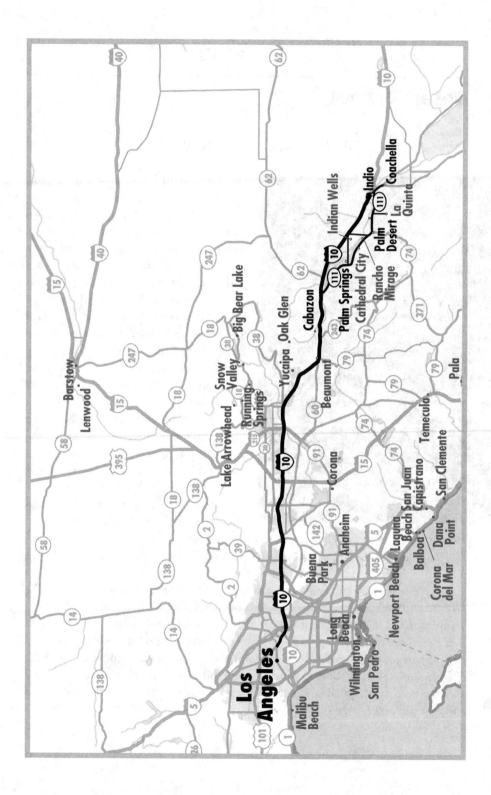

Day 1 / Morning

For the one-and-a-half-hour, 110-mile trip to the desert, head east from Los Angeles on San Bernardino Freeway I–10.

The tall, majestic gray mountains are topped with snow. After Beaumont, roadside billboards advertise **Desert Hills Factory Stores,** 48–850 Seminole Road (909–849–6641), in Cabazon. If you're a dedicated discount shopper, go ahead and take the Cabazon Main Street exit, turning left past Hadley Fruit Orchards. The sprawling outlet center showcases more than one hundred leading names in fashion and home furnishings, with prices reputed to be 30 to 60 percent below retail. The stores are open daily; Sundays are quite crowded. (Make a note to return to Hadley Fruit Orchards en route back to Los Angeles, to check out its large variety of dried fruits, nuts, and other edibles.)

Return to I–10, heading toward Palm Springs by turning left at the small road sign and left again on I–10 east. You soon feel close enough to the tall mountain ranges to almost touch them. The windy San Gorgonio Pass at the junction of Highway 111 and I–10 is the site of one of California's three large **wind farms,** where 4,500 wind turbines resembling silvery windmills spinning in the sun generate enough electricity for some 93,000 homes.

At the junction follow 111 into **Palm Springs,** curving around the tall mountain. Just past the city limits, **Palm Springs Aerial Tramway**'s cable cars, with two newer revolving tram cars, whisk you up 8,516 feet to the cool wilderness of Mount San Jacinto State Park in a fifteen-minute ride. In the brisk mountain air, you'll have breathtaking views and opportunities for hiking, cross-country skiing, and a picnic. A cocktail lounge, restaurant, and gift shop are here, too. The cars run year-round every half hour (760–325–1391; fare).

At **Palm Springs Visitors Information Center,** 2781 North Palm Canyon Drive (Highway 111) (800–347–7746), you can pick up maps and brochures, make hotel reservations in the city of Palm Springs, and purchase souvenirs. On North Palm Canyon Drive, lined with palm trees, **Loehmann's Plaza** houses the popular discount clothing store and other specialty discount stores.

LUNCH: Grill-A-Burger. 166 North Palm Canyon Drive, Palm Springs. (760) 327–8175. Sip a milkshake under a thatched umbrella and feast on one of more than nineteen gourmet hamburgers. Homemade onion rings and fries, along with a vegetarian selection and full bar, complete the menu in this tropical setting. Open Tuesday through Saturday 11:00 A.M. to 9:00 P.M., Sunday 11:00 A.M. to 4:00 P.M. Closed Monday.

Afternoon

Palm Canyon Drive is inviting to stroll, with its many shops, cafes, and galleries. There's ample parking space, and you won't find parking meters. The city still retains its village atmosphere, even though it is quite busy Saturday nights and usually crowded with college students during the Easter spring break, when adjacent desert cities are quiet. Palm trees are illuminated at night, and midweek canyon strolls are highlighted by festive street fairs and sidewalk parties. **VillageFest,** held every Thursday from 6:00 to 10:00 P.M. along Palm Canyon Drive, with streets closed to traffic, is a lively combination of old-fashioned street fair and block party. It features music, a farmers' market, sidewalk vendors, and fun.

For quick insights into the city's history, stop at the **Village Green Heritage Center,** 219–223 South Palm Canyon Drive (760–323–8297), where several small museums share a garden setting and fountain. Miss Cornelia White's House, built in 1894 and made entirely of railroad ties, displays paintings, bibles, photos of memorabilia, and the town's first telephone, complete with hand crank.

The McCallum Adobe, the town's oldest building (1885) and the family home of Judge John McCallum, the city's founder, contains photographs and the collections of the Palm Springs Historical Society. Both historical sites are open Wednesday and Sunday from noon to 3:00 P.M. and Thursday, Friday, and Saturday from 10:00 A.M. to 4:00 P.M. (Nominal admission.) Closed the end of May through October 15. Ruddy's General Store Museum, a re-creation of an old-fashioned general store of the 1930s and 1940s, displays hundreds of authentic items of that bygone era. Open October through May from Wednesday through Sunday, 10:00 A.M. to 4:00 P.M.; weekends only from July through September. (Nominal admission.)

Next door, the Agua Caliente Cultural Museum Information Center displays historical artifacts and photos of Cahuilla Indians, the city's first settlers. Open Labor Day to Memorial Day, from 10:00 A.M. to 4:00 P.M. Wednesday through Saturday and noon to 4:00 P.M. Sunday; Memorial Day to Labor Day, from 10:00 A.M. to 4:00 P.M. Friday and Saturday and noon to 4:00 P.M. Sunday. (Free.)

The stunning **Palm Springs Desert Museum,** 101 Museum Drive (760–325–7186), with its sunken sculpture garden and Annenberg Theater, presents changing exhibitions, along with its permanent collection of Western and contemporary California art. (Open 10:00 A.M. to 5:00 P.M. year-round; closed Monday and major holidays. Admission.)

To visit **Moorten Botanical Garden,** 1701 South Palm Canyon Drive (760–327–6555), follow South Palm Canyon Drive about 2.5 blocks past Lyon's Restaurant; it's on the right-hand side of the road. Wander through more than two private acres of 3,000 varieties of desert plants, including giant cacti, and birds. All plants are labeled; the dirt paths are cool and shady under the tall plants. Pick up a map showing different trails and plant locations. The old red-roofed adobe house with the sunny green lawn is the owner's residence. (Open Monday through Saturday from 9:00 A.M. to 4:30 P.M. and Sunday from 10:00 A.M. to 4:00 P.M. Closed Wednesday. Admission.)

Afterward check in at your hotel (see "Lodging"). Since this is Palm Springs, you'll probably want to enjoy some swimming and sunbathing before going to dinner.

DINNER: **Copley's on Palm Canyon,** 621 North Palm Canyon Drive, Palm Springs. (760) 327–9555. Palm Springs's newest hot spot features lobster potpie, pork chops, Caesar salad with pineapple croutons, and an excellent fish selection. New York steak with lobster mashed potatoes is also popular. Chef-owned and operated. For this hacienda-style eatery, dress elegantly causal. Open daily 5:30 P.M. to 10:00 P.M. Sunday brunch.

LODGING: **L'Horizon,** 1050 East Palm Canyon Drive, Palm Springs. (800) 377–7855; (760) 323–1858. Quiet luxury in a handsomely decorated hotel. Twenty-two rooms/suites, plus Jacuzzi suite, with TV and other amenities, situated around a large swimming pool on two beautifully landscaped, grassy acres of orange trees and flowers, all framed by Mount San Jacinto. You can't beat the location or the warm hospitality, which includes complimentary continental breakfast, plus daily *Los Angeles Times* and complimentary badminton, use of bicycles, and library. Closed from June 1 until October 1.

Day 2 / Morning

BREAKFAST: At L'Horizon. Relax over a beautifully served continental breakfast (included in your room rate) of fresh fruit juice; bagels and cream cheese; a Thermos of coffee, tea, or hot chocolate; plus fresh pastry, brought to your room or served in the private poolside patio in the desert's bright morning sun.

To see the unusual **Knott's Soak City, U.S.A.,** 1500 Gene Autry Trail (760–327–0499), drive east on East Palm Canyon Drive to Gene Autry Trail, then turn left for about 1 mile, until you see the tall slide. The sixteen-acre family water playground features water slides, inner-tube rides, food, private cabanas, and a health club. (Open daily at 10:00 A.M. from mid-March through Labor Day; weekends through October. Admission; parking fee.)

Follow South Palm Canyon Drive to its end for a visit to the magnificent **Indian Canyons,** settled centuries ago by ancestors of the native Agua Caliente Indians, the city's largest landowners. Palm Canyon, the most accessible, is remarkably beautiful, with its thousands of native *Washingtonia filifera* fan palm trees. A fifteen-minute scenic drive through the quiet foothills leads you up to a small Trading Post, crowded on Sunday; it sells jewelry, T-shirts, artifacts, and Native American souvenirs. Follow the pathway down to the canyon floor and a dramatic, 15-mile-long rocky gorge of waterfalls and mountain streams alongside a towering grove of palm trees said to be more than 1,500 years old. (Open daily year-round; admission.)

LUNCH: **Cedar Creek Inn,** 1555 South Palm Canyon Drive, Palm Springs. (760) 325–7300. Lots of greenery and airy French country decor. It's noted for innovative specialties of seafood and pasta as well as handsome sandwiches. Bread is made on the premises, and desserts are dazzling.

After lunch, why not return to your hotel for a refreshing, leisurely swim and a bit of relaxation in the warm sunshine?

Afternoon

Neighboring desert resort communities cut a distinctive swath, 40 miles long and 20 miles wide, east and south across the Coachella Valley. To get to the **Living Desert,** 47900 Portola Avenue, Palm Desert (760–346–5694; www.livingdesert.org), drive east on Highway 111 through Rancho Mirage, where Eisenhower played golf, Gerald Ford tees off, and you can stand on the corner of Bob Hope Drive and Frank Sinatra Drive—really something to tell the folks back home about.

Turn right from Highway 111 at Portola Avenue and continue for about 1.5 miles to the 1,200-acre wildlife center and botanical park, featuring rare and endangered desert animals and African wildlife. Maps guide you to the exotic horned Arabian oryx, slender gazelles, bighorn sheep clambering the hillsides, leopards, cheetahs, and other animals as well as to the aviary, picnic areas, hiking trails, and Village Watutu. During November and December, the Living Desert hosts a spectacular Wild Lights presentation. Bring the whole family to view giraffes, pandas, and all the zoo animals in lighted perfection. Drinking hot chocolate and making s'mores around a campfire lend a special touch. If you're lucky, you'll meet docents displaying live animals and birds. The Tortoise Shelf bookstore/gift shop sells cool, refreshing ice cream. (Open daily 9:00 A.M. to 5:00 P.M. year-round except Christmas Day. Admission.)

Take Portola Avenue back to Highway 111 to explore **Palm Desert,** another celebrity haunt of designer golf courses, deluxe resorts, and El Paseo Drive, a fashionable stretch of carriage trade shops, galleries, and cafes with inviting patio dining. Shopper Hopper shuttle provides free service to the major shopping area of Palm Desert (760–343–3456).

The **Coachella Valley**'s palm groves have flourished since the 1800s. Considered the "Date Capital of the World," the area produces about 99 percent of America's dates, harvested from 250,000 date-producing palms that thrive in the brilliant desert sun, intense heat, and natural underground water supply.

Continue easterly where, at Indian Wells city limits, a dramatic grove of tall date palms looms on the right side of the highway beneath the massive mountain range. Another grove is farther along. At harvesttime you can watch the agile date pickers high up in the trees. Across the highway, the deluxe high-rise Hyatt Grand Champions Hotel and Renaissance Esmeralda Resort share two well-manicured golf courses.

Among the many date ranches open to the public, **Shield's Date Gardens** roadside store, at 80–255 Highway 111, Indio (760–347–0996), has been growing, packing, shipping, and selling many varieties of dates since 1924. Here you can also purchase local grapefruit and oranges; enjoy the house drink specialty, a refreshing date milk shake; and watch a movie, *The Romance and Sex Life of the Date*. Shield's is open daily, except on Christmas.

To get to the **Fantasy Springs Casino,** 84–245 Indio Springs Parkway (800–827–2946; 760–342–5000), on Native American reservation land (about 30 miles southeast of Palm Springs), continue toward Indio on Highway 111 to Golf Center Parkway; turn left, drive over the bridge to I–10, and then turn right at the sign for the casino. The vast, twenty-four-hour casino is crowded with casually dressed patrons and features slot machines, off-track satellite horse wagering, bingo, poker, blackjack, two restaurants, and a bar.

To return to Palm Springs, go back to the first stop sign and turn left onto I–10; go past another stop sign, then turn right at the first traffic signal on Highway 111 Palm Springs. You're soon back at your hotel in time for some exhilarating swimming and relaxing before going out to dinner.

DINNER: Le Vallauris, 385 West Tahquitz Canyon Way, Palm Springs. (760) 325–5059. Better wear your Guccis to this fine French restaurant, with its romantic courtyard and flower-filled dining room. Besides pasta, fish, lamb, and seafood, menu specialties include lobster ravioli with truffle sauce and grilled breast of duck with potato pancake. (It's also a great place to see celebrities.)

LODGING: L'Horizon.

Day 3 / Morning

BREAKFAST: At your hotel. After breakfast there's time for more swimming and sunning on your last morning in the desert.

LUNCH: Las Casuelas Terrazza, 222 South Palm Canyon Drive, Palm Springs. (760) 325–2794. Enjoy your last lunch in Palm Springs at everybody's favorite spot for tasty Mexican cuisine and people-watching.

Afternoon

Try not to leave town too late in the day, particularly on Sunday, when traffic heading out of the city gets very heavy.

To return to Los Angeles, drive north on Indian Canyon Drive, following it around to North Palm Canyon Drive and the wind turbines as it becomes divided Highway 111, then I–10 west. On the way home you can stop and shop at **Hadley Fruit Orchards** (909–849–5255), about 20 miles from Palm Springs in Cabazon. Take the Apache Trail exit and park in front. Besides a wine-tasting salesroom, Hadley offers a wide selection of California dates, dried fruits, nuts, and bakery items, plus a small snack area; it's open daily from 7:00 A.M. to 9:00 P.M. To get back on I–10 west to Los Angeles, drive down the frontage road past the discount factory stores, turn left at the second stop sign, and turn right on I–10 west. Stay on it all the way to Los Angeles.

There's More

Casinos. There are several casinos in Palm Springs and the Coachella Valley, all open twenty-four hours. Here are some highlights:

Spa Resort Casino, 401 Amado Road, Palm Springs. (760) 883–1000.

Agua Caliente Casino, 32250 Bob Hope Drive, Rancho Mirage. (760) 321–2000.

Augustine Casino, 84–001 Avenue 54, Coachella. (760) 391–9500.

Casino Morongo, 49750 Seminole Drive, Cabazon. (909) 849–3080.

Trump 29, 46–200 Harrison Place, Coachella. (760) 775–5566.

Golf is the leading desert sport, with more than eighty courses to play. Deluxe resorts feature their own; other hotels can generally provide tee times for their guests at nearby private links. These golf courses are open to the public:

Mesquite Golf and Country Club, 2700 East Mesquite Avenue. (760) 323–9377. Eighteen holes.

Tommy Jacobs' Bel Air Greens, 1001 South El Cielo Road. (760) 322–6062. Nine-hole executive course, night driving range.

Tahquitz Creek Golf Resort, 1885 Golf Club Drive. (800) 743–2211; (760) 328–1005. Two 18-hole championship golf courses, with great views of Mount San Jacinto.

Horseback riding. Smoke Tree Stables, 2500 Toledo Avenue, Palm Springs. (760) 327–1372. Daily rides 8:00 A.M. to 5:00 P.M. following desert trails in mountains and Indian Canyons. Guides and group rides available.

Tours. Desert Adventures Jeep Tours (888–440–5337) takes you for guided, narrated sunrise and sunset tours of the Coachella Valley, including Indian Canyons.

Elvis Presley's Palm Springs Estate, Celebrity Tours, 845 West Chino Canyon. (888) PS–ELVIS. Tours start every half hour, 10:00 A.M. to 4:30 P.M. Tuesday through Saturday.

Celebrity Tours of Palm Springs (760–770–2700) offers guided one- and two-hour sightseeing tours to movie stars' homes, country clubs, date farms, and other attractions.

Covered Wagon Tours (P.O. Box 1106, La Quinta, CA 92253; 800–367–2161; 760–347–2161; www.coveredwagontours.com) requires reservations for its two-hour narrated tour through the Coachella Valley Preserve aboard authentic, mule-drawn covered wagons. Tour only or with chuckwagon dinner and sing-along dinner. Fee.

Offbeat shopping. In Cathedral City try Trader's Discount Place, 62–555 East Palm

Canyon Drive (760–328–4585). For one-stop bargain shoppers, this indoor swap meet has thirty-five specialty stores featuring jewelry, shoes, gift items, golf clubs, and other merchandise at reportedly good prices and values. Open Tuesday through Sunday from 10:00 A.M. to 5:00 P.M.

In Palm Springs, North Palm Canyon Drive has become home to almost a dozen antiques and art boutiques, vintage clothing shops, and furniture stores. Among them are Patsy's Clothes Closet (4121 East Palm Canyon Drive; 760–324–3825), featuring a good collection of Chanel and other designer suits, celebrity discards, and barely worn clothes from Escada and Donna Karan, and the Village Attic (849 North Palm Canyon Drive; 760–320–6165), where you can browse through 1950s furniture, lamps, tuxedo chairs, and other items.

Hot-air ballooning. Fantasy Ballooning Flights (800–GO–ABOVE) has sunrise or sunset champagne adventures. Groups, senior, and family discounts.

Palm Springs Air Museum, 745 North Gene Autry Trail, Palm Springs. (760) 778–6262. Showcases one of the world's largest collections of World War II prop-driven airplanes—bombers and fighters in flying condition—in two 20,000-square-foot hangars. Sixty-seat Buddy Rogers Theatre of the Air, memorabilia, gift shop. Special events. Open daily year-round from 10:00 A.M. to 5:00 P.M. except Thanksgiving Day and Christmas. Admission.

Special Events

Twenty-four-hour Events Line: (760) 770–1992. Reservations information.

January. Palm Springs International Film Festival. (800) 898–7256. Annual Bob Hope Chrysler Golf Classic. (760) 346–8184.

Early February. Annual Frank Sinatra Celebrity Invitational Golf Tournament, Palm Desert. Fashion show and luncheon as well. (800) PSSTARZ.

Mid-February. Annual National Date Festival, Indio. Ten days. Agricultural exhibits, and Riverside County Fair, junior fair, nightly Arabian Nights Pageant, camel and ostrich rides, exhibits. (800) 811–3247; (760) 893–8247.

Early March. Pacific Life Open at Indian Wells Tennis Gardens, Indian Wells.

Mid-March. La Quinta Annual Arts Festival. Juried show features fine art of 200 artists. Food, entertainment, children's activities. (760) 564–1244.

End of March. Annual Nabisco Championship LPGA Tour. Celebrity Pro-Am Competition, Mission Hills Country Club, Rancho Mirage. (760) 324–4546.

April. Coachella Valley Music & Arts Festival. (323) 930–7100. Desert Swing & Dixie Jazz Festival, Palm Springs. (760) 333–7932.

June. Annual Film Noir Festival, Palm Springs. (760) 864–9760.

July 4. Independence Day fireworks displays throughout the desert resorts. Call the cities for times and locations.

September 10. Annual Palm Springs International Festival of Short Films. (760) 322–2930.

October. American Heat Palm Springs Motorcycle Weekend. (800) 200–4557.

November. Living Desert Wild Lights. (760) 346–5694.

Mid-November. The Skins Game La Quinta Annual PGA match play event at Landmark Golf Club, Indio.

Early December. Festival of Lights Parade along Palm Canyon Drive. Annual Christmas Tree Lighting Ceremony, at the top of the Palm Springs Aerial Tramway. Celebrity guest and entertainment, 6:00 P.M.

Other Recommended Restaurants and Lodgings

Palm Springs

Blue Coyote Grill, 445 North Palm Canyon Drive. (760) 327–1196. A congenial, upscale downtown spot voted number one for good Southwestern and gourmet Mexican cuisines, with sizzling fajitas and mariachi Mexican entertainment.

Elmer's Pancake & Steak House Inc., 1030 East Palm Canyon Drive. (760) 327–8419. Friendly, bustling place, with prompt service, for pancakes, sandwiches, steaks, salads, and burgers. Crowded Sunday morning.

Hyatt Regency Suites Palm Springs, 285 North Palm Canyon Drive. (800) 233–1234; (760) 322–9000. Luxury hotel in the heart of downtown, with 193 one- and two-bedroom suites; swimming pool, Jacuzzi; two restaurants, lounge; golf and tennis arranged at country club.

The Willows Historic Palm Springs Inn, 412 West Tahquitz Canyon Way. (760) 320–0771. A Mediterranean-style villa built in 1927, this inn has been handsomely restored as a small luxury hotel evoking the ambience of old Palm Springs. This AAA four-diamond bed-and-breakfast has eight distinctive guest rooms with antique furnishings, private baths, cable TV, terry robes, some fireplaces, and private garden patios; swimming pool, Jacuzzi, and a dramatic two-story mountain water-fall. Guests enjoy complimentary daily three-course gourmet breakfast and late-afternoon wine tasting and hors d'oeuvres around the fireplace. Two-night minimum stay weekends and holidays.

Palm Desert

Marriott's Desert Springs Resort & Spa, 74855 Country Club Drive. (800) 331–3112; (760) 341–2211. The area's largest resort, with 884 deluxe rooms on 400 acres of lush grounds and lakes. Spectacular lobby waterfall; lagoon with gondolas. Two 18-hole golf courses, 18-hole putting course, twenty tennis courts, five swimming pools, health spa; nightclub, five restaurants.

Rancho Mirage

Westin Mission Hills Resort, Dinah Shore Drive. (800) WESTIN–1; (760) 328–5955. Has 512 deluxe rooms amid 360 acres; two 18-hole golf courses, seven lighted tennis courts; three swimming pools, whirlpools; fitness center; two restaurants, three lounges, spa, pool bar; Cactus Kid's Club; conference center.

Bangkok Five/Cuisine of Thailand, 70026 Highway 111. (760) 770–9508. Along the city's noted Restaurant Row in the Atrium Design Center. Smart-looking, chic dinner favorite for delectable Thai dishes such as *Tom Kha Kai* (spicy chicken coconut soup with lemongrass), *Thai Satai* (tender chicken, beef, or pork on skewers with curry peanut sauce), and other flavorful specialties.

The Lodge at Rancho Mirage, 68–900 Frank Sinatra Drive. (800) 223–7637; (760) 321–8282. High above the city, tucked in twenty-four quiet acres. Mobil four-star, AAA-diamond-rated elegant resort features 240 guest rooms and suites. Guest room amenities include honor bar, minirefrigerator, TV, clock radio, marble bathroom, hair dryer, small private balcony, daily newspaper. Concierge service; two restaurants, lobby lounge and bar; huge swimming pool, whirlpool and spa; fitness center, ten lighted tennis courts; access to nearby golf courses. Seasonal rates. Overnight valet parking fee or free self-parking.

Indian Wells

Hyatt Grand Champions Resort, 44–600 Indian Wells Lane. (800) 233–1234; (760) 341–1000. AAA four-diamond, Mobil four-star award winner, featuring 480 deluxe guest rooms and suites on thirty-four acres; two championship eighteen-hole golf courses, twelve tennis courts and stadium, seven swimming pools, spa, health/fitness center; three restaurants; and gift shop.

Miramonte Resort, 76–477 Highway 111. (800) 237–2926; (760) 341–2200. Tuscan-inspired resort amid eleven acres of olive groves, citrus trees, and date palms is a member of exclusive Preferred Hotels and Resorts Worldwide—the only member in the region. The 215 guest rooms include 98 luxury rooms with private terrace and marble-appointed bathroom, and eighteen junior suites with plush robes, hair dryer, refrigerator, honor bar, cable TV, coffeemaker, clock radio, in-room safe, concierge service. Restaurant, lobby lounge; boutiques; two swimming pools, sauna, Jacuzzi; spa; and fitness center. Golf concierge arranges tee times at nearby courses.

La Quinta

La Quinta Resort and Club, 49–499 Eisenhower Drive. (800) 854–1271; (760) 564–4111. The Coachella Valley's oldest hotel has been a favorite retreat for celebrities and stars since it opened in 1926. Its 900 guest rooms and suites are situated in Spanish-style casitas rambling along forty-five acres of flowers and towering palm trees. Accommodations include private patio, minirefrigerator and/or icemaker, large bathroom, TV, and other amenities. The resort has five restaurants, two lounges, forty-one swimming pools, fifty-two hot spas, eight championship golf courses, twenty tennis courts, two pro shops, fitness center, meeting facilities, pleasant shopping arcade. Seasonal rates; golf and tennis packages.

For More Information

Palm Springs Visitor Information Center, 2901 North Palm Canyon Drive (Highway 111), Palm Springs, CA 92262. (800) 347–7746; www.palm-springs.org. Provides maps, brochures, visitor guides, hotel reservations. Gay guide to Palm Springs available. Open daily.

Palm Springs Desert Resorts Convention & Visitors Bureau, The Atrium Design Center, 69–930 Highway 111, Suite 201, Rancho Mirage, CA 92270. (800) 967–3767; (760) 770–9000.

The Palm Springs Desert Resorts Visitors Center, located in the IMAX Theatre, 68–510 East Palm Canyon Drive, Cathedral City, CA. (760) 770–2882. Stop by to browse and/or purchase books, keepsakes, Frank Sinatra memorabilia, and more. Plus, here's where to pick up firsthand information about restaurants, shopping, and sightseeing. Open 10:00 A.M. to 8:00 P.M. daily.

EASTERN ESCAPE FOUR

Gambling and Glitter

Las Vegas / 2 Nights

- ☐ Gambling casinos
- ☐ Resort hotels
- ☐ Musical shows
- ☐ Shopping
- ☐ Golf and tennis
- ☐ Antique car collection
- ☐ Factory-outlet stores

This jaunt takes you 300 miles northeast of Los Angeles to the internationally famous "Gambling Capital of the World," the "City That Never Sleeps." This twenty-four-hour party town is neon-lighted, glitzy, crowded, and noisy, with fast-paced casinos offering plenty of action, mega-resorts vying for fantasy themes, showgirls in lavish musical productions, inexpensive food buffets, gourmet restaurants, trendy cafes, and magicians who make little white birds appear from red silk scarves. While in recent years Las Vegas attempted to make itself over as a family destination, it's now returning to its sexy, risqué roots with the type of attractions that originally made "Sin City" so popular. Bugsy Siegel, the playboy mobster who built the Flamingo Hotel in 1946 as a 105-room "carpet joint" where all employees wore tuxedos, said, "Come as you are—enjoy yourself!"

Day 1 / Morning

From Los Angeles take San Bernardino Freeway 10 east past Ontario/Upland to I–15 north to Las Vegas via Barstow. Look for I–15 about a half hour from downtown Los Angeles; at the I–15 TWO MILES sign, stay to the right for Barstow–Las Vegas/215 north, follow the curve, and you're on I–15 north toward the smoky lavender mountain range. The freeway curves to the left for Barstow and climbs as you enter San Bernardino National Forest. The road travels through curving, barren landscape and lots of boulders, and it climbs again as you reach Cajon Summit, an elevation of 4,900 feet.

Just south of Barstow, the midway point between Los Angeles and Las Vegas, take the Lenwood exit for lunch; gas, if you need it; and **discount shopping.** Factory Merchants Outlet Plaza (2837 Lenwood Road, Barstow; 760–253–7342), in a large cluster of white buildings, houses fifty manufacturer-owned outlet stores that claim savings from 20 to 70 percent off retail prices and include such well-known names as Bugle Boy, Evan Picone/Gant, Toys Unlimited, Bass Shoes,

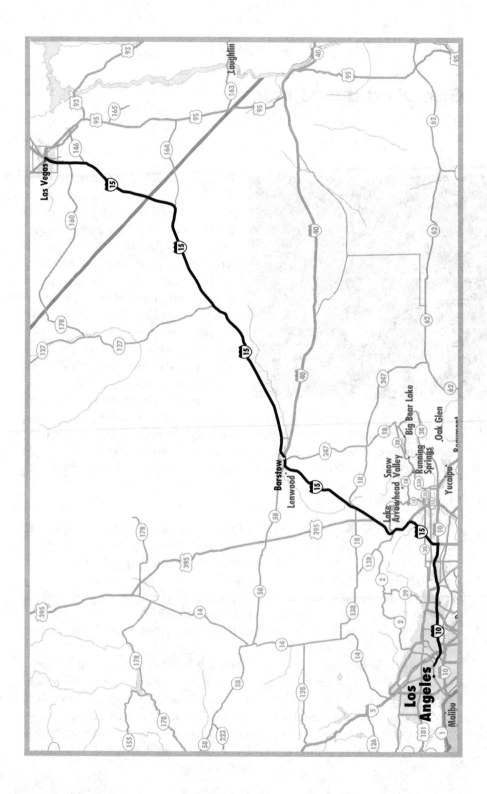

Johnston & Murphy, Levi's, Lenox, and Adolfo II. Turn left on Mercantile Avenue into the parking lot. Stores are set among grassy courtyards, redbrick paths with planters, and covered walkways in an attractive complex. (Open daily from 9:00 A.M. to 8:00 P.M.; closed Thanksgiving and Christmas.)

LUNCH: In-N-Out Burger, 1561 Lenwood Road, Barstow. (800) 786–1000. Large, busy fast-food eatery with long lines that move quickly for hamburgers, fries, coffee, or soft drinks. With many pleasant young people in the kitchen and behind the counter, service is pretty fast.

Afternoon

Many drivers prefer to fill their gas tanks here at the halfway point, even though gas is more expensive than in Los Angeles or Las Vegas, as 150 miles of long, deserted road lie ahead. After lunch return to I–15 north; it curves left for Las Vegas, and you drive through magnificent scenery, enjoying the grandeur and peace of the desert, which is ringed with mauve mountains and filled with perky Joshua trees amid the scrub. You climb to 4,000 feet again at Halloran Summit Road for quite a distance. When you cross the Nevada state line, where gambling is legal, the first thing you see is Whiskey Pete's Casino, along with other gambling halls.

The Las Vegas city high-rise skyline is visible beyond the mountains as you arrive, after a five-hour drive. Take exit 34 to the Las Vegas Strip, beneath low-flying planes from nearby Las Vegas McCarran International Airport. Drive down Las Vegas Boulevard, also known as the Strip, past many hotels with familiar names: Excalibur Hotel, a white castle with moat and drawbridge, 4,000 rooms, different colored towers, and a medieval Disneyland look; the Tropicana Resort, with lush landscaping, waterfalls, and massive Easter Island–type sculptures; a familiar New York City skyline at New York–New York; the Eiffel Tower at Paris; and majestic Caesars Palace.

Las Vegas hotels are different from others because you enter through areas of labyrinthine, bustling casinos filled with people playing slot machines, blackjack, roulette, craps, poker, keno, bingo, pan, and sports book wagering. You may find it difficult to have a drink at the bars, since those counters too are covered with video poker machines. Bars are open twenty-four hours. Though hotels have their special features and glamorous window dressings, the casinos are the focal point. Better bring a sweater along, as many of the casinos have their air-conditioning set to nearly freezing.

The tables at different casinos have different betting minimums. Slots are from 5 cents to $5.00 to a special $100 and $500 slot machine. All over the casinos you hear the steady sounds of slots whirring and beeping and the winning clatter of coins dropping, murmurs of dealers, conversation, people walking, talking, cocktail waitresses offering drinks to players—there's constant movement, noise, color, and people. Day and night run together. It's a great place for insomniacs; there are no clocks in the casinos and hardly any water fountains.

DINNER: Jimmy Buffett's Margaritaville, Flamingo Las Vegas. (702) 733–3302. This three-story restaurant is one of the largest in Las Vegas. Enjoy burgers, ribs, salads, pastas, and appetizers in this lively tropical paradise with palm trees. Great atmosphere, and dancing with live music nightly from 10:00 P.M.

LODGING: The Venetian Resort-Hotel-Casino, 3355 Las Vegas Boulevard South. (888) 283–6423; (702) 414–1000. The themed, luxe, thirty-five-story all-suites megaresort re-creates the romance of Venice, offering 4,780 spacious guest room suites with marble bathrooms, minibar, two color TVs, in-room safe, three telephones, fax machine/copier/printer. Marvel at famous Venetian landmarks of St. Mark's Square and the glittering Doge's Palace; take a gondola ride on the Grand Canal, lined with fabulous shops and cafes and tour Madame Tussaud's Wax Museum. Experience fine dining in nineteen upscale, celebrity-chef restaurants, two nightclubs, two shows in-house, two lounges, four swimming pools, Canyon Ranch Spa Club, room service; complimentary valet parking; 120,000-square-foot casino.

Day 2 / Morning

BREAKFAST: Grand Lux Café, The Venetian. (702) 414–3888. Walk downstairs to dine buffet-style at the express breakfast of eggs, sausage, bacon, hash browns, croissants, fruits, and Danish. If it's pancakes and waffles your taste buds are asking for, you'll have to request the a la carte menu, which offers extensive selections. Open twenty-four hours.

Since most visitors come to Las Vegas to try their luck, they soon join the throngs in the lively casinos. Others may prefer to relax in and around the large swimming pools. Still others like to see more of the town and drive along the Strip, to visit the different shops and hotels. Hotels are widely spaced, with many entrances through acres of convention-hall-size casino rooms—you'll find yourself doing as much walking as driving. **Caesars Palace,** with its fountains and sidewalk people movers, is one of the city's most flamboyant hotels. It has 2,418 rooms and suites, twenty-four restaurants and cafes, three swimming pools and two spas, and three casinos. Self-park in the covered structure and take the sidewalk people mover into the casinos, or park in the lot near valet parking. Valet parking is free at most hotels, and you usually tip $1.00 when the attendant delivers your car. But chances are good that there'll be a considerable wait, so you're better off parking your car yourself. At some hotels you may try to park in the fifteen-minute Registration Zone, if there's a space, for just a quick look-around.

The **Forum Shops** in Caesars Palace attract many visitors with an hourly spectacle. More than 103 upscale specialty shops and restaurants, including Gucci, Louis Vuitton, and renowned Spago encircle an elaborate fantasy rotunda of an ancient Roman piazza with tall marble columns and marble floors. In the center of an ornate, massive festival fountain reminiscent of the Trevi fountain in Rome, realistic, robotic, animated figures of Bacchus (god of merriment), Apollo, and Venus perform on the hour in an entertaining ten-minute show.

Alongside Caesars Palace, the **Mirage Resort** is another showpiece offering many diversions, including its magnificent 100-foot waterfalls cascading into rocky lagoons; its lobby atrium filled with tall, exotic trees and tropical foliage reaching to a glass dome ceiling; and its wall-length tropical fish aquarium behind the registration desk. Additionally, in a special pool you can watch five bottlenose dolphins dive and play, but there's an admission. The Three-Minute Volcano, at the Mirage's front entrance and 100 feet above the rocky lagoon, erupts every fifteen minutes at night—the earth rumbles, there's thunder, eerie red coals glow, and the water roils in the lagoon.

Hotels in Las Vegas are lit up with electric and neon lights that move, go on and off, up and down, and sideways in different, gaudy colors and shapes, and you see kitsch you never thought possible on such a large scale.

Driving toward downtown, you pass many wedding chapels in little white cottages of fanciful design and whimsy. Las Vegas is considered the "Marriage Capital of America," with no red tape, blood test, or waiting period required. More than thirty-five wedding chapels perform quickie marriages twenty-four hours a day.

Continue to Fremont Street, known as Glitter Gulch, where every inch of every building is ablaze with lights and you can take a snapshot without using a flash—at midnight! Glitter Gulch became even more spectacular when the **Fremont Street Experience,** a $70-million project, opened in December 1995 and transformed it into an exciting 5-block pedestrian mall lined by hotels and casinos. Arching overhead, a 90-foot-high electric signboard and canopy of two million lights features a dynamic, computer-generated light and sound show every hour. The lowest-price gas station in town is just below Fremont Street, on the corner of Ogden and Las Vegas Boulevard—cheaper than Los Angeles and far less than Barstow. Many fine lower-priced restaurants are also in this vital area.

LUNCH: Planet Hollywood, 3500 Las Vegas Boulevard South. (702) 791–7827. Would you like to see Dorothy's famous ruby-red slippers up close and personal? Well, this upbeat Hollywood-themed restaurant is filled with memorabilia from all the great movies. Menu features pizzas and salads, as well as burgers and sandwiches. Popular items include grilled foods, from fajitas to salmon and steak. Friendly, fun atmosphere for those who want to remember Hollywood. Souvenir shopping available at the Planet Hollywood store located next to restaurant. Sunday through Thursday 11:00 A.M. to 11:00 P.M., Friday and Saturday until midnight.

Afternoon

Las Vegas was discovered in 1829 by a party of traders who found abundant waters in its artesian springs. Later, in 1844, John C. Frémont led his first overland

The Fremont Street Experience, a neon-lit spectacular, is presented nightly.

expedition west and stopped here. His visit is commemorated with his name on many hotels and businesses. In 1855 Mormon settlers arrived and built a fort, now preserved as a historic site. Las Vegas (Spanish for "The Meadows") became a city in 1905, when the railroad made it a stop on its route east from California.

Gambling was forbidden by law in Nevada until it was legalized in 1931, during the Great Depression. The first hotel built on the Las Vegas Strip was the El Rancho Vegas, in 1940. Several others followed, and the Las Vegas Strip was on its way.

After World War II, resort building in Las Vegas began to flourish. The Desert Inn opened in 1950; the Sahara and the Sands, in 1952. The nine-story Riviera, built in 1954, was the first high-rise. The Dunes, Hacienda, Tropicana, and Stardust were built between 1955 and 1957. In 1989 the 3,049-room Mirage Hotel Casino mega-resort opened; the 4,000-room Excalibur opened in 1990. And three new major mega-resort hotel/casinos opened in late 1993: the colossal, pyramid-shaped Luxor Hotel-Casino, featuring a full-scale reproduction of King Tut's tomb; Treasure Island Adventure Resort, themed around a small Caribbean village; and the 5,005-room MGM Grand Hotel & Casino, claiming to be the world's largest hotel. In 1996 the Sands was imploded to make room for the Venetian Resort-Hotel-Casino, with its elaborate frescoes and gondola rides. The city continues to glitter and grow as more hotels and resorts explode on the scene. (See "Other Recommended Restaurants and Lodgings.")

Las Vegas also calls itself the "Entertainment Capital of the World," with such regular headline entertainers as Elton John, Britney Spears, Wayne Newton, Neil Sedaka, Celine Dion, and Tom Jones. Many hotels have their own musical production shows in which lissome, long-legged, singing and dancing Las Vegas showgirls are lavishly costumed (or half-costumed). Some visitors see two musical shows in different hotels each night and additionally watch the lounge entertainment.

If you're an antique-car buff, the **Imperial Palace Hotel & Casino,** 3535 Las Vegas Boulevard South (800–634–4441), has more than 200 antique classic automobiles on display that belonged to world leaders and celebrities. It's worth the long hike through two casinos, then up the elevator to the fifth floor. The stunning collection of gleaming cars includes a 1922 Renault, a 1931 burgundy Pierce Arrow, a 1920 Minerva, a 1929 Cord with front-wheel drive, Deusenbergs, and a 1932 Stutz Rollsten convertible. Also on display here are Adolf Hitler's bulletproof armored Mercedes-Benz and Benito Mussolini's 1939 Alfa Romeo. (Open daily from 9:30 A.M. to 11:00 P.M.; pick up a free admission ticket as you enter the hotel.)

The Fashion Show, 3200 Las Vegas Boulevard, encompasses Neiman Marcus, Saks Fifth Avenue, Dillards, Robinson-May's, Macy's, and more than 140 boutiques, restaurants, and an international food court. Additionally, most hotels have their own gift shops and exclusive boutiques. In another area about 1 mile east, the **Boulevard Mall,** 3528 Maryland Parkway at Desert Inn Road (702–732–8949), is a major shopping hub and the largest shopping center in Nevada, with 150 shops including Sears, Macy's, Dillards, JCPenney, and other department stores; restaurants; a food court and fast-food eateries; and lower prices than the Strip.

DINNER: Postrio, The Venetian. (702) 414–7770. Sit outside on the patio overlooking beautiful St. Mark's Square (no reservation needed) and feast on Wolfgang

Puck's delicious pizzas, pastas, and sandwiches. Or dine inside (reservation needed) on contemporary American fare. The fine-dining menu includes fish, poultry, steak, and other specialties. There may be a wait for the patio, but the ambience is stunning, so relax and enjoy the spectacular setting.

LODGING: The Venetian.

Day 3 / Morning

BREAKFAST: The Ultimate Cravings, The Mirage (3400 Las Vegas Boulevard South). (800) 627–6667; (702) 791–7111. A walk through the scenic lobby with its tropical foliage and waterfalls takes your cravings to The Ultimate Cravings for a delicious breakfast buffet. Pay as you enter and enjoy the no-lines perk. With ten different food stations, there's something for everyone—lox and bagels, waffles, French toast, oatmeal, breakfast pizza (your choice of egg, sausage, bacon or ham), and a stunning variety of breads, pastries, doughnuts, and muffins (including sugar-free). There are also omelette and carving stations. Saturday and Sunday champagne buffet brunch.

See more of Las Vegas or spend time in your favorite fashion before you leave for the five-hour trip back to Los Angeles.

There's More

Factory-outlet shopping. Belz Factory Outlet World, 7400 Las Vegas Boulevard South (corner Warm Springs Road). (702) 896–5599. This thirty-six-acre, enclosed, climate-controlled mall features seventy-five outlets, where you'll find savings of up to 70 percent off famous-name brands. Open Monday through Saturday from 10:00 A.M. to 9:00 P.M. and Sunday to 6:00 P.M.

Vegas Pointe Plaza, 9155 Las Vegas Boulevard South. (702) 892–9090. Open-air, Spanish-style mall of sixty stores, selling famous-name manufacturers' bargains; plus a sports/casino-style bar. Open Monday through Saturday from 10:00 A.M. to 8:00 P.M., Sunday to 6:00 P.M.

Ethel M. Chocolates Factory & Cactus Garden, 1 Cactus Garden Drive, Henderson. (888) 627–0990. Free self-tour in which you watch caramels, nut clusters, and liqueur-filled chocolates being made and receive a free sample. Afterward visit the large cacti garden. Open daily from 9:00 A.M. to 7:00 P.M.

M&M's World, 3785 Las Vegas Boulevard South. (702) 736–7611. This candy lover's delight is a treat for all. The four-story building is filled with M&Ms of every color, cheerfully displayed in tall see-through canisters. Other items—from playing cards and magnets to sweatshirts and key chains—are available. Call for days and store hours.

Hoover Dam and Lake Mead are 30 miles from the Strip; bus tours leave daily. Dedicated in 1935 by President Franklin Roosevelt, Hoover Dam is one of the world's great engineering marvels. Guided thirty-five-minute tours take visitors deep within the awesome, 726-foot-high (seventy-story-high) dam to the banks of generators and provide information on the history and inner workings of the dam. Be prepared for long lines, though the tours leave every few minutes. A three-level, 110-foot-diameter circular visitor center has a 400-car parking garage, rooftop overlook, rotating theater, exhibit gallery, and two high-speed elevators to transport guests and trim the long lines. Lake Mead, one of the largest man-made lakes in the United States, offers 550 miles of recreation, with boating, fishing, waterskiing, and camping. Admission.

Liberace Museum, 1775 East Tropicana Avenue (corner of Spencer). (702) 798–5595. Take Las Vegas Boulevard to Tropicana Avenue; turn left (east) for about 2.5 miles. The popular small museum exhibits personal items of the flamboyant entertainment personality who wore elaborate sequinned jackets and fur-trimmed capes and made the candelabra famous. Features include fifteen pianos, one covered completely with rhinestones. In the Car Gallery, ornate, customized cars are covered with gold glitz and rhinestones, and a Rolls-Royce Phantom V is covered with thousands of mirror tiles. The Costume Gallery displays jewelry and furs. Open Monday through Saturday from 10:00 A.M. to 5:00 P.M. and Sunday from 1:00 P.M. Admission.

Wet 'n Wild Water Park, 2601 Las Vegas Boulevard. (702) 871–7811. Water-oriented family recreation in flumes, wave pool, slides, water roller coaster, fountain, and lagoons. Seasonal days and hours. Admission.

Special Events

Mid-January. Las Vegas All-American Classic, Sam Boyd Stadium. (435) 673–6402, Football All-Star game, NFL Scouts attending.

Late January. Triple Mini Slot Tournament, Riviera Hotel.

Beginning to end of February. Las Vegas International Marathon, Vacation Village Hotel.

Last week in February to first week in March. $200,000.00 Slot Tournament, Imperial Palace Hotel.

March. Annual NASCAR Race, Las Vegas Motor Speedway. (800) 644–4444.

Big League Thursday, Cashman Field. (702) 386–7200. Annual Major League exhibition.

Late March. Annual Angel Planes Airfest, Boulder City Airport. Great American Train Show, Cashman Center.

Fisrt week in April. NHRA Summit. Com Nationals, Las Vegas Motor Speedway. (800) 644–4444. A must for all racing enthusiasts.

Mid-April. Annual Mardi Gras Festival, Fremont Street Experience. (800) 249–3559.

End of April. Annual City of Lights Jazz Festival, Desert Breeze Park. (702) 228–3780.

First week in May. THQ World Supercross GP Finals, Sam Boyd Stadium. (702) 895–3900.

June. Cinevegas International Film Festival, Palms Hotel and Casino. (702) 368–2890.

September. Las Vegas Stampede, Grand Central Parkway. (403) 236–2466.

NASCAR Truck Race, Las Vegas Motor Speedway. (800) 644–4444.

October. Vegoose Music Festival, Sam Boyd Stadium. (800) 594–TIXX.

Mid-October. Las Vegas International Bike Festival and Expo; various venues. (704) 792–9430.

End of October. Henderson Expo, Henderson Convention Center.

December. Billboard Music Awards, MGM Grand Garden Arena. (702) 474–4000. NFR Cowboy Christmas Gift Show, Las Vegas Convention Center. (702) 260–8605.

Beginning of December. National Finals Rodeo, Thomas and Mack Center. (702) 895–3900.

Other Recommended Restaurants and Lodgings

Las Vegas

Dining is inexpensive in Las Vegas, and the operative word is *buffet,* featured throughout the day at most hotels. The largest buffet is at Circus Circus; the longest line is the one you're standing in. Prices vary, as do the specialties offered. Brunches are also appealing, especially Sunday champagne brunch, with all the bubbly you can drink. Because of price and enjoyability, you'll usually find long buffet lines. At most buffets you pay before you enter the dining room. One way to avoid standing in line is to prepay your meal. Walk around the line to the cashier and tell him or her that you want to return in a half hour or an hour (whatever time you desire) and that you'd like to prepay your meal to avoid waiting. Get a receipt. Play the slots, watch TV, and return later—present your receipt to the cashier and you'll be seated immediately, without standing in line. Worth a try.

If you don't enjoy standing in buffet lines, try the coffee shops. The wait for your order may be interminable, but you'll be sitting down. Another alternative is McDonald's, in the basement of the Barbary Coast Hotel, across from Caesars Palace. No line, no wait.

Palms Casino Resort, 4321 West Flamingo Road. (866) 726–6773. This showplace features 440 rooms, a three-story spa salon and fitness center, seven restaurants, theater-cinema complex, and a state-of-the-art nightclub. From the open-air deck of the fifty-fifth-floor Ghost Bar, guests can enjoy 275-degree views of the glittering Las Vegas skyline. The casino is 95,000 square feet.

MGM Grand Hotel & Casino, 3799 Las Vegas Boulevard South. (702) 891–1111; reservations: (800) 929–1111. Thirty-story emerald-tower mega-entertainment resort hotel of 5,005 guest rooms, including 751 suites, offers luxurious amenities of marble bathrooms, spacious closets, and personal service. The casino is reportedly the size of four football fields; ten signature restaurants showcase famous chefs and their cuisine; two showrooms, garden swimming pool and spa, conference center, promenade shops, youth activity center.

New York–New York Hotel & Casino, 3790 Las Vegas Boulevard South. (800) NY–FOR–ME. The tallest hotel-casino in Nevada dramatically re-creates the best of the Big Apple skyline with twelve New York City–style, forty-seven-story hotel towers replicating some of Manhattan's famous landmarks, from the Statue of Liberty and the Empire State Building to the Coney Island roller coaster. The hotel towers house 2,035 art deco guest rooms, an 84,000-square-foot casino, restaurants with themed dining experiences, food court, nightclubs, lounge bars, swimming pool, Jacuzzi, health spa and fitness center, gift shops, and boutiques.

Bellagio, 3000 Las Vegas Boulevard South. (702) 693–7147. AAA five-diamond award winner. Inspired by the small village of Bellagio on Italy's scenic Lake Como, the opulent resort has an eight-acre lake at its doorstep featuring a thousand dazzling fountains dancing to music and lights. Bellagio emphasizes quality and informal elegance throughout with its flowers and gardens, 3,000 guest rooms with sweeping lake views, marble bathrooms, plush robes, and haute cuisine of award-winning celebrity-chef restaurants. World-class shopping arcade, six swimming pools, spa and sauna, and 100,000-square-foot casino. The Bellagio Gallery exhibits works by Renoir and Degas, among other artists.

Wynn Las Vegas, 3131 Las Vegas Boulevard South. (702) 770–2121. The Wynn is on a roll. Newly opened in April 2005, this fifty-story luxury hotel has plenty of "bling" to go around. Boasting 2,716 view rooms, each with two plasma screen TVs, marble bathrooms, and all the amenities. This fantasyland has twenty-two food and beverage eateries, four pools, spa, an eighteen-hole championship golf course, two nightclubs, and nightly show. Wynn Esplanade boasts high-end stores and the only Manolo Blahnik store in the United States. Saturday and Sunday champagne buffet brunch.

Paris Las Vegas Casino Resort, 3055 Las Vegas Boulevard South. (888) 266–5687; (702) 946–7000. *Bonjour* to this upbeat, thirty-four-story resort, which re-creates Gay Paree's noted landmarks from the Louvre and L'Arc de Triomphe to its signature centerpiece, the fifty-story Eiffel Tower. French decor of mirrors and crystal chandeliers is featured throughout its 2,916 rooms and 295 suites, with two-line phones, voice mail, cable TV, on-command TV, hair dryer, iron and ironing board, separate shower and bathtub, in-room safe, concierge floors, and twenty-four-hour room service. Fine dining is offered in eight French-inspired restaurants. Visitors shop along the cobblestone walkways of Le Boulevard, lined with authentic French boutiques and outdoor cafes. The casino is 85,000 square feet.

NOTE: Experienced visitors recommend joining the free Slots Clubs in the casinos; get your name on the hotel mailing list of members eligible for discounts on rooms and food, special rates, and other perks not available to nonmembers. Sign up at the Slot Club booths in your hotel's casino. Additionally, check out your hotel *Fun Books*—they contain coupons for free cocktails, discounts, and other goodies.

For More Information

LVCVA (Las Vegas Convention and Visitor Authority), 3150 Convention Center Drive, Las Vegas, NV 89109–9095. (702) 735–3611.

Las Vegas Chamber of Commerce, 711 East Desert Inn Road, Las Vegas, NV 89109. (702) 735–1616.

INDEX

About the Authors

Eleanor Harris, a knowledgeable traveler and photojournalist, is an expert on Southern California and has written about its vacation attractions for such publications as _Los Angeles_ magazine, _Travel & Leisure, National Motorist, Cruise Travel,_ and _Westways._ She is a self-syndicated columnist and former dining editor, as well as a painter, gourmet cook, architectural consultant, and sometime golfer. She lives with her husband, Ben, in Beverly Hills, where they raised two daughters.

Claudia Harris Lichtig, daughter of Eleanor Harris, is a travel writer and photographer who grew up in beautiful Southern California. She has a keen interest in travel and writing about the delights of discovering new places, as well as rediscovering old escapes. She is always on the lookout for new and exciting activities for kids and eager to put her own sunny stamp on California's colorful coastline. A graduate of UCLA and a former teacher, she lives with her husband and two children in Marina del Rey.